BERTRAND RUSSELL
and
THE BRITISH
TRADITION
IN PHILOSOPHY

Es frägt sich hier, wie kommt der
Satzverband zustande.

—WITTGENSTEIN

BERTRAND RUSSELL
and
THE BRITISH
TRADITION
IN PHILOSOPHY

by D. F. PEARS

RANDOM HOUSE   NEW YORK

CONTENTS

To Anne

PREFACE

This book is arranged in such a way that the text can be read continuously without the footnotes, and two of the chapters, which are more difficult than the others, may be omitted without much loss of continuity. The two chapters are VIII and IX, in which Russell's and Wittgenstein's views about complete logical analysis are explained and compared with one another. Most of the footnotes merely give references, but some of them take the discussion of questions of interpretation further than it is taken in the text. Occasionally that requires a long note, and in such cases the note is relegated to the end of the chapter.

The interpretation of Wittgenstein's argument for logical atomism, which is given on pp. 146-50, contradicts an interpretation which I suggested on p. 28 of *British Analytical Philosophy* (edited by Bernard Williams and Alan Montefiore, Routledge and Kegan Paul, 1966).

I am much indebted to Mr B. F. McGuinness for improvements which he suggested at many points in this book, and also for what I have learned from him about the interpretation of Wittgenstein's *Tractatus Logico-Philosophicus*.

KEY TO THE ABBREVIATIONS OF TITLES OF

WORKS WHICH ARE USED IN THE FOOTNOTES

(see also the Bibliography, p. 273)

(Inverted commas are used to distinguish the titles of articles from the titles of books.)

I RUSSELL'S WORKS

A.M.	*The Analysis of Mind*
H. KN.S.L.	*Human Knowledge, its Scope and Limits*
I.M.PH.	*Introduction to Mathematical Philosophy*
I.M.T.	*An Inquiry into Meaning and Truth*
I.T.	*Introduction to Wittgenstein's Tractatus Logico-Philosophicus*
KN.A.KN.D.	'Knowledge by Acquaintance and Knowledge by Description'
L.A.	'Logical Atomism'
L.KN.	*Logic and Knowledge*
M.PH.D.	*My Philosophical Development*
M. and L.	*Mysticism and Logic* (The book: not the essay)
M.TH.C.A.	'Meinong's Theory of Complexes and Assumptions'
M.TH. of T.	'The Monistic Theory of Truth'
MYS. and LOG.	'Mysticism and Logic' (The essay: not the book)
O.D.	'On Denoting'
O.KN.E.W.	*Our Knowledge of the External World*
O.N.A.	'On the Nature of Acquaintance'
O.N.T. and F.	'On the Nature of Truth and Falsehood'
O.P.	'On Propositions'
P.M.	*Principia Mathematica*
P. of M.	*The Principles of Mathematics*
P. of PH.	*The Problems of Philosophy*
PH.B.R.	'Reply to Criticism' in *The Philosophy of Bertrand Russell*
PH.E.	*Philosophical Essays*
PH.L.A.	'The Philosophy of Logical Atomism'
PH. of L.	*A Critical Exposition of the Philosophy of Leibniz*
R.S.-D.PH.	'The Relations of Sense-data to Physics'
R.U.P.	'On the Relation of Universals to Particulars'
U.C.M.	'The Ultimate Constituents of Matter'

II WORKS BY OTHER AUTHORS

A. and R.	F. H. BRADLEY: *Appearance and Reality*
B. and B.B.	L. WITTGENSTEIN: *The Blue and Brown Books*
F.H.B.	R. A. WOLLHEIM: *F. H. Bradley*
H.TH.KN.	*Hume, Theory of Knowledge*, ed. D. C. Yalden-Thomson
I.W.T.	G. E. M. ANSCOMBE: *An Introduction to Wittgenstein's Tractatus*
L.F.	L. WITTGENSTEIN: '*Some Remarks on Logical Form*'
N.B.	L. WITTGENSTEIN: *Notebooks 1914-1916*
N.L.	L. WITTGENSTEIN: *Notes on Logic*
PH.I.	L. WITTGENSTEIN: *Philosophical Investigations*
T.H.N	D. HUME: *A Treatise of Human Nature*
T.L.-PH.	L. WITTGENSTEIN: *Tractatus Logico-Philosophicus*
W.L.A.	J. P. GRIFFIN: *Wittgenstein's Logical Atomism*

INTRODUCTION

This book does not give a complete account of Russell's philosophy. It only covers the period from 1905 to 1919. At the beginning of that period his theory of meaning changed in a way which affected the whole of the subsequent development of his philosophy. At the end of it his theory of mind changed in an almost equally important way. Between these two changes his ideas developed with extraordinary rapidity over a very wide range of subjects. Much of his time was spent on the foundations of logic and mathematics. That side of his work will only be described in a minimal way in this book. His logical apparatus will be explained only to the extent to which it must be understood by anyone who wants to understand his reconstruction of empirical knowledge, and the symbolism of logic will not be introduced.

Russell's reconstruction of empirical knowledge is the main theme of this book. This side of his work is best seen in a fairly long historical perspective. For what he did was to take over and strengthen the type of empiricism whose most distinguished exponent had been David Hume. The framework of Hume's system was psychological: the framework which Russell substituted for it was logical. Considerable space will be devoted to describing Hume's system, in order to show how Russell's developed out of it, and, more generally, how the new logical approach to the problems of philosophy differs from the old psychological approach.

The ideas of two other philosophers, Bradley and Wittgenstein, will be presented in some detail. Bradley was the greatest contemporary representative of the kind of Idealism which Russell's philosophy was designed to supplant. Wittgenstein's philosophy, on the other hand, was very close to Russell's during this period, and so it will be presented in greater detail. They met before 1914, and the exchange of ideas between them continued, with some interruption, until after the end

of the war. Wittgenstein's first great work, the *Tractatus
Logico-Philosophicus*, was written during and immediately
after the war, and it has many points of affinity with the lectures
which Russell gave in 1918 and 1919 under the title *The
Philosophy of Logical Atomism*.

Russell's work during the period that has been chosen
really culminates in those lectures, and much of this book will
be devoted to them. The change which his philosophy under-
went in 1919 will also be described in some detail, but its
subsequent development will hardly be touched. The choice
of this restricted period of fifteen years has certain disadvantages. One, which has already been mentioned, is that the
account of the development of his ideas will be left incomplete. Another is that some of the most important criticisms
of his theories will only be mentioned very briefly.

However, these two disadvantages are not as great as they
might appear to be. Against the first there stands the complete account of his philosophical development which Russell
himself has already given.[1] Against the second it is arguable
that major criticisms of his theories are best presented in their
own historical context. Anyway, that is the policy which will
be followed here. When a criticism develops naturally out of
things that were happening on the front of the philosophical
stage during those fifteen years, it will be presented fully. But
when a criticism comes out of a corner which was not illumi-
nated until later, it will be presented briefly.

On the other side there are, of course, the general advantages of examining a shorter period more thoroughly. But
there are also two special considerations. First, by the end of
1919 Russell already had most of his more important ideas on
his work-bench. Naturally, he had not finished with them, but
they were there, and their main outlines were visible. Secondly, during those fifteen years a considerable part of the history of philosophy was the history of the development of his
ideas.

[1] *My Philosophical Development.*

CHAPTER I

PRELIMINARY REMARKS ABOUT EXISTENCE

Bertrand Russell was born in 1872. His first great philosophical work, *The Principles of Mathematics*, was published in 1903. Shortly after its publication his philosophy changed in a way that affected the whole of its subsequent development.[1] The details of this change will be given later, but its general character must be explained now, because the understanding of his philosophy depends upon it. It was a change in his theory of meaning. He had thought that every phrase in a sentence gets its meaning by denoting something. Some phrases are, of course, single words, while others are more elaborate units, like 'the daughter of Hitler'. It is not necessary at the moment to enquire how we tell where one phrase ends and another begins. The point is that Russell had believed that every phrase, long or short, must denote something, or else be meaningless. Now that theory does not imply that a word like 'dragon' denotes an actual species of animal, or that the phrase 'the daughter of Hitler' denotes an actual woman. But, when a phrase lacks an actual denotation, the theory would credit it with a denotation not belonging to the actual world. Dragons and Hitler's children are supposed to exist in another world whose discovery is generally attributed to Plato. The change in Russell's theory of meaning came when he decided not to postulate that other world. The reason for his decision was what he sometimes calls 'a vivid sense of reality'.[2] Its consequence was that he had to find some other way of explaining how phrases that lack an actual denotation acquire a meaning.

[1] See *P. of M.* Introduction to the second edition (1937), pp. ix-xii.
[2] *PH.L.A.* p. 29 (*L.KN*, p. 223).

In some cases no great search was needed. Consider the general word 'dragon'. It is evident that the idea of a dragon is made up out of other ideas of properties which do actually exist, such as the idea of leathery wings and the idea of a scaly body. The idea of a dragon is, in David Hume's terminology, a complex idea, and correspondingly the word 'dragon' is a complex symbol. The singular phrase 'the daughter of Hitler' is more difficult. It too is obviously a complex symbol, and so in one way or another it too must be able to acquire a meaning even though no such woman actually exists. But it is not so easy to explain exactly how it does acquire its meaning. Russell offered his explanation in his Theory of Definite Descriptions, which was the first product of his new theory of meaning.[8] A full account of this theory, and of the way in which Russell used it, will be given later. The briefest possible version of it would be that a proposition in which a definite description occurs entails the existential proposition that there is one and only one thing that fits the description. In this particular example the entailed existential proposition would be that there is one and only one thing that is female and begotten by Hitler. If this is right, then, in order to explain the fact that the complex symbol 'the daughter of Hitler' has a meaning in spite of the fact that, taken as a whole, it has no denotation, it would be enough to show that each of the symbols in the existential proposition has a denotation.

Although there are considerations which tell against Russell's Theory of Definite Descriptions, at least there is no doubt that it is comprehensive. That is to say, someone who used the definite description 'the daughter of Hitler' would have to admit that Russell gave a comprehensive account of what he meant. So, as far as comprehensiveness goes, Russell's account of the meaning of the phrase 'the daughter of Hitler' is as good as the account of the meaning of a word like 'dragon' which he took over from Hume. The difference

[8] See *O.D.* (*L.KN.* p. 41ff) and *PH.L.A.* ch. VI (*L.KN.* p. 241ff).

comes when we ask whether the two accounts are *correct*. It is very plausible to say that the correct way to give the meaning of the word ' dragon ' is to enumerate the essential properties of the creature. But the correctness of Russell's Theory of Definite Descriptions is more questionable.[4]

At this point two questions arise, both of which must be answered at the outset of any attempt to understand Russell's philosophy. First, how can we tell whether an account of the meaning of a phrase is comprehensive? Notice that this is not the same thing as asking how we can tell whether such an account is correct. A rough answer to the question about comprehensiveness would be that a comprehensive analysis conveys everything that people want to convey when they use the phrase. But there might be various ways of conveying everything that people want to convey, and perhaps only one of them would be the way that language actually uses. If that were so, a philosopher who based his analysis on that particular way might claim that it was the correct analysis. Whatever the merits of such a claim, it would clearly go beyond the claim that his analysis was comprehensive.[5]

The second question which must be answered is about the philosophical conclusions that can be drawn from the fact that a certain analysis of a phrase is comprehensive. Let us ask this question about a fresh example. Consider the phrase ' object in the external world '. Now Russell accepted the traditional arguments which the sceptic has always used against our ordinary belief in the external world. Consequently he felt that this belief of ours needed to be reconstructed in a new and safer form. The reconstruction which he suggested was based on sense-data. His idea was that the phrase ' object in the external world ', though it may lack an actual denotation, acquires its meaning through the phrases

---

[4] See pp. 68-9.
[5] If the criterion of correctness is faithfulness to everyday language, Russell thinks that correctness is not important. Cf. *M.PH.D.* p. 230. See pp. 68-9.

which people use to describe the sense-data which they get when they take themselves to be perceiving such objects.[6] Now suppose, as Russell supposed, that this analysis of the phrase 'object in the external world' is comprehensive. Then the second question is this : Does it follow that objects in the external world do not exist? Or rather, since that is too blunt a question, does it follow that in some sense they do not exist? If so, in what sense?

Before these two questions are answered, this last example requires some comment. Evidently it adds a complication to what was said about the complex symbols which were considered just now. For, according to Russell, it is not really enough to analyse the word 'dragon' as 'creature with a scaly body, leathery wings etc. ', since all these phrases are supposed to denote properties in the external world. An adequate analysis of the word 'dragon', or indeed of any other phrase which is applied to something in the external world, would be confined entirely to sense-data.

The complication which is introduced by this view will be unravelled later. But it is important to notice now that we have been taken down to a deeper level by Russell's analysis of the phrase 'object in the external world'. The preliminary analyses of the word 'dragon' and of the phrase 'the daughter of Hitler' might be called horizontal analyses, because they remain on one level, the level of ordinary descriptions of things in the external world. But the analysis of the phrase 'object in the external world' into descriptions of sense-data is a deep analysis, because it takes us down to things of an entirely different kind. Somewhat similarly, a house might be analysed into the bricks out of which it was built, and this analysis would remain on the level of ordinary things in the external world: but if we went further, and analysed the bricks into atoms, we should have descended to a deeper level, because atoms are things of an entirely different kind. However, this analogy is not exact, because people do not actually perceive atoms, whereas, according to Russell, the

[6] *PH.L.A.* pp. 11-12 (*L.KN.* pp. 195-6).

traditional arguments of the sceptic prove that sense-data are the only things that they ever really perceive. But the analogy would be more exact if human beings by some act of magic became fantastically small, so that atoms were the only things that they ever really perceived. Then some genius might construct the idea of a brick, or even the idea of a house, both of which would be complex ideas of vast configurations of atoms. But, of course, the analogy would still not be exact, because the construction of objects in the external world out of sense-data does not present that kind of difficulty.

Now let us take up the two questions. First consider the question about comprehensiveness, and the rough answer already given to it; which was that a comprehensive analysis of a phrase would convey everything that people want to convey when they use the phrase. This answer is rather too simple. For there is evidently a scale on which different analyses of a phrase would occupy different positions. An absolutely comprehensive analysis would convey everything that people want to convey when they use the phrase : another analysis, further down the scale, would convey less; and perhaps there might be analyses so far down the scale that they were utter failures. Now the interesting thing is that Russell did not insist on a comprehensive analysis in every case. He did insist on it when he was analysing an ordinary definite description, like 'the daughter of Hitler', in a preliminary way, and he rightly claimed that his theory achieved it. But in many cases he thought that people want to convey more than they ought to convey, so that a good analysis of what they mean would be less than comprehensive. His analysis of the meaning of the phrase 'object in the external world' into descriptions of sense-data illustrates this view : indeed, if his analysis of the phrase 'the daughter of Hitler' were taken beyond the preliminary stage, it would provide another illustration of this view. It was stated just now that he supposed that his analysis of any statement mentioning an object in the external world was comprehensive. But that was not quite accurate. What he supposed was that it was as comprehensive as it ought to be. For since he accepted the sceptic's traditional arguments, it seemed to him that when people talk about the external world they try to convey more than they really ought to convey. In such cases he thought that a good analysis would be less than comprehensive. The philosopher should use Ockham's razor[7] and cut back their meaning to its legitimate extent. It follows that he did not think that all philosophical analyses ought to be exact translations.[8]

It is more difficult to deal with the second question, which was about the conclusions that can be drawn from the fact that an analysis of a certain phrase is sufficiently comprehensive. The example used just now was Russell's analysis of the phrase ' object in the external world ' into descriptions of sense-data; the supposition was that this analysis is sufficiently comprehensive; and then the question was whether it follows that in some sense objects in the external world do not exist. Does it follow? And, if so, in what sense?

One way of answering these questions would be to say that the phrase would have a meaning even if objects in the external world did not exist. Therefore they need not exist, and the question whether they exist or not can be left open. This is the answer which Russell gives,[9] and it sounds very like his answer to the parallel questions whether dragons exist, and whether the daughter of Hitler exists. However, the likeness is deceptive, and it is essential to avoid being deceived by it. Here it is necessary to remember that the two kinds of analysis differ from one another. The preliminary analyses of the word ' dragon ' and of the phrase ' the daughter of Hitler '

---

[7] i.e., the maxim of William of Ockham: ' *Entia non sunt multiplicanda praeter necessitatem* '. See *PH.L.A.* p. 58 (*L.KN.* p. 270), and *L.A.* p. 362 (*L.KN.* p. 326).

[8] Russell's attitude to comprehensiveness is connected with his contempt for correctness when correctness is judged by the criterion of faithfulness to everyday language. He thought that, when what people mean goes beyond what they can legitimately mean, philosophers should not follow them all the way with their analyses.

[9] *PH.L.A.* p. 60 (*L.KN.* p. 273).

are horizontal, whereas the analysis of the phrase 'object in the external world' goes down to the deeper level of sense-data. This produces a big difference between Russell's two answers, which sound so alike; the answer that dragons and the daughter of Hitler need not exist in order to give those phrases meanings, and the answer that objects in the external world need not exist in order to give that phrase a meaning. The difference is this: in the first two cases nobody would doubt that Russell's analyses are comprehensive because there obviously could not be a case of perceiving a dragon which involved more than perceiving a creature with the right essential properties, and something similar is true of the daughter of Hitler; but in the third case, where his analysis takes us down to the deeper level, we might well question whether it is as comprehensive as it ought to be. Is perceiving objects in the external world really no more than perceiving sense-data? Perhaps this analysis is too economical. Possibly Ockham's razor has cut away too much of our ordinary meaning.

Let us leave such doubts on one side for the moment, and, concentrating on deep analysis, let us continue our enquiry into Russell's conclusions about existence. When he thinks that he has a sufficiently comprehensive deep analysis of a certain phrase, what exactly does he mean by his conclusion that the denotation of the phrase need not exist? This really is a very cryptic thing to say in such cases, and it needs to be weighed carefully. Consider again his deep analysis of the phrase 'object in the external world' into descriptions of sense-data. If he thinks that this analysis is sufficiently comprehensive, what can he mean by saying that objects in the external world need not exist? It sounds as if he means that the question whether they exist or not is a question to be settled by empirical investigation, just as the question whether dragons exist or not has been settled by zoologists. However, this cannot be what he means. For, if he is right in thinking that our knowledge of the external world does not really extend beyond our own sense-data, it would be no good trying to peer at an object in order to see behind our sense-data. Of course, even at the superficial level it would be no good trying to peer behind the essential properties of an animal in order to see the animal itself. But at the superficial level nobody would feel that it was necessary to do such a thing; whereas at the deeper level people might well feel that it was necessary, simply because the analysis into sense-data seems to rob them of a legitimate part of what they meant.

What then does his cryptic conclusion mean? The answer is that it must not be taken to imply that the question, whether objects in the external world exist or not, is any kind of empirical question. For he is really saying something about his *analysis* of the phrase ' object in the external world '. The clue to understanding what he is saying about his analysis is to be found in his view that it is right that his analysis should be less than comprehensive. The crucial point is that when a deep analysis of a phrase is less than comprehensive, it leaves out part of what people mean when they use the phrase. In order to get the whole of what they mean, that part would have to be put back again. That is to say, the omitted part would have to be restored in order to get the full popular idea of the thing in question. Now when Russell says that objects in the external world need not exist, his point is that *in so far as they are thought of in the full popular way* they need not exist. This is a natural comment for him to make on what he regards as the surplus and illegitimate element in the popular idea. For his reason for making his analysis of the phrase ' object in the external world ' less than comprehensive was simply that he believed that people use this phrase to convey more than they legitimately ought to convey. Consequently, if the things in question had to exist even according to the full popular idea of them, it would follow that his analysis was too parsimonious. That is why, when he is confident that he has a deep analysis which is sufficiently comprehensive in spite of being parsimonious, he says that the things in question need not exist. He means that they need not exist according to the full popular idea of them.

On the other hand, when he is discussing a horizontal analysis of a phrase which is obviously comprehensive, his remark that the denotation need not exist means something quite different and much simpler. In such a case there is no distinction between the full popular idea of the thing in question and a more parsimonious idea of it. There is only one way of thinking of the thing, and, thought of in that way, it simply need not exist in order to give a meaning to the phrase which would denote it if it did exist.

The second of the two preliminary questions still needs a little more discussion. The question was, what conclusions about existence follow from the fact that a deep analysis of a phrase is as comprehensive as it ought to be. So far, only one of Russell's conclusions has been examined, the conclusion that the things in question need not exist in order to give the phrase a meaning. But there is also another remark that he often makes in such cases; which is that the things in question may or may not exist.[10] This remark can now be easily explained. What he means is that he does not need to deny the existence of the things in question in so far as they are thought of in the full popular way. He can rest in agnosticism on this point. For his reason for adopting a parsimonious analysis was not that people are necessarily *mistaken* in believing that the things in question, thought of in the full popular way, exist, but rather that they have no good reason for this belief.[11]

Unfortunately, he does not always remain in this agnostic position. Sometimes, when he thinks that he has found a sufficiently comprehensive deep analysis of a phrase, he goes so far as to say that the things in question do not exist. For example, he occasionally says that classes do not exist.[12] He often puts this in a rather less extreme way by saying that

[10] *PH.L.A.* p. 60 (*L.KN.* pp. 273-4).
[11] *PH.L.A.* p. 28 (*L.KN.* p. 221), pp. 58-60 (*L.KN.* pp. 270-4), *L.A.* p. 362 (*L.K.N.* p 326).
[12] e.g. in the discussion at the end of lecture VII of *PH.L.A.*, p. 57 (*L.KN.* p. 268).

classes are ' logical fictions '. He means that the belief that
classes exist in anything more than the sense allowed by his
parsimonious analysis is mistaken. The extra element in the
popular idea is a mere *flatus intellectus*. This is a deviation
from his usual agnosticism, but it is an understandable one.[13]

So much for the two preliminary questions. We must now
ask what Russell hoped to achieve by his kind of analysis.
What was the point of pruning popular ideas and reaching
these rather cryptic conclusions about existence? The answer
is that he was going to use his newly invented logical apparatus
to do some reconstruction. He was going to reconstruct the
edifice of human knowledge, because it seemed to him that,
if it were left in its familiar, rather ramshackle state, it would
not be strong enough to withstand the forces of scepticism.
Not that he thought that everything could be saved from the
sceptic. As has already been pointed out, he judged that our
ordinary belief in objects in the external world could not sur-
vive the sceptic's traditional arguments. But he wanted to save
as much as possible, and he wanted what was saved to be saved
unimpaired by the collapse of what had to be sacrificed. So
his newly invented apparatus was going to be used like steel
and concrete in the reconstruction of an old building. Great
care would have to be taken in selecting the places where the
new foundations would be sunk, and in ensuring that the new
structure really could bear the load which it was required to
bear. That is to say, great care would have to be taken in
selecting the basic propositions from which all other empirical
propositions would be derived, and in ensuring that the
derivation really was valid. Those parts of the original
edifice which had been built too audaciously to be saved
would simply be abandoned to their fate. That is to say, the
surplus, illegitimate element in popular ideas would be
abandoned to the sceptic. The final result of this enterprise
might well seem very strange. People might object that they
had been given a different building. But Russell would reply
that it was all that could be saved of the original building; or,

[13] See Note A at the end of this chapter.

in other words, that it was all that they could have legitimately meant when they talked about the external world.

The change in Russell's theory of meaning began with his Theory of Descriptions, which was published in 1905 in his article *On Denoting*.[14] Its development continued well beyond 1919, which is the end of the period with which this book is concerned. In this period there was an astonishing explosion of new ideas in Russell's mind, or, rather, not a single explosion, but a chain-reaction which began with the 1905 article. His second great book on the foundations of mathematics, *Principia Mathematica*, which he produced in collaboration with A. N. Whitehead, belongs to this period, and so too does his elegant, and more popular treatment of this subject, the *Introduction to Mathematical Philosophy*. But nothing will be said here about his work on the foundations of mathematics, and his logic will be discussed only when it plays an essential part in his reconstruction of empirical knowledge.

When Russell was planning his reconstruction of empirical knowledge, he felt himself pulled in two opposite directions. On the one hand he wanted to save as much as possible. But on the other hand he wanted what was saved to be firmly based on sound foundations, and well and truly saved. Now his immediate predecessor, John Stuart Mill, who was, as a matter of fact, his godfather, seemed to him to accept received scientific doctrines in too facile a way. But if he followed the line of British empiricists further back to Hume, he found the opposite situation. Hume's strong and subtle sceptical arguments carried away too much. As for the Idealists, he never could accept their notion that the objects of knowledge are really all inside human minds.[15] That view seemed to him to represent the abandonment of any attempt at reconstruction. So his task was to achieve something like Mill's results with Hume's rigour.

The influence of Hume's *Treatise of Human Nature* on Russell's mind was powerful and persistent. In fact, as will

[14] *Mind* 1905 (*L.KN.* p. 39ff).   [15] *M.PH.D.* pp. 61-2.

be shown later, although he advanced beyond Hume's system, he was apt to forget that he had done so, and would sometimes find it difficult to emancipate himself from Hume's way of looking at things, and would relapse into it. Consequently, one good way of achieving an understanding of Russell's philosophy is to approach it through Hume's. So we shall now go back two centuries, and make a quick sketch of Hume's system.

NOTE A

The interpretation of Russell's views about existence which has emerged from the preceding discussion differs from the interpretation suggested by Mr. J. O. Urmson in his book *Philosophical Analysis*. Mr. Urmson points out that Russell's analysis of a definite description like 'the daughter of Hitler' cannot be used to support the thesis that no such woman exists (pp. 29-30). This is correct. It was only intended to support the conclusion that she *does not have to exist* in order to give the definite description a meaning. But he then goes on to impute a confusion to Russell. According to him, when Russell propounded the thesis that classes do not exist, he simply failed to notice that his parsimonious analysis of the word 'class' cannot be used to support this thesis. This is incorrect. The point of Russell's analysis of the word 'class' is that, according to him, there is a gap between its popular meaning and its legitimate meaning; whereas, if we stick to the level of objects in the external world, there is no gap between the popular meaning and the legitimate meaning of a definite description like 'the daughter of Hitler'. Consequently, anyone who denied the existence of Hitler's daughter would mean that, on this level, she happens not to exist; whereas, when Russell denies that classes exist, he means that, thought of in the full, popular way, they never exist. Admittedly, this thesis is a deviation from his usual agnosticism about the existence of anything corresponding to the extra element in the popular meaning of a complex symbol. But it does not involve a confusion between the true statement, that the analysis of a complex symbol shows that it *does not have to possess* a denotation in order to possess a meaning, and the false statement, that the analysis of a complex symbol shows that *in fact it does not possess* a denotation. See pp. 111-12.

However, although Russell was not confused on this point, he sometimes gives the impression of confusion. For instance, the passage cited by Mr Urmson (*P.M.* 2nd ed. vol I, pp. 71-2) suggests that his doubt about his analysis of the complex symbol ' class ' led him to doubt the truth of his thesis that classes do not exist. But in the interpretation of that passage it is essential to distinguish between what Russell regarded as the legitimate element in the meaning of the word ' class ' and what he was inclined to regard as the illegitimate, extra element in its meaning. Now his analysis of the word is parsimonious, and he does not feel confident about it, because it seems to him to depend on a dubious assumption (the Axiom of Reducibility: see *I.M.PH.* p. 193). His lack of confidence in his parsimonious analysis ought to lead him to doubt whether he can adopt an agnostic view about the existence of anything corresponding to the element which he has pruned away. But, by the process of thought which has been explained, it leads him to doubt his thesis that ' classes are not genuine objects as their members are if they are individuals '. However, in *I.M.PH.* (p. 184 and p. 193) he makes it clear that his position, about which he feels some doubt, is really agnostic. But unfortunately in *P.M.* (p. 72) he writes as if he were dubious not about his agnosticism about the existence of anything corresponding to the extra element in the meaning of the word ' class ', but about the dogmatic denial of the existence of any such thing. This is a slip, and not a sign of confusion in his treatment of existence. The slip is an example of mental haplography; his doubt about a doubt has been compressed into a single doubt.

CHAPTER II

HUME'S SYSTEM

According to Hume, the mind is equipped with two kinds of ideas, complex ones and simple ones. The idea of a dragon is complex, and one of Hume's examples of a simple idea is the idea of scarlet.[1] Both of these are general ideas. There are also singular ideas, like the idea of the city of Paris,[2] but in Hume's system all singular ideas are complex, and there are no simple singular ideas. It is easy to see why he thought that all simple ideas are general. The reason is that if you look at the colour scarlet, you cannot analyse what you see into different features, whereas if you look at Paris, you can; so the sense-impression of Paris, and the idea of Paris which is derived from it are both complex, and the same seems to be true of all other sense-impressions of individuals and of the singular ideas that are derived from them. Now Hume maintained that any idea in a person's mind will be derived in one of two ways from sense-impressions: either it will be a replica of an impression that he has had, or it will be compounded out of other ideas which are replicas of impressions that he has had. A complex idea might enter someone's mind in either of these two ways.[3] For example, someone might have acquired the idea of Paris by actually going there, whereas another person might only have heard the city described, and so might have built up the idea out of its various elements. Of course the description would produce this effect only in the mind of a person who already possessed the elements: for instance, he might have seen streets, and quays, and bridges in other cities. Given this condition, the indirect way of acquiring a complex idea would be effective.

---

[1] *T.H.N.* I.i.1 (vol. 1, p. 14. All page-references are to vol. 1 of the Everyman edition, unless vol. 11 is specified).

[2] *T.H.N.* I.i.1 (p. 14).   [3] *T.H.N.* I.i.1 (p. 13).

Indeed, if the thing in question did not exist, it would be the only possible way in which the idea might enter someone's mind. How else could you get the idea of a winged horse? On the other hand, simple ideas can never enter the mind in the indirect way. The idea of scarlet can only be acquired as a direct copy of an actual impression of the colour itself.

The parallelism between Hume's account of complex ideas and Russell's account of complex symbols hardly needs to be emphasised. Both are contributions to theories of meaning.[4] Both trace the branching lines which have to connect what is meaningful with the experience which gave it its meaning. But there are differences between the two accounts. One difference is that Hume deals not with symbols but with ideas, and it is not quite accurate to call ideas ' meaningful ' or ' meaningless ', because a meaningless idea would hardly count as an idea at all. However, that is not a very important difference, because ideas do have phrases annexed to them, and phrases can be meaningful or meaningless. A more important difference is that Hume claims that, when a phrase is annexed to an idea which is not derived from impressions in either of the two ways that he describes, it follows that it is meaningless : whereas Russell is prepared to allow that part of the meaning of a phrase may be less closely connected with experience, and in such cases he merely observes that he does not know whether anything in reality corresponds to that part of its meaning. Hume, in effect, held a verificationist theory of meaning, while Russell never denied that the meaning of a phrase might go beyond what was verifiable, and, if part of it crossed that line, he merely professed agnosticism about the existence of anything corresponding to that part. This is a considerable difference between the two philosophers' theories

---

[4] This is obvious in Russell's case. In Hume's case it needs to be supported by quotation. ' When he (our author) suspects that any philosophical term has no idea annexed to it (as is too common), he always asks *from what impression that idea is derived*? And if no impression can be produced, he concludes that the term is altogether insignificant.' (*An Abstract of a Treatise of Human Nature, H.TH.KN.,* p. 251).

of meaning. But an even greater difference will become apparent later, when Russell's theory of simple singular symbols is introduced.[5]

Hume did not confine his attention to horizontal analysis. For his opinion about the range of perception was similar to Russell's. Not that their theories of perception are the same. But they have one very important thing in common: Hume believed, as Russell did later, that perception never penetrates beyond the screen of the perceiver's sense-data.[6] Hume called them ' impressions ', and he located them in the mind of the perceiver. He appears to have regarded an impression as a kind of image stamped on the mind. He was not using the word ' impression ' in the way in which it is used in the sentence ' He got the impression that it was scarlet '. He was using it to denote the kind of thing that would have to be qualified by an adjective or adjectival phrase, rather than followed by a substantival clause. This raises an important question about the interpretation of his system: What sort of qualification did he consider appropriate to impressions? When someone looks at something scarlet, would his impression be a scarlet impression or an impression of scarlet? He seems to choose the second alternative when he speaks of impressions ' of colours, tastes, smells, sounds, heat and cold '.[7] But he seems to choose the first alternative when he speaks as if visual ideas actually are colours:[8] for there is no doubt that he regards visual ideas as images which copy visual impressions.[9]

His pessimistic assessment of the range of perception might have led him to a deep analysis of complex phrases like Russell's. For instance, when he had analysed the word ' horse ' horizontally into descriptions of the essential properties of horses, it might have led him to take analysis of these properties down to the level of impressions. But, though

5 See pp. 45-6.
6 *T.H.N.* I.ii.6 (pp. 71-2).
7 *T.H.N.* I.iv.2 (p. 186).
8 *T.H.N.* I.i.6 (p. 24), and I.i.7 footnote (p. 28).
9 *T.H.N.* I.i.1 (p. 12).

he was inclined to follow this route, he was not satisfied with the destination. He thought that the continued and distinct existence of objects in the external world could not be covered by an analysis into impressions. Yet, when he looked for an alternative, all that he could find was the theory that objects are equipped with properties which produce impressions in people, but which are not themselves perceived, because they lie behind the screen of the impressions that they produce. But it seemed to him that it is a fatal objection to this theory that it is unverifiable. So, unable to find a third theory, he concluded that there is no rational defence of our belief in the external world.[10] Russell did not agree.

At this point it is worth remembering that, in order to acquire knowledge, it is not enough merely to receive impressions. Something has to be done with them after they have been received. This applies to any kind of knowledge; it applies to knowledge of the external world, but it applies equally to knowledge of one's own impressions. What still has to be done after impressions have been received is to record them, and that requires a sentence, or, if not a sentence, at least a complete thought. Now it is a peculiarity of Hume's system that it does not include thoughts about impressions that are actually being received. He discusses thoughts about past impressions, which are memories, and he discusses expectations of future impressions. But on the subject of thoughts about present impressions he says nothing. This is a strange omission. He seems to have been so struck by the pictorial character of impressions that he believed that they would reveal their nature immediately. But they do not speak for themselves. We have to describe them, and our descriptions of them may be mistaken.

It is understandable that Hume should omit thoughts about present impressions. For he never worked out an adequate theory of thinking about anything. He excluded complete thoughts from his system, or, rather, he always tried to reduce

[10] *T.H.N.* I.iv.2 (pp. 182-3), and I.i.7 (p. 28).

them to isolated ideas, which are really no more than fragments of thoughts.[11] For instance, when he was discussing expectation, which is one form of belief, he tried to make do with the isolated idea corresponding to the expected impression. It is evident that in this kind of theory of thinking there is no room for thoughts about present impressions. For according to it the whole point of an idea is to represent an impression, and it would be superfluous to have an idea representing a present impression. The idea could not do anything that had not already been done by the impression. However, the theory is clearly inadequate. A proper theory of thinking would show that the idea could do something more than the present impression. It could be part of the thought which contained the person's description of his impression. For instance, he might say to himself that it was an impression of scarlet.

Hume's theory of expectation is free from this particular difficulty. For the idea of the expected impression comes first, and so it does have a function even in his system.[12] However, the theory will not do. If someone expects an impression of scarlet, Hume would say that he has an idea of scarlet in his mind. But there is nothing in his theory to explain how that idea gets its reference to the future. An explanation of this point would have to start with an examination of complete thoughts and not with isolated ideas. Here again the trouble is that Hume credits pictures with powers which they do not really possess. For his ideas are images,[13] and images are pictures, and pictures are not really articulate. Pictures have no tense.

Incidentally, the pictorial character of ideas in Hume's system gives him some difficulty when he tries to distinguish a belief about the future from a mere supposition about the future. He sometimes seems to say that, when a person expects an impression, his idea will be more vivid than when he merely supposes, for the sake of argument, that he will

[11] *T.H.N.* I.iii.7 footnote (p. 98).
[12] *T.H.N.* I.iii.7 and 8 (p. 96ff).   [13] *T.H.N.* I.i.7 (p. 28).

receive an impression.[14] But that cannot be right. For any difference in the idea would produce a difference in the content of the thought, and so could not serve to distinguish a thought which was a belief from a thought which was a mere supposition. For example, an idea of a dull red might quite well be part of a belief that an impression of dull red was about to be received. The dullness of the idea would not necessarily show that the thought was a mere supposition. Hume is aware of this difficulty, and he circumvents it by using the concept of strength in order to distinguish between an idea of belief and an idea of supposition. That is to say, his considered view is that an idea of belief is stronger and more masterful, and imposes itself on the person's mind.[15] The interesting thing is that, when an idea or image is called 'strong' in this sense, its strength is not one of its pictorial properties any more than the attachment of a painting to the wall of a museum is a pictorial property of the painting.

This sketch of Hume's system is very incomplete. His views on several important topics have not even been mentioned. There will be occasions to mention some of them later in the course of the exposition of Russell's philosophy. Meanwhile enough has been said to illustrate the main deficiency in Hume's system, which, as we shall soon see, Russell was to remedy. Its main deficiency was that it did not contain complete thoughts, but only isolated ideas. Or, to put the same point linguistically, it did not allow for sentences, but only for phrases. It was non-propositional.

[14] *T.H.N.* I.iii.7 (p. 98).   [15] *T.H.N.* I.iii.7 (p. 99).

CHAPTER III

RUSSELL'S VIEWS ABOUT
SENSE-DATA

Something must now be said about Russell's views about
sense-data. For, according to him, sense-data are the ultimate
sources both of meaning and of truth, or, if we look at the
matter from a slightly different angle, both of understanding
and of knowledge. So it is necessary to discover what
Russell thought a sense-datum is.

The phrase 'sense-datum' has been used by different
philosophers to denote very different things. The common
factor in its meaning is 'what is given by the senses', which
is contrasted with 'what is inferred'. For instance, one of
the two views about the external world which Hume rejected
was the view that the causes of our impressions, which, unlike
the impressions themselves, are not given by the senses, can
nevertheless be legitimately inferred. This common factor in
the meaning of the phrase 'sense-datum' allows it to be
applied to very different kinds of things. Indeed, what is
given by the senses may not really be any kind of thing at all.
What is given might be how things look to you, or how they
sound to you, and so on for the other senses. If a philosopher
used the phrase 'sense-datum' in this way, he would be
following one of the two uses of the word 'impression', the
use which requires a substantival clause. As a matter of fact,
this was the way in which A. J. Ayer often used the phrase
'sense-datum' in *The Foundations of Empirical Knowledge*.[1]
As so used, it does not really denote any kind of thing. Or, at

[1] See *The Foundations of Empirical Knowledge*, p. 25 and pp.
58-9.

least, it does not denote any kind of thing which could be classified as mental or physical.[2] The phrase ' sense-datum ' is a sort of atrophied noun, and it gets its meaning by inclusion in the larger phrase, ' sense-datum proposition '.[3]

But this is a late development, and it would be quite wrong to see it in the writings of 18th-century philosophers.[4] Hume, as has been said, used the word ' impression ' to denote a kind of thing which, according to him, exists in the mind, and which can be described by adjectival phrases derived from our ordinary descriptions of objects in the external world. Now the phrase ' sense-datum ' is often used in just this way. But it can also be used to denote other, different kinds of things. Sense-data might be physical things. For instance, they might be parts of the surfaces of material objects, or waves of light or sound, or even things in the nervous system of the observer. When the phrase ' sense-datum ' really does denote things, the only restriction on its application is that it must denote things which might plausibly be regarded as the only things that are ever really given to us by the senses.

Throughout the period during which Russell believed in the existence of sense-data, a period which extends down to 1919,[5] and so includes *The Philosophy of Logical Atomism*, he consistently regarded them as physical entities. He found the opposite view, that they are located in the mind, both stuffy and implausible. It seemed to him to be the result of a confusion of which Berkeley was guilty, the confusion between the thing that is perceived and the perceiving of it.[6] The perceiving does take place in the mind, but the thing that is perceived, the sense-datum itself, is located in the nervous

[2] *Loc. cit.* pp. 75-7.

[3] cf. G. A. Paul's paper ' *Is there a Problem about Sense-data?* ' *Aristotelian Society*, Supplementary Proceedings, 1936 (reprinted in *Logic and Language* [*First Series*], ed. A. G. N. Flew).

[4] Berkeley is sometimes interpreted in this way: e.g. by G. J. Warnock, *Berkeley*, ch. viii.

[5] See *M.PH.D.* p. 134ff and *O.P.* (*L.KN.* pp. 305-6).

[6] *P. of PH.* pp. 38-43.

system. So Russell's theory of sense-data differs from Hume's. While he agrees with Hume's view that our senses do not reach out as far into the external world as we ordinarily suppose, he does not think that their range is quite as restricted as Hume thought. They do reach outside the mind of the observer.

However, it is not so easy to see what Russell thinks their immediate target is. What kind of physical things did he take sense-data to be? He seems to have thought of them as events in the nervous system of the observer. That is to say, they are not things inside his mind, like Hume's impressions, but occurrences just outside his mind. But what sort of occurrences are they? The answer that he gives is that they are appearances. Perhaps the sense of sight provides the best illustration of what he means by this equation of occurrences in a human nervous system with appearances. An exploding star propagates light and colour in all directions. At every point in space to which this light penetrates there will be an appearance of a red flash. Now, according to Russell, an observer does not know exactly what those appearances are like at the places that are not enclosed by his own nervous system.[7] But at one place, the place that is enclosed by his own nervous system, he does know what the appearance of the red flash is like : it is the result which is produced for his inspection after the light-rays have struck his retinae and their effects have been scrambled in his optic nerves. This result is a sense-datum, and according to Russell it is a patch of colour.[8] When he is explaining this difficult theory, he says ' What I mean may perhaps be made plainer by saying that, if my body could remain in exactly the same state in which it is, although my mind had ceased to exist, precisely that object which I now see when I see the flash would exist, although of course I should not see it, since my seeing is mental.'[9] In

[7] R.S.-D.PH. (M. and L. p. 150).
[8] P. of PH. p. 46 and R.S.-D.PH. (M. and L. p. 147).
[9] U.C.M. (M. and L. p. 131).

that case Russell would not call the object a 'sense-datum', because there would be no mind to which it could be given. Rather, it would be the sort of thing which *could* be sensed, a '*sensibile*'. But what about the appearances of the red flash at places where there is not even a human nervous system? They too, according to Russell, are *sensibilia*, but it is important to notice that these *sensibilia* are twice removed from being actually sensed. For not only is there no human mind at the places where they occur; there is not even a human nervous system.[10]

This theory of sense-data bristles with difficulties. Of course, Russell does not think it possible for a human nervous system to remain in exactly the same state even though the mind has ceased to exist. But the trouble is that his description of the situation which would arise, if that impossible thing happened, is itself questionable. He makes it sound so like removing one's eye from the view-finder of a camera. No doubt human vision does work somewhat like photography. But does the analogy extend to what happens on your side of your retinae? Can an event in your nervous system really *be* a colour? Certainly the event would be what happened when a colour appeared to you, and *in that sense* it might be the appearance of a colour. But at this point we might use Russell's own argument, and distinguish between the appearance of what appears and its appearing. Surely only the appearing can be an event, and what is seen is the appearance in *the other sense* of that word. The effect of this distinction seems to be to put the appearance back in the world beyond the observer's retinae, and to destroy the idea that there is a kind of camera built into his brain. Russell says that he does not know that appearances at places where there are no human nervous systems are like appearances at places where there are human nervous systems. But perhaps what he ought to have said is that, if the word 'appearance' is used in such a way that an

[10] *R.S.-D.PH.* (*M. and L.* p. 150).

appearance can be seen, then it is unintelligible to suggest that appearances of things in the external world are located inside the nervous system of the observer, so that we need not even enquire whether appearances at places where there are no human nervous systems are like appearances at places where there are human nervous systems.

Perhaps the most surprising feature of his theory is that, in spite of everything else that he says about sense-data, he maintains that they are such things as patches of colour. It is not necessary, and perhaps it is hardly fair to ask how a patch of colour could be absorbed into the nervous system of the observer. For he evidently means that perceiving colours is no more than experiencing certain events in one's afferent nerves. When he equates sense-data both with appearances and with those events, he is merely making this point in an epigrammatic way. However, the analysis of the word 'appearance' reveals that the literal meaning of the epigram is only that a person who sees the colour scarlet is really experiencing an event in his own nervous system which is the appearing of that colour to him. Obviously the appearing cannot itself be scarlet. Indeed, it seems to be generally true that, whatever sense-data are taken to be, provided only that they are things inside the observer, the vocabulary for describing them cannot be the same as the vocabulary for describing things in the external world, although, of course, the two vocabularies will be connected with one another. Hume was half aware of this. For he was inclined to think that, when a person looks at something scarlet, his impression, which, according to him, would be in the mind, would be an impression of scarlet.[11] There really does not seem to be any room in a theory like Russell's for the assertion that sense-data are things like patches of colour. Yet he certainly makes it.[12]

[11] See p. 28.

[12] cf. Wittgenstein's remark: 'But don't we at least *mean* something quite definite when we look at a colour and name our colour-impression? It is as if we detached the colour-*impression* from the object, like a membrane. (This ought to arouse our suspicions.)' *PH.I.* § 276.

These doubts about Russell's theory of sense-data will not be developed here. Enough has been said to indicate the kind of place where he wanted to site the foundations of empirical knowledge. His next task was to show that these foundations would support a sufficiently comprehensive reconstruction. Now descriptions of objects in the external world will look very new and strange when they have been analysed into descriptions of sense-data. But Russell was prepared for this. In general, the use of Ockham's razor to pare away illicit elements in popular ideas is likely to produce an unfamiliar result. This may seem paradoxical, because the result is supposed to be an account of what we always meant. But a philosopher who undertakes this kind of analysis will not be surprised. For he only tries to capture the legitimate element in what we always meant.

Russell had his own version of Ockham's maxim: 'Wherever possible, logical constructions are to be substituted for inferred entities'. He calls this 'the supreme maxim in scientific philosophising'.[13] It is explained and illustrated both in *The Philosophy of Logical Atomism*[14] and in *Logical Atomism*.[15] The reason why he called certain things 'logical constructions' was that the legitimate meanings of the phrases which denoted them had to be constructed by a logical method out of descriptions whose meanings could be learned directly from experience, and the correctness of whose application could sometimes be known. In the case of objects in the external world the descriptions used in the construction were descriptions of sense-data. The reason why these logical constructions had to be substituted for the inferred entities has already been given. It is that any inference which went beyond sense-data could never be known to be correct. Of course, if the phrase in question were only given a horizontal analysis, nobody would feel any temptation to infer the

---

[13] *R.S.-D.PH.* (*M. and L.* p. 155).
[14] *PH.L.A.* p. 58ff (*L.KN.* p. 270ff).
[15] *L.A.* p. 362ff (*L.KN.* p. 326ff).

existence of an entity beyond the elements mentioned in the analysis : for instance, nobody would be tempted to infer that a horse is anything more than a creature with the right essential properties. But when a phrase is given a deep analysis, we are tempted to make an inference which goes beyond the basic elements, and which could never be known to be correct : for instance, when descriptions of objects in the external world are analysed into descriptions of sense-data, we are apt to feel dissatisfied, and inclined to infer the existence of entities beyond them. The point of substituting logical constructions for inferred entities is simply to get rid of the surplus part of the meaning of the phrase, the part which encourages the inference that can never be known to be correct.

When Russell calls his logical constructions ' fictions ', he does not mean that we only pretend that they exist. For instance, he does not mean that we only pretend that objects in the external world exist. That would be absurd. What he means is that the belief that they exist in anything more than the sense allowed by his parsimonious analysis is mistaken. But unfortunately, this explanation of his views about existence, which was given in Chapter I,[16] is not quite complete, and something must now be added to it.

He had an additional reason for thinking that things like objects in the external world have a rather inferior kind of existence. His additional reason was that their existence is fragmentary. It is necessary to keep this point distinct from the point about deep analyses which has just been discussed, and it is difficult to keep it distinct, because it arises directly out of it. Consider again the deep analysis of the phrase ' object in the external world ' into descriptions of sense-data. This analysis has two effects. The first effect, which has just been discussed, is that the surplus part of the meaning of the phrase is abandoned. The second effect, which is distinct, is that the existence of objects in the external world is shown to be fragmentary. Such objects are really only col-

[16] See pp. 18-22.

lections of sense-data which occur serially and separately.[17]

But, we might ask, what is inferior about such a fragmentary kind of existence? It is difficult to find a precise answer to this question, but Russell seems to have been influenced by two ideas. The first is the idea that the existence of a composite whole is dependent on the existence of its elements, and to that extent inferior. The second, which is prominent in Hume's *Treatise*,[18] is the idea that the most perfect form of existence requires the most perfect form of identity, which is only to be found in cases where time introduces no changes in the composition of the things in question. For instance, sense-data exist so briefly that time has no chance to introduce changes. Indeed, they are defined in such a way that anything which might be taken to be a change in a sense-datum has to be interpreted as the replacement of that sense-datum by another.[19] Anyway, whatever the exact reason for Russell's grading of the different ways in which composite wholes and their elements exist, there is no doubt that it gave him an additional motive for saying that things like objects in the external world do not really exist.

Let us now return to his attempt to get rid of inferences, and examine it more closely. Naturally he did not want to purge our knowledge of objects in the external world of all inference. He only wanted to get rid of inferences that would lift us above the level of sense-data, because he thought that they could never be known to be correct. But that leaves us with all our ordinary perceptual inferences, like the inference from what I see here today to what I shall see if I return to this place tomorrow. However, his reconstruction of empirical knowledge changes the nature of these ordinary inferences. He makes them safe by interpreting them as inferences which

---

[17] *PH.L.A.* pp. 8-9 (*L.K.N.* pp. 190-1), p. 47 (*L.KN.* p. 253), pp. 58-60 (*L.KN.* pp. 268-74).

[18] *T.H.N.* I.iv.6 (p. 239ff).

[19] cf. the discussion at the end of lecture II of *PH.L.A.*, pp. 16-17 (L.KN. p. 203).

never rise above the level of sense-data, and by discarding their surplus meaning. But there is a difficulty here. Whose sense-data are meant? Now he makes it clear that he is not thinking only of his own sense-data, as a solipsist would. He also allows himself to use other people's sense-data in the construction of the external world.[20] But in that case, when two people talk to one another, each will be saying things whose meaning has been derived from his own sense-data. How then will they succeed in communicating with one another? Each would have to know what the other's sense-data had been like. But that raises the notorious problems of other minds and private languages.[21]

Even if the foundations of empirical knowledge include other people's sense-data, it is still questionable whether the load will be spread sufficiently widely. Russell was inclined to think that an adequate reconstruction would require the inclusion of unsensed *sensibilia* as well as sense-data.[22] Of course, he was not thinking of the kind of unsensed *sensibilia* which are events in human nervous systems without minds, since, as has already been explained, it is impossible for the conditions for the existence of such unsensed *sensibilia* to be realised. He was thinking of the kind of unsensed *sensibilia* which are events in places where there are no human nervous systems. Now suppose that those events are like the events that occur in people's nervous systems, and that both are properly called 'appearances'. Doubts have already been raised about this supposition, but let us now make it. It is

---

[20] *M.PH.D.* pp. 104-5; cf. *R.S.-D.PH.* (*M.andL.* p. 157).

[21] See pp. 78-82 and p. 136. Russell takes the problem of communication rather lightly on pp. 11-12 of *PH.L.A.* (*L.KN.* pp. 195-6). He never raises the more fundamental question, whether a person could succeed in establishing a private language solely for his own use in recording his sense-data. Wittgenstein later argued that this is impossible (*PH.I. passim*: see P. F. Strawson's review of *PH.I.*, *Mind*, January 1954, N. Malcolm's review, *Philosophical Review*, October 1954, and J. J. Thomson's article '*Private Languages*', *American Philosophical Quarterly*, March 1965).

[22] *R.S.-D.PH.* (*M. and L.* pp. 157-8).

then clear why Russell allowed himself to include unsensed *sensibilia* in his foundations. For, given the supposition, they are intrinsically exactly like sense-data. They could have been sensed, and the only difference between them and sense-data is that they happen not to have been sensed. However, Russell was worried by this difference, and he did try to reduce the area of his foundations so as not to include unsensed *sensibilia*.[23] Perhaps this is why they are not mentioned in *The Philosophy of Logical Atomism.*

No account of Russell's theory of sense-data would be complete without an explanation of his later abandonment of it.[24] He abandoned it because he ceased to regard sensation as an affair between a subject and an object. This was not because he changed his mind about the object. He continued to hold the same view about what is sensed. But he ceased to regard being sensed as being *given*, because he came to think that the ego, to which what is sensed would have to be given if it were given, is itself a logical construction. Indeed, the ego has to be analysed into a series of events which actually include the appearances which were supposed to be given to it. Hence he concludes that what we sense cannot be given, and so cannot be data.

Even in *The Problems of Philosophy*[25] he is not sure that knowledge of the ego is anything more than knowledge of its history. Hume had categorically denied that it is anything more, and had even hinted that it would be unintelligible to assert that it is.[26] In 1918, when Russell wrote *The Philosophy of Logical Atomism*, he was no longer inclined to assert it, and professed agnosticism about any surplus meaning in the word 'ego'.[27] Then in 1919, in his article *On Propositions*,[28] he explicitly says that the ego is a logical construction. The result is very strange. His theory of sense-data had flattened the external world against the window-pane of perception, but

23 *O.KN.E.W.* pp. 116-17.   24 *M.PH.D.* pp. 134-5.
25 *P. of PH.* pp. 50-1.   26 *T.H.N. I.iv.* 6 (p. 238).
27 *PH.L.A.* p. 62 (*L.KN.* p. 277).
28 *O.P.* (*L.KN.* pp. 305-6).

at least it had left a detached observer within. But now the observer too vanished into the glass, and the world became a transparent wafer.[29] This led to further developments in his theory of perception, which will be described later.[30]

[29] The wafer is made out of things which Russell regarded as homogeneous, namely thoughts, sensa and unsensed *sensibilia*. According to him, these things are in themselves neither mental nor physical, but neutral between the two categories. Cut one way, the wafer yields the psychological histories of people. Cut another way, it yields the physical histories of objects in the external world. But in itself it is homogeneous and neutral. This is why the theory is called Neutral Monism. It was propounded by William James in 1904 in his article *'Does "consciousness" exist?'* (*Essays in Radical Empiricism*, p. 1ff). Russell had opposed it for 14 years before finally accepting it. On p. 28 of *PH.L.A.* (*L.KN.* p. 222) he gives one of his main reasons for opposing it, a reason which is set out more fully in the paper to which he there refers, *O.N.A.* (*L.KN.* pp. 168-9). After he had accepted the theory he developed it in his book *A.M.* (1921). For further discussion of this topic, see p. 135 footnote 41.

[30] See Ch. XI.

CHAPTER IV

RUSSELL'S LOGICAL APPARATUS

So far little has been said about Russell's reason for calling his method of reconstruction 'logical'. Allusion has been made to his logical apparatus, but its nature has not yet been explained. Perhaps the best way to understand its nature is to trace its development out of Hume's earlier psychological apparatus. In the first two chapters this line of development was traced up to a certain point, and it is now necessary to follow it through to the end. First, let us mark the point which was reached earlier. Hume lists three kinds of ideas : an idea may be general and complex, like the idea of a dragon, or the idea of a horse : or it may be general and simple, like the idea of scarlet; or it may be singular and complex, like the idea of the city of Paris. Russell classifies the three phrases which are annexed to these three kinds of idea in an exactly parallel way. The first is a complex general symbol, the second is a simple general symbol and the third is a complex singular symbol.

This classification of Russell's is, of course, a logical one. For symbols are classified as complex if they are definable, and as simple if they are indefinable, and definition is a logical operation. It is interesting to observe that Hume was aware that his classification of ideas was really a logical one. For he says that, when a complex idea is taken apart, the result will be a definition which enumerates the simple ideas out of which it was compounded.[1] He even goes on to compare this kind of analysis to microscopy, introducing the very analogy which suggested the title *The Philosophy of Logical Atomism*

[1] *An Enquiry Concerning Human Understanding*, § VII, pt. i. (ed. Selby-Bigge, p. 62).

to Russell.[2] However, Russell's use of definition is more
explicit and more sophisticated than Hume's. It is more
explicit, because Russell works with language, and on the
whole avoids entanglement in questions of psychology. It is
more sophisticated because he does not think that every
definition of a phrase provides an analysis of it. For instance,
in *The Philosophy of Logical Atomism* he says that, though
it is correct to define ' red ' as ' the colour with the greatest
wave-length ', this definition does not provide an analysis of
the word.[3] His reason for saying this is that an analysis gives
the meaning of a word, or at least the legitimate part of its
meaning, and, since the average person who uses the word
' red ' knows nothing about the physical theory of colour, a
definition based on that theory cannot have anything to do
with the meaning that the word has for him.

More will be said later about this distinction between those
definitions which provide analyses and those which do not.[4]
The point to be emphasised now is that one thing which makes
Russell's method a logical one is that he relies on definition,
which is a logical operation. He relies on the kind of definition which gives the meaning, or at least the legitimate part
of the meaning, of the phrase in question, as it is actually
used. He had high hopes of this method, because he thought
that it would provide firm and precise results instead of the
customary vague intuitions and spongy opinions which are to
be found in most philosophical books. He belongs to the long
line of European philosophers who have tried to improve
philosophical method by making it more like scientific
method.[5]

[2] *PH.L.A.* p. 1 (*L.KN.* p. 178).
[3] *PH.L.A.* p. 11 (*L.KN.* pp. 194-5).
[4] See pp. 47-8, pp. 139-40, pp. 147-51.
[5] e.g. the full title of *O.KN.E.W.* is *Our Knowledge of the External
World as a Field for Scientific Method in Philosophy*. Ch. II, which
is entitled ' *Logic as the Essence of Philosophy* ', ends with the following manifesto: ' The old logic put thought in fetters, while the new
logic gives it wings. It has, in my opinion, introduced the same kind

It is now necessary to go beyond the point that was reached in the first two chapters. The crucial step is Russell's introduction of simple singular symbols. In Chapter II it was remarked that Hume refused to allow the existence of simple singular ideas. The explanation which was given of his refusal was that, if you look at the colour scarlet, you cannot analyse what you see into different features, whereas, if you look at the city of Paris, you can : so the impression of Paris is complex, and therefore the idea of Paris will be complex too, and this seems to apply to all other singular impressions and to the singular ideas that are derived from them. Now Russell agreed with the first part of this conclusion, but not with the second part. His agreement with the first part of it is evident in the passage in *The Philosophy of Logical Atomism* where he says that the name 'Piccadilly' is definable,[6] and therefore a complex symbol. It is also evident in the important passage in which he treats proper names of people in a similar way.[7] He says that a proper name of a person ' is really a sort of truncated or telescoped description', and that, if you want to draw out what someone means when he uses the proper name, you must discover how he would describe the person, and then substitute that description for the proper name : for example, the name ' Moses' might be replaced by the description ' the person who, as a child, was found by Pharaoh's daughter in a floating cradle '. But Russell did not agree with the second part of the conclusion given above. He did not agree that all singular symbols are complex. Some of

---

of advance into philosophy as Galileo introduced into physics, making it possible at last to see what kinds of problems are capable of solution, and what kinds must be abandoned as beyond human powers. And where a solution appears possible, the new logic provides a method which enables us to obtain results that do not merely embody personal idiosyncrasies, but must command the assent of all who are competent to form an opinion.' (pp. 68-9).

[6] *PH.L.A.* p. 9 (*L.KN.* p. 191).

[7] *PH.L.A.* p. 41 (*L.KN.* p. 243).

them, he thought, are simple, and he called these simple
singular symbols 'logically proper names'.[8]

This is a difficult doctrine. It appears to mean that a symbol
might be applied to a particular thing without picking up any
descriptions of that thing in the way in which the name
'Moses' picks up descriptions of the man. But how could it
avoid picking up descriptions? How could the person who
used the symbol fail to have some description in mind? Yet,
if he did, that would make his symbol complex, just as it
makes the name 'Moses' complex. A hint of a solution to
this problem of interpretation is contained in something that
Russell says in *The Philosophy of Logical Atomism*,[9] if that
passage is read together with a parallel passage in his paper
On the Nature of Acquaintance.[10] In the first of the two
passages he says that, when the word 'this' is applied to a
sense-datum, it is a logically proper name. In the second he
says that it would be wrong to suppose that in such a case the
word "'this' *means* 'the object to which I am now attending.'": and then he goes on to explain that "'this' is not
waiting to be defined by the property of being given, but is
given; first it is actually given, and then reflection shows that
it is that which is given." His point is that, in such a case,
whatever we say about the denotation of the word 'this' will
be expressed in a proposition, even if we only say that it is
given, and this proposition must have a sense, and it will have
a sense only if the word already denotes something, quite
independently of anything that might be said about the thing
that it denotes. That is to say, when the word 'this' is a
logically proper name applied to a sense-datum, its denotation
must exist with an intrinsic nature of its own, which is independent of, and prior to anything that is said about it.
Russell calls the denotation of a logically proper name a 'particular'. Since the intrinsic nature of a particular does not
include anything that can be said about it, it cannot be put

[8] *PH.L.A.* pp. 14-15 (*L.KN.* pp. 200-1).
[9] *PH.L.A.* p. 15 (*L.KN.* p. 201).   [10] *O.N.A.* (*L.KN.* p. 168).

into words, but only named.[11] As he remarks, his particulars are very like the individual substances of traditional philosophy.[12]

There is one point about this line of thought which needs to be emphasised before anything more is said about it. By itself it could not lead to the conclusion that the word 'this' denotes something intrinsically simple, even when it refers to one of your sense-data. The most that it could prove is that in such a case *you have to treat its denotation as if it were simple*. To put this point more plainly, the most that it could prove is that in such a case, if you were to say everything that you could say about your sense-datum, you would have to treat it as the unanalysable subject of everything that you had said. But it does not follow that another person might not have been able to say more about it, perhaps because his powers of discrimination were greater than yours. If that were a possibility, what you had had to treat as simple would not be intrinsically simple.

Russell does not appear to have denied this. For, as we shall see later, the most likely interpretation of his doctrine is that there are singular symbols whose denotations we have to treat as simple, whether or not they are intrinsically simple. His parallel doctrine, that there are simple general symbols, should be interpreted in the same way. At least this seems to be the implication of his remarks about the physical theory of colour which have already been mentioned.[13] For, if the word 'red' can be defined as 'the colour with the greatest wavelength', then, although this definition is not in fact an

---

[11] *R.S.-D.PH.* (*M. and L.* p. 147). The logical point which Russell makes in this important passage is also made by Wittgenstein, *T.L.-PH.* 3.221. In that passage Wittgenstein presents it in an entirely general way, without any reference to sense-data. See pp. 152-3.

[12] *PH.L.A.* p. 17 (*L.KN.* p. 203). The version of Russell's argument for 'particulars' which is given here will have to be generalised later, so that it will also apply to the sort of case in which a complex individual is analysed into a set of 'particulars'. See pp. 122-3.

[13] See p. 44.

analysis of the word, it could *become* its analysis. All that is
needed is that there should be creatures endowed with greater
powers of discrimination than we possess, so that, when they
looked at something red, their visual apparatus would achieve
what we can achieve only with the aid of scientific instruments. Now Russell's logical atomism is the combination of
the two theses, that there are simple singular symbols, and
that there are simple general symbols. So, if the interpretation of them which has just been suggested is correct, his
logical atoms would not be unsplittable, although we have to
treat them as if they were unsplittable. This interpretation
will be defended later.[14]

Russell's thesis that there are simple general symbols may be
temporarily shelved, so that we may concentrate on his thesis
that there are simple singular symbols. In order to understand this thesis properly, we need a fuller account of his
logical apparatus. In particular, we need to understand his
Theory of Definite Descriptions. But, before that theory is
explained, it is necessary to guard against a well known
source of misunderstanding in Russell's exposition. The
trouble is that he explains the theory on the level of objects
in the external world, and then uses it in a more recondite
way, which ultimately takes him down to the deeper level of
sense-data. When he is talking in a popular way, he treats
people and objects in the external world as if they were simple
entities : or, to use his terminology, he treats them as if they
were particulars, and he treats ordinary proper names as if
they were logically proper names. For example, in *The Philosophy of Logical Atomism* he sometimes treats Sir Walter
Scott as if he were a simple entity.[15] He does so in order to
explain the difference between the ordinary proper name
'Scott' and the definite description 'the author of Waverley'.
He is giving a preliminary explanation of this contrast as it
exists in our everyday language about the external world. His

[14] In Ch. VIII and Ch. IX.
[15] e.g., *PH.L.A.* pp. 42-3 (*L.KN.* pp. 244-6).

point is that we often do treat people and objects in the external world as if they were simple entities. But, as we have seen, he does not think that Scott is an entity that has to be treated as simple, and he marks the provisional character of this part of his exposition by saying that, though ' Scott ' is not really a name, it can be used as a name.[16] He means that, though the ordinary proper name ' Scott ' is not a logically proper name, it can be used as if it were a logically proper name. That is to say, sometimes when a person uses the name ' Scott ' *he will be thinking of its actual denotation directly without the intervention of any descriptions: in his thought the denotation will not be split up into its elements.*

Let us add this complication to the distinction that was drawn just now between singular symbols whose denotations are intrinsically simple and singular symbols whose denotations have to be treated by us as simple, whether or not they are intrinsically simple. The result is a three-fold classification of singular symbols. There are singular symbols whose denotations are known by us to be complex, and the point that has just been made is that Russell allows that we may on occasion treat the denotations of these symbols as if they were simple; there are singular symbols whose denotations have to be treated by us as simple, whether or not they are intrinsically simple; and there are singular symbols whose denotations really are intrinsically simple. The last two classes may overlap, because a denotation which has to be treated by us as simple may in fact be intrinsically simple. This three-fold classification of singular symbols must be borne in mind throughout this chapter and the next five.

The first step towards understanding definite descriptions like ' the author of Waverley ' is to notice that they are explicitly complex, whereas ordinary proper names are only implicitly complex. Indeed, as we have just seen, an ordinary proper name, in spite of the fact that it is a complex symbol, can sometimes be used to denote a person directly without the intervention of any descriptions. Naturally, this special use of

[16] *PH.L.A.* p. 43 (*L.KN.* p. 246).

an ordinary proper name, in which it masquerades as a logically proper name, would be impossible if the person did not
exist. So it looks as if the crucial question about a complex
symbol is the question what happens when the thing which it
aims at denoting does not exist. For instance, what happens
to the definite description 'the daughter of Hitler'? Now,
as was pointed out in Chapter I, this question must be
answered in a way that allows us to understand how the phrase
acquired a meaning. It is no good saying that, if the daughter
of Hitler does not exist, she subsists in the other world.
Russell says that 'a vivid sense of reality' ought to prevent
us from accepting such a thesis. That is true. But the real
objection to it is that it is absolutely useless as an explanation.

The explanation which he suggests is that, though the
definite description looks as if it has to denote an entity, it
really entails a proposition, the proposition that Hitler had one
daughter. Of course, if this proposition happens to be true,
the definite description will succeed in denoting the entity
which it aims at denoting, namely Hitler's only daughter. But
his point is that this success is not necessary in order that the
definite description should have a meaning. All that is necessary is that the elements out of which it was compounded
should have denotations. Now, since it entails a proposition,
in this case the proposition that Hitler had one daughter, the
elements which constitute this proposition will be the elements
out of which it was compounded. So if it has a meaning in
spite of the fact that the thing which it aims at denoting does
not exist, the explanation will be that it acquired its meaning
from the denotations of the elements that constitute the proposition which it entails.

It is hardly necessary to emphasise that Russell was not
merely trying to rid himself of the superstition that Hitler's
daughter must enjoy a shadowy existence like Homer's dead
heroes, or, rather, like his living heroes. He was trying to give
a precise and adequate explanation of the fact that the definite
description has a meaning in spite of the fact that, taken as a

whole, it has no denotation. What does very much need to be emphasised is his apparently insignificant point that under analysis the definite description expands into an entailed proposition. This is really the most important feature of his theory.[17]

In order to see how important it is, let us recall Hume's version of atomism. His version was criticised because it did not allow for complete thoughts, but only for isolated ideas; or, to put the same point linguistically, because it did not allow for sentences, but only for phrases. Hume described the elements which constitute propositions without ever putting them together to make propositions, rather as if someone told us everything about cog-wheels except how they work. What Russell did was to transform this static system into a dynamic one, in which the elements are actually connected up and functioning in propositions.

Perhaps this has not been made very clear in the account so far given of Russell's Theory of Definite Descriptions. For in the preliminary remarks about existence definite descriptions were introduced as if they were isolated phrases. The motive for introducing them in that way was to make the connection with Hume's atomism, and to show how Russell's atomism developed out of it. But the additional point about Russell's theory which has just been emphasised is enough to bring out the dynamic character of his system. That point is that, according to him, a definite description entails a proposition, and it could hardly do that unless it occurred in another proposition. That is to say, the definite description ' the daughter of Hitler ' could hardly entail that Hitler had one daughter unless it occurred in another proposition, perhaps in the proposition that the daughter of Hitler is a soprano. For entailment is a relationship that holds between propositions.

So Russell's analysis of definite descriptions is an analysis of the complete propositions in which they occur. Part of it has already been given. It is that the proposition that the

[17] *PH.L.A.* p. 3 (*L.KN.* p. 182), p. 41 (*L.KN.* p. 243).

daughter of Hitler is a soprano entails that Hitler had one daughter. The other part is, of course, that the proposition entails that she is a soprano. Taken together, these two entailments exhaust the meaning of the original proposition. This account of Russell's Theory of Definite Description is still not sufficiently exact.[18] But it does bring out the most important point about the theory, which is a point about the first part of the analysis. Because Russell examines definite descriptions in their place in propositions, and actually functioning, he is able to give an account of them which is a great improvement on Hume's account of singular complex phrases. He is not forced to analyse the singular phrase ' the daughter of Hitler ' in exactly the same way as the general words ' soprano ' or ' dragon '. When he traces the meaning of the phrase ' the daughter of Hitler ' back to its roots in our experience, he finds a new kind of complexity. He is led back to elements which are already combined to form a proposition. Hume had treated all complex phrases as static blocks, and so it never occurred to him that some of them might actually contain the life and movement of propositions. It was Russell's dynamic analysis that suggested this possibility to him. Now a singular phrase, if it succeeds in denoting, will denote a thing, and a proposition, if it is true, will correspond to a fact. So the point on which Russell improved Hume's account of singular complex phrases can be presented as a point about things and facts. ' The analysis of apparently com-

---

[18] Three things have to be done in order to make it exact. First, an account of Russell's analysis of existence is needed: this is given in Ch. v. Secondly, his analysis of the stipulation of uniqueness has to be explained: the explanation is given in Ch. xiv. The third requirement is an account of his logical symbolism, which, in the final analysis, welds all the entailments of a proposition like ' The daughter of Hitler is a soprano' together again to form a single proposition. This third task will not be undertaken, because it would involve the introduction of logical symbolism, which is something that is avoided throughout this book. The final welding together and reconstruction as a single proposition can be seen in *O.D.* (*L.KN.* p. 44).

plex *things* such as we started with ' [Piccadilly, Rumania, Twelfth Night and Socrates] ' can be reduced, by various means, to the analysis of facts which are apparently about those things. Therefore it is with the analysis of facts that one's consideration of the problem of complexity must begin, and not with the analysis of apparently complex things '.[19]

[19] *PH.L.A.* p. 9 (*L.KN.* p. 192).

THE FORMAL TREATMENT OF EXISTENCE

The next thing to be done is to give a more precise account of Russell's Theory of Definite Descriptions. This will require an explanation of his treatment of the idea of existence. For the first part of his analysis of definite descriptions really uses the idea of existence. Perhaps this is not obvious when the first part is presented in the way in which it has just been presented. We do not actually use the verb ' to exist ' when we say that the proposition that the daughter of Hitler is a soprano entails that Hitler had one daughter. But what this entailment means is that the daughter of Hitler exists. So the first part of Russell's analysis uses the idea of existence, and his treatment of existence must now be explained.

As usual, it is instructive to start from Hume's account of the same idea. Hume's account was dominated by a very striking fact about existence, the fact that, if it is considered as a property of things, it does not seem to make any difference to them. Of course, a thing may be non-existent, but in that case we cannot say that there is a thing which lacks the property of existence, because there is no thing. Nor can we say, when a thing does exist, that its existence makes a difference to it, because it was not there waiting for existence to be added to it like a coat of paint. In short, if existence is considered as a property of things, it seems to suffer from a kind of inconspicuousness, which, given the importance of existing, is rather peculiar. Hume was very struck by this inconspicuousness of the idea of existence. ' To reflect on anything simple,' he says, ' and to reflect on it as existent are nothing different from one another. The idea of existence, when con-

joined with the idea of any object, makes no addition to it.'[1]
The original impressions from which the idea of the object
was derived did not include a separate impression of existence.
There might be impressions of its shape and of its colour, but
its existence would be something which would not appear
separately on the screen of impressions.

However, the inconspicuousness of the idea of existence is
not really enough to establish Hume's thesis that ' the idea of
existence, when conjoined with the idea of any object, makes
no addition to it.' Indeed, this thesis cannot be correct. For
there is a great difference between thinking that an object
exists, which is a proposition, and merely having in one's
mind an idea of it, which is not a proposition; and the only
possible explanation of this difference is that existence is a
separate idea, which does make an addition to the idea of the
object. This conclusion is reinforced by the consideration
that you can have the negative thought that an object does not
exist. This thought could not be explained by a philosopher
who accepted Hume's thesis. For it too would require the
presence of the idea of the object in the thinker's mind, and
according to Hume that idea, in itself, without any addition,
would constitute the positive thought that the object did exist.
But people do succeed in thinking that some things do not
exist.

So Hume ought to have retraced his steps, and looked more
closely at the premiss from which he deduced his incorrect
conclusion. His premiss was that existence does not seem to
make any difference to things. But it is important to include
in this premiss the proviso that existence is being considered
as a property of things. That is to say, the full statement of
his premiss is that existence, considered as a property of
things, does not seem to make any difference to them. But
this suggests a possibility that did not occur to him. Perhaps
existence ought not to be considered as a property of things.

Russell's account of existence starts from this point. If
existence is not a property of things, what is it? Is it a

[1] *T.H.N.* I.ii.6 (p. 70ff), I.iii.7 footnote (p. 98).

property of something else? Or is it not a property at all? His answer to these questions is, very roughly, that existence is a property of properties. This way of putting his answer is not at all exact, and an accurate version will be given in a moment. Meanwhile the rough version will serve to bring out the general character of his treatment. His main point is that the existence of a thing can be affirmed only through its properties. For example, the proposition that Sir Walter Scott exists cannot assert the existence of the man directly, but can only assert it through some supposed property of his, perhaps through the authorship of Waverley. Now, as was explained in the last chapter, Russell allows that the ordinary proper name ' Sir Walter Scott ' can sometimes be used as if it were a logically proper name; this special use is made of it when the speaker is thinking of the denotation directly without the intervention of any descriptions. So his main point about existence can be put by saying that in the proposition that Sir Walter Scott exists, it cannot be the case that the ordinary proper name is being used as a logically proper name. If it were being so used, it would derive its meaning directly from its denotation without the intervention of any descriptions, and in that case the proposition would be meaningless if the denotation did not exist. But that is absurd, since the proposition clearly has a meaning even if the man does not, and never did exist.[2] Therefore, it must be the case that his existence

[2] The verb ' to exist ' is used by Russell in a timeless way (see p. 66. But if tensed verbs are used, there is seldom any need to make any reference to future existence, because an ordinary proper name is very unlikely to derive its meaning from a future denotation.

Russell's point about the meaning of ordinary proper names is not the point that was made just now against Hume's treatment of existence. That point was that Hume's treatment of existence was deficient, because it did not contain any way of distinguishing between the affirmative thought that an object exists and the negative thought that it does not exist. The point that is being made now is that, even when that deficiency has been remedied by allowing that in all such thoughts the idea of existence occurs separately, it is still possible to give a mistaken account of the idea of the object, or a mistaken account of the singular symbol which is used to pick out the object.

is being affirmed through some property. This argument reinforces Russell's thesis that ordinary proper names are very often 'truncated or telescoped descriptions'. For it proves that it *must* be possible to replace them by descriptions whenever they occur in propositions affirming or denying existence.[3]

Russell's main point about existence is that it does not qualify things directly, as ordinary properties like shapes and colours qualify them. If it did qualify them directly, you could pick out a particular thing with a singular symbol used as a logically proper name, and then go on to ascribe existence to it, as you might ascribe an ordinary property to it. But in fact this cannot be done. For logically proper names and all singular symbols which are used as logically proper names get their meanings directly from their denotations, so that the mere occurrence of such a singular symbol in a proposition is enough to convey that its denotation exists. Consequently it would be a kind of tautology to go on to ascribe existence to it, and a kind of contradiction to go on to deny existence of it.[4]

The mistake is to treat the singular symbol as a logically proper name, and its effect is to make negative existential propositions meaningless. This effect looks deceptively like the effect of Hume's mistake, but it is not the same.

This point of Russell's is a point about singular symbols which we know to be complex: such symbols cannot be used as logically proper names when they are the grammatical subjects of existential propositions. Naturally, it is equally impossible for singular symbols which actually are logically proper names to occur as the grammatical subjects of existential propositions. See p. 120.

[3] *PH.L.A.* pp. 40-1 (*L.KN.* pp. 241-3). The exact nature of the logical relationship between ordinary proper names and definite descriptions which licenses the substitution is controversial. See pp. 75-80. Cf. J. R. Searle *'Proper Names'*, *Mind*, 1958.

[4] Cf. *PH.L.A.* p. 47 (*L.KN.* p. 252). Russell says that such ascriptions and denials of existence are nonsense. He means that the ascription would be a kind of tautology, and the denial a kind of contradiction; but not the kind of tautology or the kind of contradiction that Wittgenstein describes, *T.L.-PH.* 4.46ff. For a proposition containing a logically proper name or a singular symbol used as a logically proper name does not *assert* or *entail* that the thing that is

So existence does not qualify things directly. What then does it do? The only way to answer this question is to see how assertions and denials of existence actually work. Now they always work through properties. Sometimes this indirect method of operation is explicit, as it is in the proposition that the author of Waverley exists. But, if it is not explicit, it is implicit, as it is in the proposition that Scott exists. Existence can get a grip on particular things only through their properties. Therefore it is not a property of things, but a property of properties.

Before we take another step, it is essential to be clear about the direction in which we are moving. That is to say, it is essential to see the direction in which Russell's logical apparatus is taking us. It was pointed out in the last chapter that he explains his Theory of Definite Descriptions on a popular level, and then uses it in a recondite way which ultimately takes him down to the level of sense-data. Now his theory of existence is involved in his Theory of Definite Descriptions. and one might get the impression that, taken together, the two theories necessarily lead us down to the level of sense-data. But that is not so. There is nothing in the logical apparatus itself which makes that destination inevitable. This point is easy to miss, because he does in fact use his logical apparatus in order to reach that destination. But, when he so uses it, he has to bring in the sceptic's traditional arguments against our ordinary belief in the existence of objects in the external world. If he had not brought in those arguments, he would not have had to identify particulars, which are the denotations of logically proper names, with sense-data. For his logical apparatus is primarily concerned with understanding and meaning, and its function is to trace in an orderly and systematic way the lines that connect symbols with the things from which they ultimately derive their meanings, and, if he

---

denoted exists. It conveys in some other way that it exists; if it did not exist, the logically proper name would be meaningless. According to Wittgenstein, it *shows* that it exists (*T.L.-PH.* 4.1211 and 3.203).

had not been convinced by the sceptic's arguments, those things need not have been sense-data.

When Russell was confronted by the sceptic's arguments, he stood at a major point of bifurcation. If he had rejected them, his logical atomism might have developed entirely on the level of objects in the external world. For instance, he might have maintained that the denotations of logically proper names are material particles. That is to say, he might have maintained that we have to treat material particles as simple entities, and then, of course, the next question would be whether they are intrinsically simple. There would be nothing surprising about a version of logical atomism which kept to the level of things in the external world. Wittgenstein, who used the same logical apparatus as Russell, certainly considered this possibility in the *Notebooks*,[5] in which he worked out the ideas that he later published in the *Tractatus Logico-Philosophicus*, and it is arguable that the logical atomism of the *Tractatus* actually is of this kind.[6] If Russell had taken this turning, his preliminary, popular analysis of ordinary existential propositions would not have been substantially different. He would still have said that in them ordinary proper names cannot be used as names, and he would still have meant that they cannot be used as logically proper names. The only difference is that he would have meant that they cannot be used like the singular symbols for material particles, rather than that they cannot be used like the singular symbols for sense-data.

Even on the level of complex objects in the external world there is a great deal of room for analysis, and it is essential to be clear about the kind of analysis that Russell is suggesting for ordinary existential propositions. So let us recall the distinction which was drawn in the last chapter between the three kinds of singular symbol. In what has been said so far about Russell's analysis of ordinary existential propositions it is evident that he has not made any use of the kind of singular

---

[5] *N.B.* p. 67 and p. 81.
[6] This is argued by Dr J. P. Griffin, *W.L.A.*, pp. 49ff.

symbol that denotes things that are intrinsically simple. But he has mentioned logically proper names, which are singular symbols whose denotations have to be treated by us as simple, whether or not they are intrinsically simple. However, he *need not have mentioned* logically proper names. For the existential propositions which he is analysing contain ordinary proper names, and so far his point has only been that ordinary proper names, though they may sometimes be treated as if their denotations are simple, cannot be treated in this way in existential propositions. That is to say, his point has been that, though ordinary proper names are the kind of singular symbols which, in general, allow us an option between the two treatments, they do not allow us the option when they occur in existential propositions. In order to make this point, he has had to explain what counts as treating the denotation of an ordinary proper name as if it were simple. But his explanation has been that, if you thought of the denotation directly, without the intervention of any descriptions, you would be treating it as if it were simple. Of course, this explanation can be expressed in a way which brings in logically proper names : we can say that to treat the denotation of an ordinary proper name as simple is to use the ordinary proper name as if it were a logically proper name. Indeed, this form of the explanation was used just now. But Russell *does not have to use* this form of the explanation. He can make his point about ordinary existential propositions without mentioning logically proper names, and so without even raising the question what the denotations of logically proper names are.

The fact that Russell has not yet had to make any use of logically proper names is, of course, explained by the method of exposition which is being used here. For his analysis of ordinary existential propositions is here being expounded in a preliminary and popular way on the level of complex objects in the external world. In order to understand his analysis at this level, we only need to understand what counts as treating the denotation of a singular symbol as if it were simple. To treat the denotation of a singular symbol as if it were simple is to think of it directly, without the intervention of any descriptions. The main reason for following this order of exposition is that it is easier to understand Russell's logical apparatus at this level, leaving the descent to the deeper level until later. No doubt, this is why he himself introduces his logical apparatus in this way in *The Philosophy of Logical Atomism*.[7]

Let us now return to the description of Russell's logical apparatus, and continue the explanation of his formal treatment of existence. We need a more exact account of his analysis of existential propositions than the one that was given just now. Two corrections have to be made, and both of them will require some explanation. First, it is not quite right to say that existence is itself a property of properties. For the particular property of properties that is meant is the property of having an instance, and saying that a property has an instance is not always the same thing as saying that it exists, since there are properties that have no instances. So the thesis ought not to be that existence is a property of properties; rather, it ought to be that the proposition that a certain individual exists is tantamount to the proposition that a certain property has one instance. For example, the proposition that God exists means that a certain set of properties,

---

[7] *PH.L.A.* p. 3 (*L.KN.* p. 182), pp. 42-3 (*L.KN.* pp. 244-6). But there is also another reason why Russell introduces his logical apparatus in a popular way. The popular version, which makes no reference to things which we have to treat as simple, is the version which he formulated first. See *O.D.* (*L.KN.* p. 41ff). The version which he expounds in *PH.L.A.* developed later. In *PH.L.A.* the two versions occur side by side, and Russell has to distinguish between singular symbols whose denotations we may treat as simple in spite of the fact that we know them to be complex, and singular symbols whose denotations we have to treat as simple.

Wittgenstein's comment on this stage in the development of Russell's logical apparatus is this: 'Russell's " complexes " were to have the useful property of being compounded, and were to combine with this the agreeable property that they could be treated like " simples ".' *N.L.* (*N.B.* App. 1 p. 99).

taken together, has one instance. General existential propositions can be translated in a similar way: the word ' instance ' merely has to be used in the plural. This point about the translation of existential propositions is incorporated in Russell's theory. But the way in which he incorporates it is rather strange, and the explanation of it involves the second correction to the inexact version of his theory. So let us now move on to that.

The second way in which the accuracy of that version has to be improved is connected with Russell's policy of always analysing phrases as they actually occur in propositions and never in isolation. In this particular case he takes the adjectives signifying the supposed properties of the things whose existence is in question in their context in a proposition, and not by themselves. For example, unicorns might be described as ' equine and equipped with one horn ', and he would take these adjectives in the context of the proposition ' This is equine and equipped with one horn '. Then, in order to get a translation of the proposition that unicorns exist, he makes two moves. First, he strikes out the word ' this ' and leaves a blank in the proposition : the result, '— is equine and equipped with one horn ', is what he calls a ' propositional function '.[8] His second move is to introduce the concept of ' satisfying a propositional function ' :[9] an individual satisfies a propositional function, if and only if the insertion of its name in the vacancy in the propositional function produces a true proposition. Then the meaning of the proposition, that unicorns exist, is that the propositional function '—is equine and equipped with one horn ' is satisfied. In this translation no mention is made of properties. Their place has been taken by propositional functions. This is an advantage, because the version which mentioned properties was too narrow, and the theory needed to be broadened so as to include relations.[10] For a singular existential pro-

---

[8] *PH.L.A.* p. 33 (*L.KN.* p. 230).

[9] *PH.L.A.* p. 35 (*L.KN.* p. 233).

[10] Henceforth the word ' property ' will be used to mean ' quality ' and will be contrasted with the word ' relation '.

position, like the proposition 'There is an island to the north of this cape', relies on a relation, and such examples are common. The necessary broadening of the theory is secured by Russell's version, because propositional functions can be constructed out of phrases signifying relations as well as out of phrases signifying properties.

Russell distinguishes between the various ways in which a propositional function may be satisfied. Two of them concern us here. First, a propositional function may be satisfied by one and only one instance, and, secondly, it may be satisfied by one or more instances. There is, of course, also the case in which it is not satisfied by any instances. That case provides a translation of the negative existential proposition that unicorns do not exist. This means that the propositional function '— is equine and equipped with one horn' is not satisfied by any instances; or, to put this the other way round, it means that there is nothing which is equine and equipped with one horn. Russell sometimes puts this in a third way, and it is here that we encounter the strangeness of expression that was mentioned just now. He sometimes says that in such a case the propositional function is impossible.[11] This is a strange choice of adjective. The idea behind it is that, if the propositional function is not satisfied by any instances, then a particular thing *cannot* satisfy it.[12] However, it is odd to use the word 'impossible', and it should be remembered that he only means that the propositional function is not satisfied by any instances.

The translation of affirmative general existential propositions, which has already been given in a rough version, is produced in a similar way. The proposition 'Lions exist' means that there is at least one thing which has the right properties and relations. Alternatively, if we construct a propositional function out of the words signifying those properties and relations, we may say that the proposition

[11] *PH.L.A.* p. 33 (*L.KN.* p. 231).
[12] See *PH.L.A.* pp. 48-9 (*L.KN.* pp. 254-5), where Russell explains his use of the word 'possible' in a parallel way.

means that that propositional function is satisfied by one or more instances or, as Russell rather strangely says, that it is possible. Finally, there are unique existential propositions, like the proposition 'The Loch Ness monster exists'. This means that there is one and only one thing which has the right properties and relations : or, alternatively, that the relevant propositional function is satisfied by one and only one instance; or, to put this in the strange way, that it is possible in respect of one and only one thing.[13]

Earlier in this chapter it was stated that Russell's main point about existence was that it does not qualify things directly, in the way in which shapes and colours qualify them. We can now add that he thought that it does not even qualify things indirectly through their properties and relations. For under analysis existence is transformed into a property of propositional functions, the property of having instances, which Russell calls 'possibility'. This theory is, in part, a precise formulation of the rather vague philosophical thesis that existence is not a predicate. Of course, it is not enough to say that it is not a predicate. For what this means is that it is not an ordinary predicate, and it is necessary to explain how ordinary predicates work, and how existence differs from them. Kant provided part of the explanation in his critique of the ontological proof of the existence of God.[14] He pointed out that, whereas ordinary predicates may be included in the definition of a thing, existence cannot be included. You cannot say of anything that it must exist because it has been defined as existing. For a definition can only give a description of a thing as it would be if it did exist, and the question whether it does exist is the question whether there is something that satisfies that description.

[13] *PH.L.A.* p. 45 (*L.KN.* p. 249). There is an obvious connection between Russell's use of the word ' possible ' and the word ' some ', and between his use of the word ' impossible ' and the word ' none '. See *PH.L.A.* p. 33 (*L.KN.* p. 231). He uses the word ' necessary ' in a way that is similarly connected with the word ' all '. See pp. 249-50.

[14] *Critique of Pure Reason, Transcendental Dialectic*, Bk. II Ch. iii. §4. (Everyman edition, p. 346ff).

But why can a definition only give a description of a thing
as it would be if it did exist? The answer to this question is
implicit in Russell's theory. It is that, if existence could be
included in the definition of a thing, it would also be possible
to ascribe it to the thing when you discovered it in the same
way that you might ascribe a colour or a shape to it. That is
to say, it would be possible to say ' This thing is serpentine,
and it is equipped with flippers, and it exists '. But the
addition of the last clause in that sentence, as has already been
explained, produces a kind of tautology.[15] Therefore existence
cannot be ascribed in the same way as other predicates, and
so it cannot be included in the definition of a thing. So
Russell's theory explains the source of the difference between
existence and ordinary predicates. But it does something more
than this. It also includes an account of the way in which
the concept of existence actually works.

It must be admitted that existence does sometimes look very
like an ordinary predicate, and Russell has to explain how it
manages to acquire this deceptive appearance. His explanation of the illusion, when it is produced by the use of an
ordinary proper name, has already been given; the ordinary
proper name is not being used as a logically proper name, but
as a description, which yields the usual propositional function. But there is also another kind of case in which existence
looks like an ordinary predicate. If someone wonders whether
what he sees is an hallucination or a real chicken, and he
decides that it is an hallucination, he may well say ' This does
not exist ', and in this proposition the word ' this ' looks
like the logically proper name of a sense-datum, and it is not
very easy to avoid treating the phrase ' does not exist ' as an
ordinary predicate. Russell discusses this kind of case in
The Philosophy of Logical Atomism, and he points out that
hallucinations exist in their own right, and are perfectly real,
and that, when people say that they do not exist, all that
they mean is that they are not correlated with other sense-
data in the usual way.[16] But this is not quite enough to dis-

[15] See p. 57.   [16] *PH.L.A.* pp. 49-50 (*L.KN.* pp. 256-8).

pose of the difficulty. Certainly the man who said 'This does
not exist' was not denying that the hallucinatory sense-datum
existed in its own right, and, if we accept Russell's account of
perception, we shall say that he was only denying that it had
the usual correlations. But we still need to understand how his
denial works. Can he really be attaching the phrase 'does
not exist' to the logically proper name of a sense-datum? The
explanation must be that he is doing no such thing. The word
'this' must here be interpreted in the way in which Russell
interprets ordinary proper names in existential propositions.
It stands for the definite description 'the chicken which I
seem to see'. It is quite understandable that in such a case
the demonstrative pronoun should point through the sense-
datum at the putative object in the external world.

Time also plays a part in making existence look like an
ordinary predicate. For example, the proposition 'He no
longer exists' may be used to announce a person's death, and
the verb in it really does look like an ordinary predicate of the
now dead person. In such a case it is not possible to say that
the personal pronoun always stands for a definite description.
For the speaker may be using it as a logically proper name :
that is to say, he may be thinking about the dead person
directly, without the intervention of any descriptions. Russell's
way of dealing with this difficulty is to avoid using the verb
'to exist' in the way in which it is used in this proposition,
to refer to a specific time.[17] If Russell says 'It does not exist'
he is denying the thing's existence in past, present and future.
This convention prevents us from using propositions like 'He
no longer exists'. When existence is denied, it is denied for
all time. Now all time includes any moment at which the
speaker might have been thinking of the thing as existing
directly, without the intervention of any descriptions. Therefore, if his denial of existence is correct, he cannot have been
thinking of the thing directly, without the intervention of any
descriptions : or, to put this point in the way in which it was
put earlier, it would be a kind of contradiction to use a symbol

[17] *PH.L.A.* *pp.* 44-5 (*L.KN.* p. 248).

as a logically proper name and then go on to deny the existence of its denotation. Similarly, according to Russell's convention, when the existence of a thing is affirmed, the affirmation is not restricted to any particular period of time, and so it would be a kind of tautology to pick out the thing with a symbol used as a logically proper name and then go on to affirm its existence.

The adoption of this convention is, of course, only a matter of convenience. Russell could have allowed the verb ' to exist ' to refer to specified periods of time. Indeed, he could have used a much more elaborate system of temporal reference than is provided by English tenses. If he had done this, his account of logically proper names would have been more complicated. He would have had to distinguish in some way between the periods within which logically proper names aim at their denotations : some would locate their targets in the present, and others would locate them in the past,[18] and perhaps there might be a distinction between pointing into the remote past and pointing into the recent past. Then his thesis would have been that a logically proper name could not occur in an existential proposition unless its temporal reference differed from the temporal reference of the verb. Naturally, this thesis would have had to be extended to all singular symbols used as logically proper names.

After this long discussion of existence we can at last return to Russell's Theory of Definite Descriptions. Let us recall the point that had been reached in the exposition of that theory. The proposition that the daughter of Hitler is a soprano had been analysed as a conjunction of two propositions, the first one being the proposition that Hitler had one daughter, and the second one being that she is a soprano. Then it was pointed out that the first proposition in this pair involves the idea of existence, because it means that the daughter of Hitler exists. The discussion of existence, which began at that point, can now be used to take the exposition of the Theory of Definite Descriptions one stage further.

[18] See p. 56 footnote 2.

What is needed is a more exact account of the proposition that the daughter of Hitler exists. This is provided by Russell's transformation of existence into the property of being satisfied, which is a property of propositional functions. Now two of the ways in which a propositional function might be satisfied have been explained. It might be satisfied by one and only one instance, or by one or more instances. Evidently the first kind of satisfaction is needed here. The proposition means that the propositional function '— is female and begotten by Hitler' is satisfied by one and only one instance, or, in Russell's other words, is possible in respect of one and only one thing. Alternatively, its meaning may be presented the other way round : There exists one and only one thing which is female and was begotten by Hitler.

The exposition of Russell's Theory of Definite Descriptions is still not quite finished, and the final stage of his analysis will be given later.[19] But it has been taken as far as it needs to be taken for the moment. Already it is possible to see that, whether or not the theory is correct, there is no doubt that it gives a comprehensive account of the meaning of propositions containing definite descriptions.[20] That is to say, everything that people convey when they use propositions containing definite descriptions is conveyed by Russell's analysis of them. The question whether his analysis is correct or not is, in part, an independent question, and it will not be investigated in this book. In order to answer it, we should first need to establish a standard of correctness. If the standard were conformity to everyday usage, a correct analysis would have to convey what it does convey in the way in which it actually is conveyed when people use definite descriptions. When Russell's analysis is judged by this standard, it is arguable that

[19] See p. 243 for Russell's analysis of satisfaction by one and only one instance. A complete exposition of the theory would also need to include an account of the way in which, in the final analysis, Russell's logical symbolism welds all the entailments together again to form a single proposition. This will not be provided in this book. See p. 52 footnote 18.

[20] See pp. 14-15.

it is found wanting. The case for this verdict has been put by Mr P. F. Strawson.[21] It rests, in the first place, on the contention that the fact that there is nothing which fits a definite description does not usually lead us to say that the proposition containing it is false, so that it cannot be right to say that a proposition containing a definite description *entails* an existential proposition. Russell does not think this criticism damaging,[22] because, if the correctness of an analysis is judged by this standard, he does not care about correctness. He only demands that an analysis should convey absolutely clearly everything which is legitimately conveyed. If this involves some departure from the conventions of ordinary speech, so much the worse for ordinary speech.

The discussion of this controversy is beyond the scope of this book. But there is one point which might be made about it. The question at issue is really more interesting than it might at first appear to be. It would be very boring if it were merely a matter of preference, one side treating everyday usage as sacred, and the other treating it as anathema. But behind the preferences it is possible to discover a more subtle issue. If a philosopher changes the logical structure of language at one point, that may lead to consequential changes at other points.[23] So it is a very real question whether consistency in carrying out the whole programme of changes would involve a sacrifice of comprehensiveness, or at least some inconvenience at other points. No doubt the untidy logic of everyday language is not the only system which would enable us to convey everything that we want to convey. But a change which makes part of the system neater may not seem to be an improvement when its effect on the whole system is realised. On the other hand, the untidiness of everyday logic

[21] '*On Referring*', *Mind*, 1950, and *Introduction to Logical Theory*, ch. vi. § 10.

[22] *M.PH.D.* pp. 241-3.

[23] cf. Wittgenstein *T.L-PH.* 3.342: 'Although there is something arbitrary in our notations, *this* much is not arbitrary—that *when* we have determined one thing arbitrarily, something else is necessarily the case. (This derives from the *essence* of notation.)'

seems to need a good theory to discipline it. How many kinds of implication ought there to be? It is not even clear how many kinds there are.

However, there is no doubt that Russell's analysis of definite descriptions is comprehensive. In fact, one of the advantages of his theory was that it provided him with a model of a comprehensive analysis. But it was a model which was to be used with discrimination. For, as was explained in Chapter I, he does not think that all analyses have to be comprehensive. According to him, all that is necessary is that, if an analysis is not comprehensive, and so does not conform to the model, its non-conformity should be justified. The justification would be that part of the popular meaning of the phrase that is being analysed is illicit.

The Theory of Definite Descriptions is also something more than a model of a comprehensive analysis. It is an instrument to be used in producing other analyses, which will take us below the level of objects in the external world, and which will often be less than comprehensive. The next thing to be done is to explain how the instrument was to be used.

CHAPTER VI

LOGIC AND KNOWLEDGE

How is this logical apparatus to be applied to human knowledge? That is the question. Now there are various kinds of knowledge, and this chapter will be concerned with knowledge by acquaintance, *a priori* knowledge and, to a lesser extent, factual knowledge. A person is said to have knowledge of a thing by acquaintance if he has come across it in his experience and remembers it, or, alternatively, if he is experiencing it at the moment.[1] The thing may be an individual,[2] or it may be a property or a relation. There are various kinds of *a priori* knowledge. One kind is knowledge of the truths of logic and mathematics, but that kind will not be discussed here. Another kind, which will be discussed, is knowledge of propositions whose truth is guaranteed by definitions of complex symbols. Factual knowledge is empirical knowledge of contingent facts.

Knowledge by acquaintance and *a priori* knowledge are both involved in learning and understanding the meanings of symbols, and it is chiefly this aspect of them that will be considered in this chapter. But knowledge by acquaintance is also connected with factual knowledge, and the connection is very close, although factual knowledge is knowledge of a different kind. The connection is that, if a person knows a

[1] Notice that Russell allows that a person may now have acquaintance with a thing because he has come across it in the past. See *O.N.A.* (*L.KN.* pp. 127-39, and pp. 165-6). This vital point is often missed by students of Russell's theory of knowledge: e.g. by J. O. Urmson, *Philosophical Analysis*, p. 86 and p. 134. The result is a very bizarre interpretation of Russell's analysis of sense-datum propositions. See pp. 181-2.

[2] This word is used here to mean ' a particular which may or may not be one which we have to treat as simple ', because the word ' particular ', according to Russell's usage in *PH.L.A.*, always means a particular which we have to treat as simple. See *PH.L.A.* p. 14 (*L.KN.* p. 199).

thing by acquaintance, it is very likely that he will know some fact about it.[3] Now it is enormously important to keep this aspect of knowledge by acquaintance severely apart from its connection with learning and understanding the meanings of symbols. If this distinction is not maintained, theory of meaning and theory of truth will tend to merge into one another.[4]

Knowledge by acquaintance is the central pillar of Russell's epistemology, and his account of it is given in *Mysticism and Logic*, and, in a shorter and more popular version, in *The Problems of Philosophy*.[5] It is contrasted with knowledge by description. The simplest way of presenting the contrast between these two kinds of knowledge is to say that you know the daughter of Hitler by description if you know that there is such a person, but have never come across her in your experience; and that you know her by acquaintance if you have come across her. Notice that knowledge by description, which is merely knowledge that something uniquely fits a definite description, is the recessive member of the pair. That is to say, if you know a thing by description, and then come across it later, Russell tends to say that you know it by acquaintance, rather than that you know it in both ways. If the distinction is drawn in this simple way, it can readily be applied at the level of sense-data. You know your own sense-data by acquaintance, or at least those of them that you are actually having or can remember, and you know other people's sense-data by description. This immediately raises the problem of other minds, which was mentioned in Chapter III.[6] For it is impossible to know other people's sense-data by acquaintance, whereas, at the level of objects in the external world, if you merely happen not to have come across a thing in your experience, it is not impossible for you to achieve acquaintance with it, provided that it exists.[7]

There is, however, a complication in Russell's exposition of

[3] *P. of PH*. p. 46.   [4] See Ch. XI.
[5] *M. and L*. p. 209ff, and *P. of PH*. p. 46ff. Cf. *O.D.* (*L.KN*. p.
[6] See p. 40.   [7] cf. *PH.L.A.* pp. 11-12 (*L.KN*. pp. 195-6). 41ff).

the distinction between the two kinds of knowledge. He often illustrates it by taking the case of a person who begins by knowing a thing by description, and later achieves acquaintance with it. Now knowledge by acquaintance also occurs in cases in which it is not preceded by knowledge by description. But, if you do take the case in which it is preceded by knowledge by description, as Russell often does, you will get a complication. Suppose that you begin by knowing the daughter of Hitler by description, and that you then meet a woman who is in fact the daughter of Hitler, although you do not know that she uniquely fits that description. Russell says that in this case you still only know the daughter of Hitler by description, and that, in order to convert your knowledge into acquaintance, you must not only meet Hitler's daughter, but also know that that is who she is. It is evident that this complication is brought in by the supposition that you begin by knowing an individual by description. For, without this supposition, there would be no reason to select any particular description and say that you have to know that the individual fits that description before you know it by acquaintance, unless, of course, someone else knows the individual by description, and is discussing the question whether you know it by acquaintance. But if you have a sense-datum, you immediately know it by acquaintance, and there is no need to ask whether it fits a certain description, because there is no particular description waiting to have this question asked about it. Hence Russell makes little use of the complication, and from now on it will be largely ignored.

So knowledge by description is contrasted with knowledge by acquaintance. But how is it related to the other two kinds of knowledge that were mentioned at the beginning of this chapter, factual knowledge and *a priori* knowledge? This question is not easy to answer. Indeed, there is no general answer to it, because what is known by description might be the denotation of a singular symbol, or it might be the denotation of a general symbol,[8] and the answer to the question will depend on which of the two it is. Let us, therefore, examine

8 *KN.A.KN.D.* (*M. and L.* pp. 213-14).

the two cases separately, bearing in mind that in this chapter and in the next four we shall be concerned with meaning rather than with truth, so that our interest in knowledge will be primarily interest in knowledge as a source of understanding meanings.

Take singular symbols first. If you know the island five miles to the north of this cape by this description, you know that the relevant propositional function is satisfied by one and only one thing, and that is a perfectly straightforward piece of factual knowledge. Of course, as Russell points out,[9] it does not enable you to assert any empirical propositions about the island. For instance, you will not be in a position to say whether it is inhabited, unless you have some other source of knowledge, perhaps someone else's testimony, since you yourself are not acquainted with it. But this presents no difficulty, and it is clear that in this kind of case knowledge by description of the denotation of a singular symbol is factual knowledge.

If the singular symbol is an ordinary proper name instead of a definite description, the situation is not quite so simple. Suppose that you hear someone assert a proposition containing the name ' Bismarck '. According to Russell, since you are not acquainted with Bismarck,[10] you will not understand his name unless you can replace it by a definite description which you do understand, and if you do not understand his name, you

---

[9] *KN.A.KN.D.* (*M. and L.* p. 217).

[10] Russell says that Bismarck himself is the only person who has ever been acquainted with Bismarck (*KN.A.KN.D.* [*P. of PH.* pp. 54-7: *M. and L.* pp. 216-18]). This extreme thesis would follow either from his earlier view, that a person has an ego, or from his later view that a person is only a series of thoughts and experiences. But his theory of knowledge by acquaintance and knowledge by description can be expounded in a popular way at the level of objects in the external world. If it is expounded in this way, the fact that you happen to have been born too late to have met Bismarck will deprive you of the acquaintance with him which you might otherwise have had. Cf. *PH.L.A.* pp. 11-12 (*L.KN.* pp. 195-6). The two views from either of which the extreme thesis would follow were described at the end of Ch. III.

will not understand the proposition in which it occurred. Let us suppose that the definite description which you substitute for his name is ' the German statesman responsible for the Franco-Prussian war ', which you do understand. Then, if you know Bismarck by description, you will at least have to know that one and only one thing fits this definite description, and this piece of knowledge is factual, exactly like the knowledge that there is one and only one thing which is an island five miles to the north of this cape.

However, in order to know Bismarck by description, it is not enough to know that there is one and only one thing which fits the definite description ' the German statesman responsible for the Franco-Prussian war '. It is also necessary to know that Bismarck is correctly described as the German statesman responsible for the Franco-Prussian war. This is where the complication comes in. Notice that it is more or less the converse of the complication which was mentioned just now, and put on one side. For in that case Russell's point was that, in order to know the daughter of Hitler by acquaintance, it is not enough for you to be acquainted with the woman who in fact uniquely fits that description : you must also know that she does uniquely fit it. And now in this case the point is that in order to know Bismarck by description, it is necessary to know that he is correctly described as the German statesman responsible for the Franco-Prussian war, in addition to knowing that one and only one thing fits this description.

This is a complication for us, because we are trying to answer the question whether knowledge by description of Bismarck is factual knowledge or *a priori* knowledge. We have seen that it involves two pieces of knowledge, the first of which is clearly factual. But is the other piece factual? Is the knowledge, that Bismarck is correctly described as the German statesman responsible for the Franco-Prussian war, factual knowledge? At first sight it looks as if it must be factual, because it is only a contingent fact that Bismarck pursued such a policy. On the other hand, when Russell deals with ordinary proper names, he says that they are ' truncated or telescoped descriptions ',[11] and this strongly suggests that the substitution of a definite description for an ordinary proper name is a piece of logical analysis which preserves the meaning of the original proposition. That is to say, it suggests that he regarded the result of this substitution as a more explicit version of the original proposition, and not as a different proposition. This interpretation is supported by the programme which he announces on the first page of *The Philosophy of Logical Atomism*, which is to get down to particulars and simple properties and relations by logical analysis. If this interpretation is correct, his view would be that the piece of knowledge that we are examining, the knowledge that Bismarck was the German statesman responsible for the Franco-Prussian war, is *a priori* knowledge. According to him, it will be true by definition, and the definition will give the analysis of the complex symbol ' Bismarck '.

On this interpretation, Russell's account of ordinary proper names runs into obvious difficulties. Who is to choose the definite descriptions which are going to have an *a priori* connection with the name ' Bismarck '? Or will any definite description which Bismarck uniquely fits qualify for this treatment? Moreover, whatever definite description is chosen, after it has been tied to the name ' Bismarck ' with an *a priori* knot, the mistaken belief that Bismarck never fitted that description would require a very special interpretation. It would not be a contingent proposition, and it would not be an ordinary violation of a definition, like the proposition that a pentagon has six sides. These are all well known objections to the thesis that ordinary proper names pick up the definite descriptions which apply to their denotations and incorporate them in their connotations.

However, this interpretation of Russell's account of ordinary proper names is not sufficiently subtle. The reason for impugning it involves certain details of his logical apparatus which have not yet been given. These details will now be

[11] See p. 45; *PH.L.A.* p. 41 (*L.KN.* p. 243); cf. *PH.L.A.* p. 15 (*L.KN.* 200-1).

filled in, and that will put us in a position to improve the interpretation of his account of ordinary proper names. It will also enable us to answer the main question with which we are concerned at the moment, which is the question whether he believed that knowledge by description of individuals is factual knowledge or *a priori* knowledge.

Let us go back to the text of *Knowledge by Acquaintance and Knowledge by Description* and see what he says about knowledge by description of Bismarck. The first question which needs to be answered is this : How exactly is the definite description 'the German statesman responsible for the Franco-Prussian war' related to the ordinary proper name 'Bismarck' *when that name is used as a logically proper name?* In order to get the answer to this question, let us suppose that someone who met Bismarck in the flesh would be acquainted with him.[12] Then, if such a person said that Bismarck was an astute diplomatist, he might be using the proper name 'Bismarck' as a logically proper name. But you, who were born too late, could not match this performance. The best that you could do would be to use the ordinary proper name as the abbreviation of a description : for you could not possibly be thinking of the denotation of the ordinary proper name without the intervention of any descriptions. This was explained in Chapters IV and V. The point that has to be added now is that Russell says that, in these circumstances, you do not assert *the same proposition* as the proposition asserted by the person who, because he was acquainted with Bismarck, was able to use his name as a logically proper name. You certainly *want* to assert the proposition that he asserted, but it is a feat that you cannot achieve. What you do instead is to describe the individual whom he picked out in the superior way, by using the name 'Bismarck' as a logically

[12] As has already been mentioned (p. 74 footnote 10), Russell makes acquaintance with Bismarck more difficult than this. But the less stringent requirement is good enough for the present purpose, which is to give a general account of Russell's theory of knowledge by acquaintance and knowledge by description.

proper name. This leads Russell to say that, instead of expressing his proposition, you *describe* it;[13] which is a way of saying that, instead of expressing his proposition, you do the best that you can do in that direction, which is to express another proposition linked to his by a definite description which is uniquely fitted by the individual whom he picked out by using the name 'Bismarck' as a logically proper name.

In this passage the point that is important for us is that Russell says that your proposition, which contains the definite description, is not the same as his proposition, which contains the ordinary proper name used as a logically proper name. They are two different propositions because they express two different thoughts. He is thinking directly of Bismarck, without the intervention of any descriptions, and you are thinking directly of the denotations of the words used in your definite description, and only indirectly, and by aspiration, of Bismarck.

This reason for maintaining that you and he are asserting two different propositions supplies us with a method of answering the question about the connection between the ordinary proper name 'Bismarck' and the definite description 'the German statesman responsible for the Franco-Prussian war'. For another person, who used the name 'Bismarck' as an ordinary proper name in the proposition 'Bismarck was an astute diplomatist', might have a different definite description in mind, perhaps the description 'the first Chancellor of the German empire'. If he did, he would be thinking directly of the denotations of the words used in this definite description, and so, since these denotations differ from the denotations of the words used in your definite description, he too would be asserting a different proposition from yours. But if the pro-

[13] *KN.A.KN.D.* (*M. and L.* p. 218). This strange way of expressing the point is echoed by Wittgenstein in *N.L.* (*N.B.* App. 1, p. 99), where he says that part of the analysis of a statement about a complex is 'a statement *about the proposition* which describes the complex completely' [my italics—D.F.P.]. Wittgenstein later gave up this way of expressing the point, and ceased to regard this part of the analysis of a statement about a complex as a meta-statement (*T.L-PH.* 2.0201).

position 'Bismarck was an astute diplomatist' has two different analyses, it must really be two different propositions : that is to say, the sentence must be ambiguous. So Russell's view is that a sentence which contains an ordinary proper name not used as a logically proper name is ambiguous. The proposition which it expresses when one person uses it may not be the same as the proposition which it expresses when another person uses it. But if this is so, how will the two people succeed in communicating with one another? Russell's answer to this question is given in a passage in *Knowledge by Acquaintance and Knowledge by Description* : ' What enables us to communicate in spite of the varying descriptions we employ is that we know there is a true proposition concerning the actual Bismarck, and that, however we may vary the description (so long as the description is correct), the proposition described is still the same.'[14]

We now have the answer to the question about Russell's view of the connection between the ordinary proper name ' Bismarck ' and the definite description ' the German statesman responsible for the Franco-Prussian war '. According to him the connection is indeed *a priori*, because, provided that the speaker is using the ordinary proper name as an abbreviation of the definite description, the proposition containing the definite description will be the analysis of the proposition containing the ordinary proper name. But the *a priori* connection is momentary and immediately revocable. It exists only while the speaker asserts his proposition with that definite description in mind, and it fixes the meaning of what he then says.[15] Nobody else is obliged to respect it. Indeed the speaker himself may break it a few seconds later and set up another momentary *a priori* connection between the ordinary proper name ' Bismarck ' and a different definite description. That is what Russell means by his thesis that ordinary proper names

[14] *KN.A.KN.D. (M. and L.* p. 218). Cf. *PH.L.A.* pp. 11-12 *(L.KN.* pp. 195-6).
[15] Wittgenstein interprets Russell's account of ordinary proper names in this way. *PH.I.* § 79.

are ambiguous.[16] Whatever the merits of this thesis, it at least avoids the obvious objections to the thesis that proper names pick up all the definite descriptions that apply to their denotations and incorporate them permanently in their connotations.

We also have the answer to the question whether Russell thought that knowledge by description of an individual is factual or *a priori*. When someone knows Bismarck by description as the German statesman responsible for the Franco-Prussian war, he has two pieces of knowledge. First, he knows that this definite description is fitted by one and only one individual, and this piece of knowledge is, as we saw earlier, factual. Secondly, he knows that Bismarck is correctly described as the German statesman responsible for the Franco-Prussian war, and, though this piece of knowledge is factual, he can use it momentarily as an *a priori* truth : that is to say, he can use the ordinary proper name ' Bismarck ' as an abbreviation of the definite description. So, when he uses the name Bismarck as an ordinary proper name, he needs the second of his two pieces of knowledge, because, if he did not possess it, he would not understand the meaning of the name. The first of his two pieces of knowledge plays a different rôle. It is part of what he asserts when he says that Bismarck was an astute diplomatist. For, when the ordinary proper name ' Bismarck ' is analysed, it turns into a definite description; and, when the definite description is analysed, it expands into a proposition in the way that has already been explained. That is the answer to the question whether Russell believed that knowledge by description of an individual picked out by an ordinary proper name is factual or *a priori*.

The next thing to be done is to ask the same question about knowledge by description of properties and relations. But,

[16] Perhaps in a perfect language a proper name would have the same connotation for all people at all times (cf. Frege, *Sense and Reference* [*Translations from the Philosophical Writings of Gottlob Frege* by Geach and Black], p. 58 footnote), but Russell thought that this would be a very tiresome convention for everyday language (*PH.L.A.* pp. 11-12, *L.KN.* pp 195-6).

since Russell's account of understanding the meaning of singular complex symbols which denote individuals known by
description is rather elaborate, it is worth pausing in order to
recapitulate what has been said about it.

It is easiest to start with the case in which someone uses an
ordinary proper name of an individual not known to him by
acquaintance. If he understands the meaning of the name, he
must know the individual by description. He will then form
in his own mind a temporary *a priori* connection between the
name and the definite description, and the definite description
will be the analysis of the name as then used by him. This
analysis, however, is not unique, since any other definite
description which is applicable to the individual might have
been used instead. Therefore ordinary proper names are
ambiguous. Nevertheless, in any given case there will be one
and only one correct analysis of an ordinary proper name.
Now it is possible that this analysis could itself be analysed.
One way in which it might be suggested that this could be
done would be to replace the definite description by the ordinary proper name *used as a logically proper name.* Of course,
the original speaker, who was not acquainted with the individual, could not use the ordinary proper name as a logically
proper name. But someone else, who had the necessary acquaintance, could use it as a logically proper name, and it
might be suggested that, if he did use it in this way, what he
said would be a more fully developed analysis of the original
proposition. But the interesting thing is that Russell rejects
this suggestion. According to him, the proposition containing
the ordinary proper name used as a logically proper name is a
different proposition from the proposition containing the
definite description, and so it cannot be its analysis. However,
though it cannot be regarded as the last stage in the analysis of
the original proposition, it is related to it in an important
way. It is the proposition which we all want to assert, but
which most of us are prevented from asserting because we
lack the necessary acquaintance. Like the magnetic pole it
explains the direction in which our definite descriptions point,

and justifies our belief that we really do communicate with one another.

This justification of our belief in our powers of communication about people may not be so good as it looks. If people belong to the external world in the way in which we ordinarily believe that they do, it is a convincing justification. For in that case many people had the necessary acquaintance with Bismarck, and many of those who did not have it might have had it. But suppose that we abandon the assumption which has been maintained so far in this exposition of Russell's account of knowledge by description of individuals, the assumption that other people could have been acquainted with Bismarck. Suppose we say, as Russell does, that Bismarck was a psychological entity or series of entities, with which only Bismarck could be acquainted. Then the situation immediately deteriorates, and Russell's justification of our faith in our powers of communication about people is no longer adequate. Similarly, as was pointed out earlier,[17] if objects in the external world are logical constructions out of sense-data, we might well doubt our ability to communicate with one another about them.

Now let us ask whether knowledge by description of properties and relations is *a priori* knowledge or factual knowledge. This is much easier to answer than the same question about knowledge by description of individuals. For the division between *a priori* and factual knowledge of properties and relations is much more clear-cut. If you know hexagonality by description, you may know that it is the property of having six straight sides, or you may know that it is a property of bees' cells. In the first case your knowledge would be clearly *a priori*, because it is guaranteed by a definition, and in the second case it would be clearly factual, because it lacks that sort of guarantee. It is worth emphasising the contrast between the clarity of the distinction between *a priori* and factual knowledge of properties and relations and the obscurity of the parallel distinction between *a priori* and factual knowledge of

[17] See p. 40, footnote 21.

individuals. In the case of properties and relations there is no need to introduce the difficult concept of a momentary *a priori* connection between a complex symbol and its analysis, and the whole matter is much more straightforward. Nor is this surprising. For the definition of general complex symbols is a natural and easily understandable operation, and it was only to be expected that, when Russell tried to find an analogous operation which could be performed on singular complex symbols, he would encounter difficulties.

However, knowledge by description of properties and relations is not entirely straightforward. It exhibits the same complication that was noted in the case of knowledge by description of individuals. If you know a property like deciduousness by description, you really possess two distinct pieces of knowledge : you know that it is correctly described in a certain way, and you know that there is a property which uniquely fits that description. Now in this chapter we are concerned with knowledge primarily as a source of understanding meanings, and so the kind of knowledge by description of properties that interests us is *a priori* knowledge. For, if you only knew a contingent fact about deciduousness, perhaps that it is a property of all the vegetation on a certain island, you could hardly claim to understand the meaning of the word. Similarly, if all you knew about hexagonality was that it is a property of bees' cells, you would not understand the meaning of that word. In both these cases you would need *a priori* knowledge about the properties denoted by the words in order to understand their meanings. According to Russell, this *a priori* knowledge would be expressed in the definitions which give the analyses of the words.[18]

This thesis of Russell's looks entirely acceptable when it is illustrated by examples like these two. Deciduousness and hexagonality are properties which can be neatly defined, and so, if you relied on *a priori* knowledge by description in order to learn the meanings of the words denoting them, that knowledge would be expressed in definitions. But it must be

[18] *PH.L.A.* pp. 10-11 (*L.KN.* pp. 193-5).

remembered that Russell's thesis is a universal one. It is meant to apply not only to examples like these two, but also to every case in which the meaning of a word denoting a property or relation can be learned through *a priori* knowledge by description. So it is worth interrupting the exposition of his account of knowledge by description of properties and relations, in order to point out that this thesis is more questionable than it might appear to be.

In fact, the questioning of this thesis is one of the major points of bifurcation in the development of recent philosophy. Russell took the thesis over from Hume, but its ancestry goes back much further. When Wittgenstein criticises it in *The Blue Book*,[19] he ascribes it to Socrates. Wittgenstein points out how seldom the meaning of a word can be caught in a definition, unless it is a piece of technical terminology. But if a word lacks a definition, it does not follow that its meaning cannot be explained in words at all. There are other ways of using words to explain its meaning. You would not use a definition in order to teach someone the meaning of the word ' game '. No doubt the statements that you made in the course of the lesson would be *a priori* truths of a kind, but they would not be definitions. They would be much less systematic than definitions. Now, if the meanings of words can often be explained in other ways, perhaps the philosophical analyst should not confine himself to seeking definitions. Perhaps he should cast his net more widely.

In the last three decades many philosophers have done this, and their results have been more realistic but less systematic. A discussion of the merits and demerits of this philosophical method is beyond the scope of this book. The method has been mentioned because it developed partly out of doubts about the thesis that a verbal explanation of the meaning of a word should always take the form of a definition. Russell, of course, is not unaware of the possibility of explaining the meanings of words in less systematic ways. His insistence on definitions is not meant to reflect what actually happens. It is

[19] *B. and B.B.* pp. 18-20. Cf. *PH.I.* § 66ff.

really the expression of a view about the way in which philosophy ought to be done. He thinks that philosophical analysis should tighten the connections between words, and improve the structure of language by making it more systematic. Here, of course, scientific language is the model to which all language has to conform, and, if the correctness of an analysis is judged by its conformity to everyday usage, he does not care about correctness.[20]

Let us now return to the exposition of his views about knowledge by description of properties and relations. According to him, knowledge of the definition which gives the analysis of deciduousness is necessary if you are going to understand the meaning of the word. Is it also sufficient? Or do you also need the other piece of knowledge that is involved in knowledge of the property by description? That is to say, do you also need the knowledge that there is a property which uniquely fits the description given in the definition? This question cannot be answered in a straightforward way, because the answer to it depends on what it would mean to say that there was a property which uniquely fitted that description. It might mean that there actually were individuals possessing the property, and presumably, if the property was deciduousness, that is what it would mean. But, as was pointed out earlier, it need not mean this.[21] For it could merely mean that the property was not an impossible one. Squaring the circle might be used to illustrate the kind of impossibility that would be meant : this feat cannot be performed, in spite of the fact that you can give a sort of definition of it. In certain cases it is worth saying that the definition of a property is all right, and that it might have instances, even if in fact it has none, and one way of saying this is to say that the property exists.[22]

If the proposition that the property exists is interpreted in this way, it often ought to be known by anyone who understands the meaning of the word denoting it. But it is very doubtful if it is always necessary that he should know it. For

[20] See p. 15 footnote 5, p. 18 footnote 8, and p. 47 footnote 21.
[21] See p. 61.   [22] Plato's Theory of Forms expresses this idea.

sometimes the impossibility of a property, like the impossibility of squaring the circle, will be far from obvious, and understanding the meaning of a phrase is a matter of degree, and it is not always clear how high the standard ought to be. If, on the other hand, the proposition that the property exists is interpreted in the first way, it is certain that a person who understands the meaning of the word need not know it. People can think of properties which, though they are possible ones, have never had instances, and perhaps never will have instances. Of course, if someone ascribes a property to an individual, he should believe that the property has at least this one instance. But this belief could hardly be a necessary condition of his understanding the meaning of the word denoting the property, since he could not believe the proposition, unless he *already* understood its meaning, including the meaning of that word.

It is worth pausing for a moment at this point, in order to reflect on the parallelism between knowledge by description of properties and knowledge by description of individuals. In order to understand the meaning of an ordinary proper name, which denotes, or purports to denote, an individual with which you are not acquainted, you need to know its analysis. But you do not need to possess the other piece of knowledge which is included in knowledge by description of the individual: you do not need to know that there is such an individual. That is part of what you assert when you put the ordinary proper name into a proposition. Similarly, in order to understand a complex general symbol, which denotes, or purports to denote, a property with which you are not acquainted, you need to know its analysis. But you do not need to know that the property has any instances. So, if the statement that the property exists is interpreted to mean that it has instances, that is a piece of knowledge which you do not have to possess in order to understand the complex general symbol. It is part of what you assert when you put the complex general symbol into a singular proposition.

Knowledge by description of relations does not require

separate treatment. So we may now sum up Russell's account of understanding the meanings of complex general symbols denoting things known by description. If a person understands the meaning of such a symbol in spite of not being acquainted with its denotation, he must know its denotation by description. For instance, if the denotation is a property, he must know the property by description. But it is not enough for him to know any description which is uniquely fitted by the property. He must know the description through which it is defined and analysed. In some cases he ought also to know that this definition does not contain a fault which would make it impossible for anything to fit it. But he need not know that the property has instances. This account of understanding the meanings of complex general symbols denoting things known by description contains one or two details which Russell does not fill in. But that is only because he treats knowledge by description of properties and relations in a more cursory way, and concentrates on the more difficult topic of knowledge by description of individuals.

No amount of knowledge by description would produce any understanding of the meanings of complex symbols unless it were supplemented by knowledge by acquaintance. It would be no good knowing the definition of deciduousness unless you understood the words used in its definition, and, in order to understand them, sooner or later you would need some acquaintance with properties or relations. Similarly, it would be no good knowing that Bismarck is correctly described as the first Chancellor of the German empire unless you understood what this phrase means, and so in this direction too you must eventually reach a point where you will rely on acquaintance with properties and relations. This is the meaning of Russell's principle : ' Every proposition which we can understand must be composed wholly of constituents with which we are acquainted '.[23] Here the word ' constituent ' is applied to any individual, property or relation, through which you understand a proposition, and the principle states

[23] *KN.A.KN.D.* (*M. and L.* p. 219; *P. of PH.* p. 58).

that the set of things with which you are acquainted must be wide enough to enable you to understand every phrase in the proposition. Now, when a proposition contains one or more complex phrases, there will be various alternative sets of constituents through which you might achieve understanding of it. For instance, you may understand the word 'hexagonal' because you are acquainted with the property which it denotes; but another person might not be acquainted with the denotation of the word, and so he would have to analyse it until he reached denotations with which he was acquainted.

It is important to notice that, when Russell uses the phrase 'constituent of a proposition' in this way, the same proposition may have different constituents for different people. This relativity in the constitution of a proposition is merely a consequence of the fact that a proposition may contain a complex symbol. For the meaning of a complex symbol may be learned in different ways. It is important to notice it, because Russell also uses the phrase 'constituent of a proposition' in another way, which probably precludes relativity of constitution. According to this other usage, the constituents of a proposition are the things mentioned in the proposition's analysis when that analysis has been taken as far as it is humanly possible to take it. If the phrase is used in this way, it is arguable that the constituents of a proposition will not vary from person to person. The argument would be that the analysis of a proposition is complete when it reaches a point at which all the things that are mentioned in it have to be treated as simple, and that point certainly does not depend on variations between people.

However, this argument only establishes that the *kind of point* at which an analysis becomes complete does not vary from person to person. It is still possible that, even when Russell uses the phrase in his second way, he would allow the *particular constituents* of a proposition to vary from person to person. If so, the cause of the variation would be different from the cause of the variation when the phrase was used in the first way. In this case they would vary because each person's acquaintance is necessarily restricted to his own sense-data, so that his complete analysis of a proposition would be necessarily different from anybody else's complete analysis of the same proposition. If this was Russell's view, it may be that Wittgenstein was rejecting it when he said that ' a proposition has one and only one complete analysis '.[24] However, it may be that Russell never denied this. For he may have thought that the result of the restriction of each person's acquaintance to his own sense-data is merely that each person is only able to give a small part of the complete analysis of a proposition. Alternatively, he may have thought that the result is that any sentence about an object in the external world will turn out to be ambiguous when the analysis of the proposition which it expresses is taken down to the level of sense-data.

When the phrase ' constituent of a proposition ' is used in the second way, it is not necessary to be acquainted with all the constituents of a proposition in order to understand it. Of course, in order to understand the complete analysis of the proposition, you certainly do need acquaintance with all of them. Can you, in fact, achieve this acquaintance? The answer to this question depends on the view which Russell took about complete analyses. If a complete analysis mentions other people's sense-data as well as yours, and so does not vary from person to person, you cannot achieve it, because you are necessarily debarred from acquaintance with other people's sense-data. If, on the other hand, it does vary from person to person, you can achieve it, because you will only need acquaintance with your own sense-data. Whichever of these two views Russell held, there is no doubt that he did not think that, in order to understand a proposition, you need to be acquainted with its constituents, in the second sense of that word. For if the proposition contains complex phrases, as it sometimes will do, you will be able to understand it without even knowing what its complete analysis is. It is only the

[24] *T.L-PH.* 3.25.

understanding of the complete analysis itself that depends on acquaintance with those constituents.[25] For the complete analysis actually mentions those constituents, and, since they are things that have to be treated as simple, you must be acquainted with them in order to understand the symbols denoting them.

It is also true that, in order to understand a proposition, you do not have to be acquainted with all of its constituents, when the phrase is used in the way in which Russell uses it in his principle. But in this case the reason why you do not need acquaintance with all of them is different. The reason is that the phrase now applies not only to things which we all have to treat as simple, but also to things which we need not treat as simple, and these are things with which a person who understands a proposition need not be acquainted. For instance, if a proposition mentions a complex property, he may happen to be acquainted with it, and then it would be a constituent of the proposition for him : but he need not have been acquainted with this constituent, because he might have been acquainted with the simple properties mentioned in its definition.[26]

[25] Throughout this discussion it is being assumed that Russell required that all the individuals mentioned in the complete analysis of a proposition would have to be picked out by logically proper names. This assumption might be questioned. For it is arguable that he relaxed this requirement, and allowed them to be picked out by definite descriptions, if the person providing the analysis was not acquainted with them. See pp. 112-15.

[26] In *O.D.* (*L.KN.* pp. 55-6). *M. and L.* and *P. of PH.* the phrase ' constituent of a proposition ' is used in the first of the two ways. Let us call this ' the loose use '. When it is used in this way, it applies to things which *the person for whom it is a constituent* may treat as simple, because he is acquainted with them (see p. 61, footnote 7). The second use of the phrase, which is stricter, developed out of the loose use (see *PH.L.A.* pp. 40-1 [*L.KN.* p. 242]). The confusing thing is that the two uses occur side by side in *PH.L.A.* If you affirm or deny the existence of a thing, it cannot be a constituent of your proposition in the loose sense : i.e. it cannot be a thing through acquaintance with which you understand your proposition (see p. 57, footnote 4). But the constituents of a proposition, in the stricter sense,

It is worth pausing at this point, in order to relate Russell's principle to Hume's account of the derivation of ideas from impressions. Suppose we take Russell's principle, and add to it his thesis that in perception the only individuals with which we are acquainted are sense-data, and the only properties and relations with which we are acquainted are those of sense-data. Then the total result will be one half of Hume's theory about the derivation of ideas from impressions. For, if we leave aside Hume's thesis that some ideas are absolutely simple, what he says about complex ideas is that either they are replicas of complex impressions, or they are compounded out of simpler ideas which are replicas of simpler impressions. Russell's principle expresses this half of Hume's theory. Or perhaps this is a slight exaggeration. The truth is that it is a sophisticated linguistic version of half Hume's theory. It uses the elaborate mechanism of knowledge by description in order to build up the meanings of propositions from a foundation established by knowledge by acquaintance.

It is easy to lose one's sense of direction in such a welter of details, and it might be useful to emphasise the line that has been followed in this chapter, pointing out how selective it has been, and what has been temporarily put on one side. The plan has been to examine the contributions made by knowledge by description and knowledge by acquaintance to the under-standing of the meanings of symbols. Consequently, we have been mainly concerned with the *a priori* element in knowledge by description, and with pure acquaintance, detached from the descriptions of its objects which nearly always come with it. In other words, factual knowledge has been kept in the background. The reason for this policy is that, given Russell's programme and method, it is necessary to consider knowledge as a source of meaning before considering it as a source of

---

are the things that would be mentioned in the fully analysed version of the proposition. The existence of these things can never be denied in a proposition which contains their logically prope rnames (or unanalysable general symbols). See p. 120.

truth. His programme was to reconstruct the edifice of human knowledge in a way that would save those parts of it that can be saved from the sceptic, and his method was to analyse the propositions in which factual knowledge is expressed, consolidating their legitimate meaning, and discarding their surplus meaning. This method puts meaning before truth, and so in this chapter knowledge as a source of meaning has been examined first. The examination has shown that Russell regarded knowledge by acquaintance as the ultimate source of all meaning, and knowledge by description as the distributor which conveys meaning to those complex symbols that denote things with which a person is not acquainted. What has not yet been examined is factual knowledge, and something will be done to remedy this deficiency in Chapters XI, XII, XIII and XIV.

Another topic that has been repeatedly postponed is Russell's theory about things which have to be treated by us as simple. That theory corresponds to Hume's view that some ideas and impressions are simple, which is the other half of his theory about the derivation of ideas from impressions. So far it has received very little attention because it is easier to follow Russell's order of exposition, and to start with complex things which we may or may not treat as simple. Russell's theory about things which we have to treat as simple will be examined in Chapter VIII.

The separation of the *a priori* element in knowledge by description from its factual element has been fairly completely described. But not enough has been said about the parallel attempt to separate pure acquaintance from the descriptions which nearly always accompany it, in order to present it as a source of meaning rather than of truth. Something can be done to remedy this deficiency immediately.

First, it is important to clear away a misunderstanding of Russell's theory about knowledge by acquaintance. He is sometimes credited with the view that acquaintance with an individual, and the connected ability to pick it out with a singular symbol used as a logically proper name, lasts only so long as the individual is actually being perceived. But there is no evidence whatsoever for this interpretation. His view is that acquaintance with individuals can continue when they are no longer being perceived, just like acquaintance with properties and relations, so that a person who has perceived an individual and still remembers it can continue to pick it out with a singular symbol used as a logically proper name.[27] According to him this would be an example of pure acquaintance which does not work through the mediation of any description, just like the acquaintance with an individual which a person enjoys while he is actually perceiving it.

But what exactly does Russell mean when he talks about pure acquaintance? Suppose that you, having seen Piccadilly, use its name as a logically proper name.[28] What does Russell think will be going on in your mind? You certainly may have a description of the place in your mind, but, if so, according to him, you will not have to form a momentary *a priori* connection between the description and the name, as you would have to do if you were not acquainted with Piccadilly. For the name will be in direct semantic connection with its denotation, and so you will be able to treat the denotation as simple, in spite of the fact that it is not the kind of thing that you have to treat as simple. When you treat it as simple you will be rehearsing what necessarily happened when you actually saw Piccadilly and noticed that the description applied to it. For at that moment you could not treat the connection between the name and the description as an *a priori* one.

It must be admitted that this is a rather negative account of what would be going on in your mind. It tells us what would not be going on, rather than what would be going on. Moreover, it invites the objection that, if you are looking at

[27] See p. 71, footnote 1.
[28] See *PH.L.A.* p. 11 (*L.KN.* p. 195). This example, of course, is an example of something in the external world. But that does not matter, because the logical point is entirely general. See p. 74, footnote 10.

Piccadilly, you must at least have one description of it in mind, *viz.* ' the thing which I am not looking at ', and that you must be thinking of it as so described : or, to express this in the terminology that was used just now, you must form a momentary *a priori* connection between this description and the name. And, if such a connection has to be formed when you are looking at Piccadilly, later, when you remember Piccadilly, it will have to be formed again, this time with the verb in the description altered to the past tense. So in this kind of case, in which you do not have to treat the denotation as simple, there does not seem to be any such thing as pure acquaintance without the mediation of any description.

It is not clear what Russell's answer to this objection would have been. He might have answered that pure acquaintance can be proved to occur when you have to treat its object as simple, so that it must be possible for it to occur when you do not have to treat its object as simple. His argument for the thesis that it occurs in the first kind of case was given earlier.[29] Applied to this example, it would be that, when you have examined Piccadilly and said everything that you can say about it, you will have to treat it as the unanalysable subject of everything that you have said.[30] However, this argument might now look less convincing. For momentary *a priori* connections seem to allow the possibility that the name must always be connected in this way with one description, but not always with the same one, and certainly not with all of them at once.

During the period with which this book is concerned, Russell did not admit that this is a possibility. He admitted it later, when he abandoned the thesis that the only individuals mentioned in a complete analysis would be individuals which we have to treat as simple.[31] But during this period he

[29] See pp. 46-7. See also Ch. VIII.

[30] This argument needs to be generalised, so that it will also apply to the sort of case in which a complex individual is analysed into a set of particulars. See pp. 122-3.

[31] *M.PH.D.* p. 161ff.

thought that he could not abandon it because it seemed to him that, if he allowed that a name was always connected with one or more descriptions, it would be impossible to explain how it acquired its connection with the first description. That does seem to require that its denotation should be self-contained, and independent of any description, or at least of any description that you could apply to it. For, if such a denotation was not already there, waiting for your acquaintance, you could never formulate the first proposition which you used to describe it. Therefore, afterwards, as long as you remember that self-contained denotation, you remain acquainted with it and your acquaintance with it is quite distinct from any factual knowledge about it which you may happen to have acquired.

It is beyond the scope of this book to examine the reasoning which has since led Russell and many other philosophers to reject this thesis. Russell's main reason for abandoning it is the well known difficulty about individual substances which is being emphasised here. If you think of a particular deprived of all its properties and relations, it is not clear that there could be anything in reality which would correspond to your intellectual achievement, if indeed it is an achievement.[82] Now Russell was always aware of this difficulty,[83] and he maintained the thesis that is being expounded here in spite of it, because he thought that the arguments on the other side are stronger. His philosophy never was a static system in which all forces had been balanced and resolved. Here, as at many other points,[84] it is fascinating to observe the tensions which were later going to lead to further developments.

This particular tension can be traced back to the assumption that the meaning of a symbol is the thing that it denotes. This assumption looks plausible for general symbols,[85] because, when properties and relations are analysed, they do not

[82] *M.PH.D.* p. 164.
[83] *See PH. of L.* (2nd edition) p. 60 (first published 1900).
[84] See Ch. XI–XIII.
[85] But it has been challenged by P. T. Geach, *Mental Acts*, Ch. 10.

dwindle to mere logical points without magnitude. But when it is extended to singular symbols, it produces the notorious difficulty about individual substances. Perhaps, then, it is a mistake to extend it to singular symbols. This is the starting point of nearly all later theories about singular symbols, including Russell's.[86]

There is also another, connected line of thought which has led many philosophers to reject Russell's doctrine of simple singular symbols. Whatever the correct account of the meaning of a singular symbol may be, perhaps it is a mistake to make the identification of an individual which is picked out by such a symbol depend entirely on the meaning of that symbol. Perhaps the context of utterance also contributes to its identification.[87] This is a suggestion which Russell has never accepted. Even later, when he abandoned his earlier view that there are individuals which we have to treat as simple, he merely extended his treatment of ordinary proper names to all singular symbols. So he still makes the identification of individuals picked out by singular symbols depend entirely on their meaning. He has never made any use of the context of utterance, because that would go against his whole idea of philosophical analysis. According to him, the analysis of a proposition must include everything which would have to be known by anyone who understood what was being said. Nothing should be left to the context. Here, of course, his model is an absolutely scientific language. If you discovered an inscription written in such a language on a stone in a desert, you would only need a dictionary and a book of grammar and syntax in order to understand what it said.[88]

[86] cf. Wittgenstein, *PH.I.* § 40.
[87] cf. Strawson, ' *On Referring* ', *Mind*, 1950.
[88] See pp. 135-6.

CHAPTER VII

LINES OF ANALYSIS

Anyone who hears knowledge mentioned will think first of knowledge of truths, and it requires some effort to concentrate on knowledge as a source of understanding meanings. But meaning comes before truth, and Russell's account of knowledge by description and knowledge by acquaintance is primarily an attempt to trace back our understanding of the meanings of phrases to its source in our experience. So it is necessary to keep this aspect of knowledge on the front of the stage until the description of philosophical analysis, as Russell conceived it, has been completed. Now, according to him, the lines connecting phrases with the sources of their meanings point in a certain direction, and they continue in that direction until they reach the place where analysis terminates. The easiest way to plot them would be, first, to follow them far enough to determine their direction, and then to try to discover how far they continue. A general account of their direction has already been given : they point towards the simpler elements in human experience from which our understanding of meanings is derived. But this account leaves out many details. It suggests a very clear and uncomplicated pattern of analysis, whereas in fact the lines diverge and connect like roads in an industrial area. This network must now be described.

What is said in a proposition is that certain things are combined in a certain way. There must be at least two things which are combined, but there may be more. Let us take the least complicated case, where there are two things, an individual and a property. Then the proposition will say that the individual and the property are combined in the way that we call ' possession '. It is worth remarking that, if you assert the proposition, you do not thereby put the two things together. Of course, we may say that you put them together in thought, but that is not the kind of combination that you mean. What you mean is that they are combined in fact, and your saying that this is so does not make it so. The question whether it is so is, of course, the question whether your proposition is true. This may seem too obvious to be worth pointing out. But it is quite easy to confuse the fact with what is constructed in thought, which may or may not be a fact.

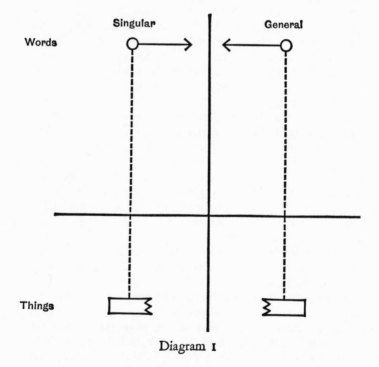

Diagram I

This diagram illustrates the working of a proposition which ascribes a property to an individual. The horizontal axis divides words from things, and, when the speaker puts the two phrases together, he is putting the two things together in thought, and that is how they will be in fact, if his proposition is true. The dotted lines connecting the phrases with the things are intended to show that in this case the speaker is acquainted with the things. For example, his proposition might be ' This one is deciduous ', and he might say this while actually looking at a tree and remembering from past experience what deciduousness is. Of course, he need not be acquainted either with the individual or with the property. If he is acquainted with them, as he is in this case, he will treat them as if they were simple, even if he is aware of their complexity. If he is not acquainted with them, he will have to know them by description.

Let us take next the case of someone who is neither acquainted with the particular tree nor with deciduousness. Such a person could not use a demonstrative phrase like ' this one ' in order to pick out the tree. So let us suppose that the tree has what few trees have, a proper name, ' Avar ', and that the proposition which he asserts is ' Avar is deciduous '. Now, if he had been acquainted with the two things, the tree and deciduousness, they would have been connected by dotted lines with their names. But he is not acquainted with them, and so the dotted lines will no longer appear in the diagram, and the question is what will take their place. How should knowledge by description be represented diagrammatically? The interesting thing is that, when what is known by description is a property or a relation, the lines of analysis will follow one pattern, and, when it is an individual, they will follow another, entirely different pattern.

Consider first this person's knowledge by description of the property deciduousness. The word ' deciduous ' means ' losing foliage periodically ', and, even if he had never come across an instance of this complex property, he would understand the word if he could define it, and if he was acquainted with the three elements mentioned in its definition. Perhaps he would also need to know that the definition determined a possible property, but that extra piece of knowledge is minimal in this case. Let us illustrate this part of the analysis of the proposition.

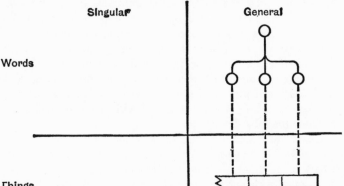

Diagram II

It is worth noticing the pattern formed by these lines. The property is split up into its elements, and each element is connected with a word which occurs in the definition. The connection is that the speaker is acquainted with these elements, because he has come across them separately in other instances. What he is asserting is that the three elements are present in the instance about which he is talking: the tree loses something, namely foliage, in a certain way, namely periodically.

If we illustrate the speaker's knowledge by description of the tree, we shall find that the lines form a different pattern. In fact, the analysis of a singular complex phrase differs from the analysis of a general complex phrase in three conspicuous ways. The first difference was mentioned in the last chapter. It is that the connection between a proper name like 'Avar' and a definite description like 'the oldest living tree' is a momentary and revocable *a priori* connection. So let us use a broken line to represent it.

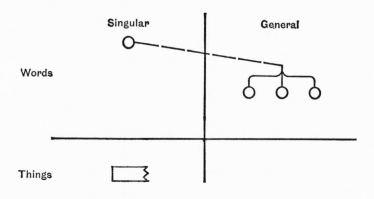

Diagram III

In this diagram the circles on the right hand side do not represent the three general words that occur in the analysis of the word 'deciduous'. They represent the three general words that occur in the analysis of the definite description 'the oldest living tree'. Now we still need to connect this definite description with the individual which the speaker hopes that it denotes. This is where the second difference in the pattern of analysis begins to appear. For we cannot just connect each of the three general words in the definite description with the properties that they denote and leave it at that. Of course, the speaker does have to be acquainted with the three properties, or, alternatively, with the elements mentioned in their definitions. So it would not be mistaken to connect the three general words with the three properties. But it would not give a complete picture of this part of the analysis of the proposition. For there would still be no connection shown between the definite description and the individual. The connecting lines would take us across to the right hand side of the diagram and leave us there. There would be nothing to illustrate the fact that the speaker was talking about the individual.

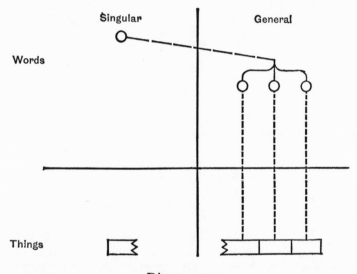

Diagram IV

This diagram shows what is lacking. Somehow or other a connection has to be established between the complex of three properties and the individual. Russell makes the connection through the word 'something'. According to the Theory of Definite Descriptions, what the speaker means is that there is something which alone possesses this complex of properties. Now the word 'something' is not at all like the name of an individual. Something is not related to nothing as John is to James. Consequently, in order to exhibit the connection, we need a new conventional sign. Let us use a figure with a discontinuous boundary to represent the word 'something'.

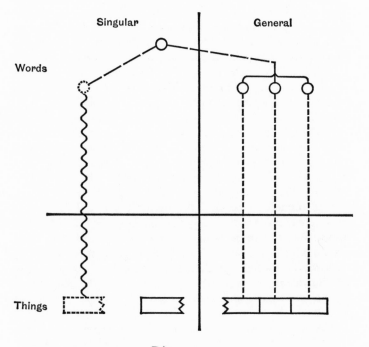

Diagram **v**

This diagram gives a complete picture of knowledge by description of an individual. It exhibits the details of the second difference between the analysis of a singular complex phrase and the analysis of a general complex phrase. The circle which symbolises the word 'something', and the rectangle below the horizontal axis with which it is connected both have discontinuous boundaries. This is because the word 'something' is unspecific. What the speaker says is that something uniquely possesses the set of properties,[1] and, although the mean-

[1] Each of these properties is complex, and would require further analysis.

ing of the word 'something' is not exactly a blank, it is very closely related to a blank. For if you want to explain the meaning of the word 'something', the first thing that you will do is to create a propositional function by making a vacancy in a proposition. In this particular case the propositional function might be '— is a tree, and living, and not younger than any other tree'. Then your next step would be to say that this propositional function is satisfied by at least one thing, and there you would have an explanation of one meaning of the word 'something': or you might take one more step, and say that the propositional function is satisfied by one and only one thing, and that would give you an explanation of the other meaning of the word 'something', which is the meaning that is needed in this case.[2]

The connection between the dotted circle and the dotted rectangle is made with a wavy line because it is a new kind of connection. Understanding of the meaning of the word 'something' does not come from acquaintance with any individual. Indeed, the dotted rectangle does not symbolise an individual. It represents a place which might be occupied by an individual, and which, according to the speaker, is

[2] See pp. 63-4. Russell's interpretation of 'something' is 'at least one thing' (*PH.L.A.* p. 34 [*L.KN.* pp. 231-2]), but it can also mean 'some one thing'. In Russell's logic the second meaning is expressed by saying that a propositional function is satisfied by one and only one thing. This makes the difference between the two meanings explicit.

It is worth noticing that in this particular case there are two different propositional functions that might be used. One is the propositional function which is suggested above: '— is a tree, and living, and not younger than any other tree'. Alternatively, we might use the propositional function: '— is a tree, and living, and neither younger than nor an exact contemporary of any other tree'. If we used this one, there would be no need for an explicit stipulation of unique satisfaction. For this propositional function could not be satisfied by one thing unless that thing were the only thing that satisfied it. Russell's example 'the first Chancellor of the German empire' offers a similar choice between two propositional functions. See *P. of PH.* p. 55 (*M. and L.* p. 217).

occupied by one and only one individual. In order to grasp the meaning of the word 'something', the speaker has to understand the process of generalising. He has to understand how to make a vacancy in a proposition, and how to put restrictions on the filling of the vacancy. In this particular case he has to understand what it means to say that in fact the vacancy is filled by one and only one individual. This is an entirely different thing from acquaintance with an individual, which is the other way of achieving understanding of the meaning of an ordinary proper name.

However, although analysis reveals that 'something' is a very special kind of word, it can figure as the grammatical subject of a proposition. That is why the dotted rectangle has a broken end. It can be combined with the complex of three properties, which, of course, also has to be shown with a broken end. So in spite of its unspecific nature it is *in this respect* like the individual which is symbolised by the continuous rectangle immediately beside it. Now one of the things that the speaker says is that in fact it is combined with the complex of three properties : 'There is one and only one thing which is a tree, and living, and not younger than any other tree'. According to him that is how things are in reality. Under analysis his definite description expands into a proposition. This feature is peculiar to the analysis of singular complex phrases. There is nothing like it in the analysis of general complex phrases which was illustrated in Diagram II.[3] This is the second difference between the two patterns of analysis.

It is worth pausing before going on to consider the third difference between the two patterns. For the second difference explains some rather puzzling things which Russell says about definite descriptions. For instance, in the longer version of his paper on *Knowledge by Acquaintance and Knowledge by Description*, the contrast between a definite description and an ordinary proper name used as a logically proper name is pre-

---

[3] There is, however, another way in which Russell sometimes analyses general complex phrases. See Note B, pp. 240-1.

sented in a way that is not entirely easy to understand.[4] Russell says that the meaning of the name 'Scott' is the man himself, and, provided that he is assuming as he often does that the name is being used as a logically proper name, this is his usual doctrine. But it is not so easy to follow him when he goes on to argue that the definite description 'the author of Waverley' cannot be interpreted in the same way, because, if it were, its meaning would be a subordinate complex.[5] What is a subordinate complex?

A subordinate complex is a complex of properties or relations, like the one that is illustrated in Diagram II. So his point is that, when a general symbol occurs as the grammatical predicate, as it does in the proposition 'This one is deciduous', the speaker will be talking about the property which is the denotation of the general symbol and so, if this property is complex, as deciduousness is, he will be talking about a complex of properties, each of which is the denotation of one of the general symbols which occur in the analysis of the word 'deciduous'. But when a set of general symbols follows the word 'the', as it does in a definite description, they have to be interpreted in a different way. For in this case the speaker will not be talking about the properties which are the denotations of the general symbols which occur in the definite description : he will be talking *through* this complex of properties *about* the individual which uniquely possesses them, if indeed there is such an individual.[6] So the definite description must be broken up in the analysis, and not treated as a subordinate complex. Diagram v exhibits the relationship between the denotations of the general words and the denotation about which the speaker is talking : the denotations of the general words appear on the right hand side, and the indi-

[4] *KN.A.KN.D.* (*M. and L.* pp. 223-9).
[5] *KN.A.KN.D.* (*M. and L.* p. 223 and p. 229).
[6] *KN.A.KN.D.* (*M. and L.* p. 227).

vidual denoted by the definite description, if indeed there is one, appears on the left hand side.[7]

Russell also says another rather puzzling thing about definite descriptions. He calls them 'incomplete symbols', but he does not always make it entirely clear what an incomplete symbol is. He contrasts incomplete symbols like 'the author of Waverley' with ordinary proper names like 'Scott', and here again he is assuming that the name 'Scott' is being used as a logically proper name.[8] This contrast is the nucleus out of which his concept of 'an incomplete symbol' grows, but it is not altogether easy to understand exactly how it grows out of it.

First let us establish the initial contrast. The point of it is that a symbol denoting something which has to be treated as simple, unlike a definite description, has a meaning all by itself: and so, if you are not acquainted with its denotation, you will not understand its meaning even though you understand the meanings of all the other words in the language.[9] The meanings of other words are no help at all, because the word whose meaning you want to understand is indefinable.

Notice two points about this contrast. First, an ordinary proper name like 'Scott' is really an incomplete symbol, because its denotation does not have to be treated as simple. When Russell contrasts the name 'Scott' with an incomplete symbol like 'the author of Waverley', he is presenting his

[7] In this explanation of Russell's argument it has been assumed that, when someone asserts the proposition 'This one is deciduous', he is talking about deciduousness as well as about the individual tree. This is not the only way of using the phrase 'to talk about'. According to another usage, the question which of the two things the speaker is talking about would be settled by the context: for example, the conversation might have been about deciduousness, in which case that is what the person who asserted the proposition would be talking about. But the adoption of this usage would merely complicate the exposition of Russell's argument without making the central point any clearer.

[8] *PH.L.A.* p. 47 (*L.KN.* p. 253).

[9] *PH.L.A.* p. 42 (*L.KN.* p. 244). Cf. Wittgenstein *T.L-PH.* 3.261.

point in a provisional and popular way. He is supposing that the name ' Scott ' is being used as a logically proper name, and his point is that logically proper names really are to be contrasted with incomplete symbols. Secondly, the contrast applies not only to singular symbols but also to general symbols.

However, he treats general symbols in a rather cursory way, and concentrates most of his attention on singular symbols, presumably because their analysis presents a more difficult problem. Consequently, his concept of ' an incomplete symbol ' tends to pick up features which are peculiar to singular complex symbols. For instance, the analysis of a definite description of an individual exhibits the very striking peculiarity which we have just been examining. It involves the breaking up of what appears to be a subordinate complex. When the definite description is analysed, it expands into a proposition. Now this leads to a radical reconstruction of the original proposition. Suppose that the original proposition was ' The author of Waverley built Abbotsford ' : under analysis this will become ' There is one and only one individual who wrote Waverley, and he built Abbotsford '. It is no good looking for an analysis of a definite description which could be substituted for it without any other change in the proposition. Straightforward substitution is possible only when a complex property occurs as a grammatical predicate, and then only if the word denoting it is not part of a definite description. In such a case the analysis illustrated in Diagram II can be carried out. But the analysis of the proposition ' The author of Waverley built Abbotsford ' radically changes its structure; or rather, it would be more accurate to say that it reveals its real structure, which is radically different from its apparent structure. Although this feature of the analysis of singular complex symbols is not shared by the analysis of general complex symbols, Russell's concentration on singular complex symbols leads him to incorporate it in the concept of ' an incomplete symbol '. Hence in *The Philosophy of Logical*

Atomism he says that incomplete symbols 'have absolutely no meaning whatsoever in isolation, but merely acquire a meaning in a context '.[10]

The next stage in Russell's account of incomplete symbols brings in an idea which was examined in the first chapter of this book. In *The Philosophy of Logical Atomism* he says that practically all the symbols that we apply to the familiar objects of everyday life, like tables and chairs, and people and places, are incomplete symbols, and that the objects themselves are 'logical fictions', most of them being 'either classes, or series, or series of classes '.[11] What exactly does this statement mean? Does it mean that some things to which incomplete symbols are applied are 'logical fictions', while other things to which incomplete symbols are applied are not 'logical fictions'? Or does it mean that anything to which an incomplete symbol is applied is a 'logical fiction'? If the second of these two interpretations is the right one, his

[10] *PH.L.A.* p. 47 (*L.KN.* p. 253). There are two possible ways of interpreting the first part of this statement. Either it merely refers to the initial contrast between complete and incomplete symbols, which is drawn on p. 42 of *PH.L.A.* (see previous footnote), or, alternatively, Russell is using the phrase 'have absolutely no meaning whatsoever in isolation' in such a way that it not only refers to the initial contrast, but also refers to the contrast between symbols which can be replaced by their analyses in a straightforward way and symbols whose analyses involve radical reconstruction of the propositions in which they occur. The second interpretation is the more natural of the two. Russell's slide from the first contrast to the second is perplexing, but understandable. It is even more perplexing, but still understandable that in some of his discussions of incomplete symbols he takes the first contrast for granted (e.g. *P.M.* 2nd ed. p. 66ff). There is an excellent discussion of the second contrast by G. E. Moore, ' *Russell's Theory of Descriptions* ', in *PH.B.R.* p. 219ff.

It is important to observe that, although a definite description is an incomplete symbol, the proposition which expresses the analysis of 'The author of Waverley built Abbotsford' is, in an entirely different sense, complete. The completeness of propositions will be explained later. See pp. 203-6.

[11] *PH.L.A.* p. 47 (*L.KN.* p. 253).

concept of 'an incomplete symbol' will have grown in a new direction.

In order to get an answer to this question, let us consider again the phrase 'object in the external world'. When Russell says that objects in the external world are 'logical fictions', he means that the popular idea of them contains more than it really ought to contain, and so makes it impossible to infer their existence legitimately. This fault will be corrected by philosophical analysis of the phrase, which will discard the surplus and illegitimate part of its popular meaning, and substitute logical constructions for inferred entities. The meaning of the phrase will be reconstructed by definitions connecting it with human experience. So the phrase is a typical incomplete symbol, because it does not have meaning all by itself; and the things to which it is applied are 'logical fictions', because there can be no reason to suppose that they exist in the full way that is suggested by the popular idea of them. So here is one clear example of an incomplete symbol which, according to Russell, is applied to 'logical fictions', and it is not the only one.

But are all things to which incomplete symbols are applied 'logical fictions'? It would be natural to give a negative answer to this question. For definability, which makes a symbol incomplete, is not necessarily accompanied by the phenomenon which makes a thing a 'logical fiction', namely the gap between popular meaning and legitimate meaning. This point was made in Chapter 1. A definite description is analysable, but there is no gap between its popular meaning and its legitimate meaning, and so its analysis will cover the whole of its one and only meaning.

However, Russell did not give a negative answer to the question whether all things to which incomplete symbols are applied are 'logical fictions'. This is made absolutely clear in a passage in *The Introduction to Mathematical Philosophy*, where he is discussing the definition of the word 'class'.[12] He says:

[12] *I.M.PH.* pp. 181-2.

' We must seek a definition on the same lines as the definition of descriptions, i.e. a definition which will assign a meaning to propositions in whose verbal or symbolic expression words or symbols apparently representing classes occur, but which will assign a meaning that altogether eliminates all mention of classes from a right analysis of such propositions. We shall then be able to say that the symbols for classes are mere conveniences, not representing objects called " classes ", and that classes are in fact, like descriptions, " logical fictions ", or (as we say) " incomplete symbols ".'

This passage shows that it is part of Russell's concept of ' an incomplete symbol' that the things to which such symbols are applied must be ' logical fictions'.

This further growth of Russell's concept of ' an incomplete symbol' can be defended up to a certain point. For there is some analogy between the thesis, that the daughter of Hitler does not have to exist in the so-called platonic way in order to give that definite description a meaning, and the thesis, that objects in the external world do not have to exist in the full way that is suggested by the popular idea of them in order to give that phrase a meaning. But the analogy breaks down, because there is no popular interpretation of definite descriptions which suggests ' platonic' existence. So when Russell says that classes do not exist what he means is utterly unlike what would be meant by someone who said that the daughter of Hitler does not exist.[13] However, it may be possible to explain why his concept of ' an incomplete symbol' grew in this direction. The explanation seems to be similar to the explanation of the other stage in its growth. It is probable that he was thinking primarily of a special class of incomplete symbols. He probably had in mind the sort of controversial concept whose deep analysis was his ultimate objective. His preoccupation with this goal might naturally have led him to say things about all incomplete symbols which only applied,

[13] See Note A, pp. 24-5, where the difference between the two meanings is explained.

or at least only fully applied, to those incomplete symbols in which he was primarily interested.

Let us now return to the point of origin of this digression, which has been concerned with some of Russell's more puzzling remarks about definite descriptions. It had just been stated that there is a third difference between the analysis of general complex symbols and the analysis of singular complex symbols. This difference was mentioned in the last chapter, and it is apparent in Diagrams I and V. Diagram I is an illustration of the proposition 'This one is deciduous', asserted by someone who is acquainted both with the thing and with the property. In this case the singular symbol is used as a logically proper name, and the thing with which it is connected is symbolised by a continuous rectangle. Now the ordinary proper name 'Avar', which was introduced later, might also be used as a logically proper name. However, we supposed that it was being used as a truncated definite description, and then the question was how it acquires a connection with the thing which the speaker hopes that it denotes. In Diagrams IV and V the continuous rectangle representing the individual has been shown apparently waiting for the name 'Avar' to establish a connection with it. But, according to Russell, the connection never is established, or at least never is established in the way in which the analogous connection is established on the right hand side of Diagram II, which illustrates the analysis of a complex general symbol occurring as a predicate not inside a definite description. For the phrase 'loses foliage periodically' really is the analysis of the phrase 'is deciduous', and, if the speaker treats the elements mentioned by the words in this analysis as if they denoted simple entities, it will be an analysis containing general symbols used as simple general symbols. But, as Diagram V shows, you cannot produce a parallel analysis on the left hand side. That is to say, when you analyse the ordinary proper name 'Avar', used as a truncated description, you never reach a stage at which your analysis will contain a singular symbol used as a logically proper name of the individual which you hope that 'Avar' denotes. Another person, who was acquainted with the individual, might pick it out with a singular symbol used as a logically proper name. But the best that you can do in that direction is to produce a definite description denoting it.

This is illustrated by the fact that in Diagram v the dotted circle representing the word 'something' is connected with a dotted rectangle, and not with the continuous rectangle. It might be thought that Diagram v shows an unfinished stage in the analysis of the ordinary proper name 'Avar' used as a truncated description, and that that is the only reason why the analysis illustrated does not contain a singular symbol used as a logically proper name of the individual which you hope that 'Avar' denotes. The next step, it might be suggested, would simply be to replace the definite description by a singular symbol used as a logically proper name. Then the continuous rectangle would acquire the connection for which it appears to be waiting. But this suggestion would be mistaken. The analysis shown in Diagram v may be unfinished, but it seems that it cannot be finished in that way. Russell makes this clear in the passage in his longer essay on *Knowledge by Acquaintance and Knowledge by Description*, which was discussed in the last chapter.[14] He says that, if you lack the necessary acquaintance, then, although you want to assert a proposition containing a singular symbol used as a logically proper name, you cannot do so. The best that you can do is to *describe* that proposition. That is to say, the best that you can do is to assert *another* proposition linked by a definite description of the individual to the one that you want to assert but cannot assert. It follows that he did not regard the proposition containing the singular symbol used as a logically proper name as the final analysis, or indeed as any stage in the analysis of the original proposition. It functions instead as a sort of magnetic pole which explains the direction in which our definite descriptions point, and justifies our belief that, in spite of the differ-

[14] *KN.A.KN.D.* (*M. and L.* p. 218). See pp. 77-82.

ent descriptions that we use, we really do communicate with one another.

If this is Russell's view, as it seems to be, it is curious that he never mentions it in *The Philosophy of Logical Atomism.* What he says there is that ' in a logically perfect language the words in a proposition would correspond one by one with the components of the corresponding fact, with the exception of such words as " or ", " not ", " if ", " then " which have a different function.'[15] Here the exceptions are, of course, logical words, and a full list of them would include the word ' some '. He then goes on to say that in such a language ' there will be one word and no more for every simple object, and everything that is not simple will be expressed by a combination of words, by a combination derived, of course, from the words for the simple things that enter in, one word for each component.' He admits that this language would be extremely inconvenient to use, and that its vocabulary would be very largely private to one speaker.[16] But in this passage, and in many others, he quite evidently assumes that the propositions of everyday life all have analyses which consist entirely of words belonging to this perfect language, *i.e.* of words whose denotations have to be treated by us as simple. Now this assumption is not flatly incompatible with the view which he expresses in *Knowledge by Acquaintance and Knowledge by Description.* For, even if an analysis stops at the stage illustrated in Diagram v, all the non-logical words in it might be symbols corresponding to properties or relations which we have to treat as simple. But it is rather odd that he does not point out that in this kind of case one of the components of the fact which the speaker *wants* to state, namely the individual, will not have a logically proper name in the analysis to denote it.

It is an interesting question whether Wittgenstein felt the difficulty which led Russell to adopt the view which he propounds in *Knowledge by Acquaintance and Knowledge by*

[15] *PH.L.A.* p. 13 (*L.KN.* pp. 197-8).   [16] See p. 40, footnote 21.

Description. Wittgenstein's analysis of a singular complex symbol begins, like Russell's, with the substitution of a definite description, interpreted according to Russell's theory,[17] and it ends, like Russell's, with a version of the original proposition which contains only 'simple signs' corresponding to the objects of the thought.[18] Did Wittgenstein feel Russell's scruple about the substitution of 'simple signs' for definite descriptions? Or was he confident that such a substitution would not produce a different thought from the thought expressed by the proposition containing the definite description? Anyway, there is no doubt that Russell's scruple was justified. For, according to him, the substitution of a logically proper name for a definite description of an individual necessarily produces a different proposition.[19]

[17] See Note A.
[18] *T.L-PH.* 3.2—3.23. [19] See p. 120, footnote 9.

NOTE A

See *Wittgenstein N.L.* (*N.B.* App. 1, p. 99), *T.L.PH.* 2.0201 and 3.24. This interpretation of these three passages is disputed by J. P. Griffin. He argues that Wittgenstein had an 'alternative theory of Descriptions' (*W.L.A.* p. 61ff): 'Describing a complex is giving the form of the objects which constitute it.' Now describing a complex is usually taken to be ascribing certain properties to the particular which constitutes it, or ascribing certain properties and relations to the particulars which constitute it (see p. 45 and pp. 93-5; the generalisation, which is needed in order to cover the case in which a complex is analysed as a set of related particulars, is given on pp. 122-3). But Griffin argues (*loc. cit.* pp. 57-9) that Wittgenstein always analyses a macroscopic property or relation as a set of *parti-*

culars arranged in a certain way, and that this arrangement is a form
(rather like Locke's analysis of secondary qualities [see Locke, *Essay
Concerning Human Understanding*, bk. II, ch. 8, and *T.L-PH.* 6.3751].
A somewhat similar suggestion is made by G. E. M. Anscombe *I.W.T.*
pp. 98-102, but, unlike Griffin [see p. 59], she does not identify
Wittgenstein's objects with material particles, so that, according to
her, Wittgenstein's analysis is not so like Locke's). On this interpretation Wittgenstein would not regard a description of a complex which
mentioned macroscopic properties and relations as fully analysed. Its
analysis would have to be continued until it only mentioned particulars and their arrangements (in Wittgenstein's terminology, ' objects' and their ' configurations ').

The chief objection to this interpretation of the three passages is
that the theory attributed to Wittgenstein is not an *alternative* to
Russell's Theory of Definite Descriptions. For, according to the attributed theory, the particulars involved in the analysis of a complex
would not always be named. Very often their arrangements would be
specified, but they themselves would be left unspecified (see Griffin, *loc.
cit.* p. 63). How, then, could reference be made to one of them? Only,
it appears, through an existential proposition containing a stipulation of
unique satisfaction (see p. 64). So we have not been offered an
alternative to Russell's Theory of Definite Descriptions, but only an
alternative way of analysing the macroscopic properties and relations
which occur in a Russellian analysis of a definite description.

The chief argument in support of Griffin's account of Wittgensteinian analysis is based on *T.L-PH.* 3.2—3.23, where it is made
absolutely clear that completely analysed propositions contain nothing
but names (Griffin, *loc. cit.*, pp. 44-5). But how is the analyst supposed
to reach this stage? If no Russellian definite descriptions lay on his
route, he would not have to choose between substituting names for
them and stopping his analysis at a point at which it still contained
existential propositions with stipulations of unique satisfaction. But
Griffin does not seem to have found an alternative route which would
allow Wittgenstein to circumvent Russellian definite descriptions.
Indeed, *T.L-PH.* 3.24 does not even suggest that Wittgenstein thought
that he had circumvented them.

If this is so, Wittgenstein encountered the difficulty that Russell
encountered on p. 218 of *M. and L.* How did he overcome it? The
apparent absence of any solution to this problem in *T.L-PH.* might
suggest that Wittgenstein must have had an alternative to Russell's
Theory of Definite Descriptions. There are also other arguments
which might be used to support this thesis (see Griffin, *loc cit.*, pp.
41-7: see especially the use that he makes of *PH.I.* § 60, which is
discussed on p. 127 footnote 19). However, one would have thought
that, if Wittgenstein really believed that he had found an alternative

route, which circumvented Russell's Theory of Definite Descriptions, he would not have shrunk from announcing the discovery in his usual way (see *T.L.PH.* 3.331, 5,5302, 5.54—5.5423). So perhaps, when he said that elementary propositions only contain names, his main point was that, though they may contain definite descriptions, they may not contain any singular or general words denoting complex things. Admittedly, this is not a very satisfactory suggestion. But it may be that the situation was not very satisfactory.

CHAPTER VIII

THE DESTINATION

The exposition of Russell's logical atomism, which has been given so far, has taken the subject in a rather unusual order. In Chapter IV three types of singular symbol were distinguished : singular symbols whose denotations may be treated as simple, in spite of the fact that we know that they are complex; singular symbols whose denotations have to be treated by us as simple, whether or not they are intrinsically simple; and singular symbols whose denotations really are intrinsically simple. The second and third of these classes of singular symbol overlap, and, of course, the same three-fold classification also applies to general symbols.[1] The order of exposition has been rather unusual, because it has concentrated so far on the first of the three types of singular symbol, whereas most accounts of Russell's system begin with the second type. Indeed, it might look as if it were necessary to begin with the second type. For that type includes logically proper names, while the first type includes ordinary proper names used as logically proper names, and it might look as if it were impossible to understand the latter without first understanding the former.

However, that would be an illusion. To use an ordinary proper name as a logically proper name is merely to use it to denote an individual directly, without the intervention of any descriptions.[2] This explanation of singular symbols of the first type is quite independent of the explanation of singular symbols of the second type. So the order of exposition that has been followed is a perfectly natural one. There are various reasons why it has been adopted.[3] One reason is that it is better to establish the general character of Russell's empiricism before going into its special features. His principle,

[1] See pp. 48-9.　　[2] See p. 60.　　[3] See p. 61, footnote 7.

that every proposition which we can understand must be composed wholly of constituents with which we are acquainted,[4] may lead in the end to the thesis that there must be symbols of the second type, but in itself it is no more than a general affirmation of empiricism. That is to say, it corresponds to Hume's thesis that all our ideas are derived from impressions, and that the derivation is often indirect, because complex ideas are often made up out of simpler ideas, derived from impressions which did not occur together; but it does not include his thesis that some ideas are absolutely simple.

In order to complete the exposition of Russell's logical atomism, something more must now be said about symbols of the second type, whose denotations have to be treated by us as simple. For, as was pointed out earlier,[5] Russell's analysis terminates with symbols of this type. Indeed the phrase ' logical atomism ', as he uses it, means the thesis that the philosophical analysis of ordinary propositions will go so far and no further.[6] This is perhaps the point of greatest difference between Russell's logical atomism and the version of logical atomism developed by Wittgenstein in the *Tractatus*, according to which a complete analysis consists wholly of symbols of the third type, whose denotations are intrinsically simple.

Perhaps it would be best to begin by recapitulating what has been said about singular symbols of the second type. There were two main points, the first of which was about Russell's characterisation of them, and the second of which was about the argument used by him to establish that they must exist. He characterises them as symbols which we are unable to analyse, and from this it follows that we cannot understand their meanings without acquaintance with their denotations, and that it neither makes sense to deny the existence of their

---

[4] See p. 87.   [5] See p. 48.

[6] This statement is not affected by the point discussed at the end of the last chapter. It remains true, whether or not Russell believed that definite descriptions containing unanalysable general symbols could be replaced by unanalysable singular symbols. The evidence for this interpretation of Russell's logical atomism will be given later in this chapter.

denotations nor to assert it. He tries to prove that they must exist by using the argument that any individual which is mentioned in a proposition can always be treated as the unanalysable subject of everything that we can say about it.[7] This unanalysable subject will be denoted by a symbol which is simple in the second of the three ways that have been distinguished. These points now need expansion and comment.

First, there might be some uncertainty about what is meant by the thesis that it makes no sense to deny or affirm the existence of a thing which we have to treat as simple. What this means is that the denial and the affirmation do not make sense if the thing whose existence is in question is picked out by a symbol belonging to the second of the three types that were distinguished. For example, it does not make sense to use a logically proper name in order to pick out an individual, if you then go on to say that that individual does not exist.[8] If you did that, you would be denying the existence of something whose existence was actually required in order to give your denial a sense, and that is just what you could not do. The thing whose existence you denied would be a constituent of your denial in the stricter of the two senses of the word ' constituent '. In this sense of the word, a constituent of a proposition is a thing that would be mentioned in the completely analysed version of the proposition. Such a thing must exist if the complete analysis has a sense. Now your denial would be, as it stood, completely analysed, and so it would use a logically proper name to pick out the thing whose existence it then went on to deny.[9] That could not be done. Nor, of course, would the affirmation be much better.[10] However, there is something else which you could perfectly well

---

[7] See p. 46. This argument needs to be generalised. See p. 122ff.

[8] See pp. 56-7.

[9] See p. 90, footnote 26. This is enough to show that Russell's scruple about substituting a logically proper name for a definite description was justified. For such a substitution in a negative existential proposition would convert a contingent proposition into a kind of contradiction.

[10] See p. 57.

do. You could formulate *another* proposition, which used a definite description in order to pick out the individual, and *this* proposition might deny or affirm the existence of the individual which in the original proposition was picked out by a logically proper name. Naturally, if the individual did exist, your denial would be false. But that does not affect the present point, which is that your denial, so long as it used a definite description, would make sense.

There is a common misunderstanding of Russell's system which might lead to a different interpretation of his thesis about affirming and denying the existence of individuals which we have to treat as simple. He is often credited with the view that these individuals, which he calls 'particulars', cannot be described. If this interpretation means that, according to him, particulars cannot have properties or relations ascribed to them, and cannot be picked out by definite descriptions mentioning their properties and relations, it must be wrong. For particulars are picked out by logically proper names occurring in propositions which then go on to say something about them, perhaps that they have certain properties;[11] consequently, it must also be possible to use definite descriptions mentioning their properties in order to pick them out.[12] However, Russell does say that, when someone is acquainted with a particular, he can name it but not assert it, and this remark might give the impression that his point is that such a person could not ascribe properties to the particular, or use definite descriptions in order to pick it out.[13] But that is not what he means. He means that, when the speaker has said everything that he can say about the particular, it will be the unanalysable subject of everything that he has said about it.[14] If the speaker refrained from saying everything that he could say, the subject of what he did say would be a complex individual, and so the symbol applied to it would expand under analysis into further propositions men-

[11] *PH.L.A.* p. 14 (*L.KN.* pp. 199-200).
[12] Wittgenstein allows that this is possible, *T.L-PH.* 2.02331.
[13] *R.S.-D.PH.* (*M. and L.* p. 147).   [14] See p. 47.

tioning the properties which he had refrained from mentioning. But, when everything has been said about it, the subject cannot be analysed any further in this way. It is a particular which can be named but not asserted. But that does not mean that it cannot have properties ascribed to it, or that it cannot be picked out by definite descriptions mentioning those properties. So there is a way in which its existence can be affirmed or denied. A definite description must be used to pick it out.

Let us now return to Russell's two main points about symbols belonging to the second of the three types which have been distinguished. These are symbols whose denotations we have to treat as simple, and his first point about them was that their meanings can be understood only through acquaintance with their denotations, and that they cannot occur as the grammatical subjects of existential propositions. That is how he characterises them. Secondly, he attempts to prove that there must be such symbols. These two points need to be expanded and generalised, in order to produce a comprehensive account of his idea of a complete analysis. So far, they have been explained only within a narrow field. They have been applied only to individuals, and not to properties and relations; and they have been applied only to cases in which a complex individual is analysed as a particular possessing a number of properties, and not to cases in which a complex individual is analysed as a set of particulars related in various ways. These two restrictions must now be removed, and his two points about symbols of the second type must be generalised.

The second restriction is easily removed. All that is needed is an alteration to Diagram v. Instead of supposing that Avar is a complex individual consisting of a particular possessing three properties, we can suppose that it consists of two particulars related to one another in a certain way, and each possessing a different property. Wittgenstein used an example of this kind when he wrote about his own version of logical

atomism long after he had abandoned it.[15] He illustrated his
earlier view by taking a proposition mentioning his broom,
and by suggesting that, under analysis, it would turn into a
proposition about the two connected parts of the broom, the
broom-stick and the brush. This gives us two properties, the
property of being a broom-stick, and the property of being a
brush, and one relation, adhesion. So, if we use Russell's
Theory of Definite Descriptions, as Wittgenstein did in the
Tractatus, we find that the complex symbol which was applied
to the broom expands under analysis into two propositions:
'There is one and only one thing which is my brush', and
'There is one and only one thing which is a broom-stick and is
joined to my brush'. If we ignore the possessive pronoun for
the moment, we get another, rather more elaborate version of
the kind of pattern that was illustrated in Diagram v.

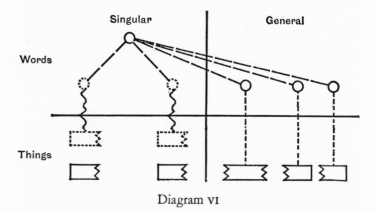

Diagram VI

In this diagram things work very much as they did in Diagram v. Of course, the word 'something' has to occur
twice, because two particulars are involved. Also on the right
hand side, in addition to the two properties, the property of
being a brush and the property of being a broom-stick, we have
had to illustrate the relation which connects them. Otherwise

[15] *PH.I.* § 60.

Diagram vi is like Diagram v. However, there is one word which has not been illustrated in Diagram vi, the word ' my '. This possessive pronoun is very important, because it makes it reasonable to stipulate that the propositional functions are each satisfied by one and only one thing. If the possessive pronoun were left out, it would be mad to make a stipulation of unique satisfaction. Nobody would say that there is one and only one thing which is *a* brush.

But how should the word ' my ' be illustrated in the diagram? What it denotes is not really a property, but a relation to an individual. For the first of the two propositions means that there is one and only one thing which is a brush and is possessed by the speaker. So we have to add another relation on the right hand side, possession, and another individual on the left hand side, the speaker.

Diagram vii only illustrates the first of the two existential propositions in the analysis: ' There is one and only one thing which is my brush '. The relation on the right hand side is not adhesion but possession, and the individual on the extreme left is the speaker. It is worth pausing for a moment to ask exactly why these two extra elements were not needed in Diagram v. The reason is that in that case the complex of three properties mentioned in the definite description was sufficient in itself to make it likely that the denotation, if there were one, would be unique. It is unlikely that there would be more than one thing which was living, and a tree, and not younger than any other tree.[16] But it is very unusual to find a definite description which relies, as that one did, entirely on properties and relations. Nearly always the mechanism of denotation will use another individual as a reference-point. and the definite description will say that there is one and only one thing which is related in a specific way to the reference-

---

[16] See p. 104 footnote 2, where it was pointed out that a different propositional function might have been used in the analysis of the definite description, *viz*; '—is living, and a tree, and neither younger than nor an exact contemporary of any other tree.'

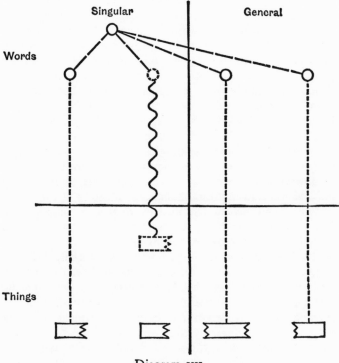

Diagram VII

point. 'The first Chancellor of the German empire', 'the King of France', and most of Russell's other examples work in this way.

The fact that nearly all definite descriptions use the mechanism of denotation that is illustrated in Diagram VII is important. It is particularly important when the individual used as a reference-point is the speaker himself. For it raises a doubt about Russell's account of the demonstrative pronoun ' this '. Russell says that, when the word ' this ' is applied to a sense-datum, it is being used as a logically proper name, and

' does not *mean* " the object to which I am now attending " :
for it is not waiting to be defined by the property of being
given, but is given; first it is actually given, and then reflection shows that it is that which is given.'[17] But could I really
know my sense-datum without the intervention of the basic
description ' given to me at a specific time '? What does the
phrase ' pure acquaintance with a sense-datum ' mean? No
doubt, when all the *other* descriptions of my sense-datum have
been peeled off it, there will still be something left to be
known. But will there be anything left when the basic description of my sense-datum has been removed? Of course, it will
still confront me, but what knowledge will it have left to give
me? Perhaps the last Chinese box will be hollow too.

However, this doubt may be put on one side, until we have
finished generalising the account of Russell's views about
symbols whose denotations we have to treat as simple. The
first stage in generalising it was to show that they apply to
cases in which a complex individual consists of particulars
related to one another in a certain way. This stage is illustrated
in Diagrams VI and VII. Of course, the analyses which these
diagrams illustrate need not be complete, since we might be
able to analyse the symbols that occur in them. But, if we
suppose that their denotations have to be treated by us as
simple, we shall have a picture of a new type of Russellian
complete analysis of a complex individual. This type plays
an enormously larger part in Russell's system than the type
illustrated in Diagram V. For Russell believed that objects in
the external world should be analysed into sets of sense-data[18]
and *sensibilia*, and such an analysis would conform to the type
illustrated in Diagrams VI and VII.[19]

[17] *O.N.A.* (*L.KN.* p. 168), which was discussed on p. 46.
[18] He abandoned sense-data in 1919. See pp. 41-2.
[19] J. P. Griffin (*W.L.A.* pp. 44-7) seems to assume that Russell
always analyses a complex as a single particular possessing certain
properties. This assumption certainly makes a Russellian complete
analysis look much more different from the kind of analysis that

The generalisation of this account of Russell's views about symbols denoting things which we have to treat as simple must now be taken one stage further. So far, we have only examined singular symbols belonging to this type. But there are also symbols of this type which denote properties and relations. Now symbols denoting things which we have to treat as simple are characterised by him in two ways. First, he says that we cannot understand their meanings without acquaintance with their denotations; and the second thing that he says about them, which follows from the first, is that it neither makes sense to deny the existence of their denotations nor to assert it. Both these theses apply in a fairly straightforward way to properties and relations. For instance, according to him, the word 'red' is a general symbol of this type, and so its meaning can be understood only through acquaintance with the denoted property.[20] It follows that, if someone denied that the property existed, his denial would not make sense. For, whether he meant that the property had no instances, or that it was an impossible property,[21] his denial could not be true, because, if it were true, it would lack sense, and, if it lacked sense, it could not be true. And, if he asserted that the property existed, the situation would be little better, because his assertion would be either senseless or a sort of tautology.[22]

The parallelism between Russell's views about singular symbols denoting things which we have to treat as simple and his views about general symbols of this type does not extend beyond this point. For he does not use the same argument to prove that there must be general symbols denoting things

Wittgenstein describes in *PH.I.* § 60 than it really is. However, the main reason why Griffin's estimate of the difference is so high is his view that Wittgenstein used 'an alternative theory of descriptions'. See Note A, pp. 115-17. It should also be remembered that a Russellian complete analysis certainly does not always use definite descriptions to pick out individuals. See p. 133.

[20] *PH.L.A.* pp. 10-11 (*L.KN.* 193-4).   [21] See p. 85.
[22] See p. 57 and p. 121.

which we have to treat as simple. Indeed, it would be quite impossible to argue that, when a complex property like deciduousness is specified as the property of losing foliage periodically, the property itself will be the unanalysable subject of this specification. For the specification is an analysis which exhausts the meaning of the word ' deciduous ', so that nothing can possibly be left over. It states that deciduousness is identical with the elements into which it has been analysed. These elements do not constitute a property of deciduousness, but, rather, they are deciduousness, and they constitute a property of the tree. The analysis of the singular complex symbol ' Avar ' elicits one or more unanalysable subjects, but the analysis of the complex property ' deciduous ' does not elicit any further unanalysable subjects.[23] Nor is it surprising that the parallelism should cease at this point. For, as has already been indicated,[24] general symbols and singular symbols are not so very alike.

So, when Russell set out to establish that there must be general symbols denoting things which we have to treat as simple, he had to use a different argument. His argument was that the analysis of a general symbol, which consists in setting forth its definition, and then setting forth the definitions of the words which occur in that definition, could not proceed to infinity. This is not the same thing as arguing that there must be properties and relations which are intrinsically simple. Russell's argument could only establish that there must be properties and relations which we have to treat as simple; it could not establish that any kind of creature would have to treat them as simple. The difference between these two conclusions may look slight. But really it is considerable. It is produced by the fact that a difference in sensory powers might

---

[23] In all the cases that have been examined so far properties and relations have been picked out by specific general words. The matter becomes more complicated when they are picked out by definite descriptions. See Note B, pp. 240-1.

[24] See pp. 99ff.

lead to a difference in the kind of meaning that some general symbol has. For instance, the word ' red ', as we use it, is unanalysable. It has that kind of meaning. The definition of the word which is provided by the physical theory of colour is not its analysis. Nevertheless, it might become its analysis. For our sensory powers might change in such a way that we could perceive directly what we can now detect only with the aid of scientific instruments, and, if that happened, we might come to equate the meaning of the word ' red ' with the specification given in the scientific definition. The result would be that, although the word would continue to be applied to exactly the same things, it would cease to be one of our unanalysable general symbols.[25] Evidently, it is much more difficult to prove that there must be general symbols which would be unanalysable for any kind of creature. For the proof of that thesis would have to establish that the denotation of the symbol could never be the subject of the kind of general statement which might be treated as its definition, and ultimately as its analysis.[26]

However, Russell only argues that the process of setting forth the definitions which give our analyses of general symbols must come to a halt somewhere. This is a plausible thesis, because, if it did not come to a halt anywhere, the meanings of our general symbols would be indeterminate. Even if we agreed in our application of them, we should not be able to explain fully and finally what we meant. This disadvantage looks very different from the disadvantage which would result if there were no singular symbols denoting things which we have to treat as simple. For, if there were no singular symbols of that type, that is to say, no logically proper names, the consequence would be that, when we had said everything that we could say about an individual, there would be nothing that we could treat as the unanalysable

[25] See pp. 47-8.
[26] The argument for the existence of intrinsically simple things will be examined in Ch. IX.

subject of everything that we had said about it. So in the case of singular symbols the trouble would be that there would be things which we could not say. But in the case of general symbols the trouble would not be that there were things that we could not say : rather, it would be that we could not fully and finally explain the meanings of things which we do say. However, the difference between the two cases must not be exaggerated, or rather, the difference as it appeared to Russell must not be exaggerated. For, though it may look large to us, it looked much smaller to him, because he believed that, if there were no logically proper names, we would be equally unable to give a full and final explanation of the meanings of our singular symbols. The reason why he believed this was that he thought that there is an element of vagueness in a proposition which uses a complex symbol in order to pick out an individual. In such a case the speaker has not asserted the proposition which he really wanted to assert.[27] A complete analysis would often remove this vagueness by replacing the complex symbols by one or more logically proper names, and, if Russell waived the scruple which was discussed at the end of the last chapter, it would always remove it in this way. Consequently, if there were no logically proper names, the vagueness could not be removed, and so we could not give a full and final explanation of the meaning of any proposition.[28] That is why the difference between the two cases did not seem so great to him.

Whatever the merits of this reason for requiring logically proper names in the complete analysis of a proposition, Russell's reasoning about simple general symbols is certainly plausible. If the meanings of complex general symbols could be given only by definitions,[29] and if definitions ran on to infinity, the meanings of complex general symbols could never be given completely. This could not prove that there are general

[27] *KN.A.KN.D.* (*M. and L.* p. 218). See pp. 77-81.
[28] See Note A at the end of this chapter.
[29] See pp. 83-4 for doubts about this.

symbols denoting things which are intrinsically simple, but it
might seem to prove that there are general symbols denoting
things which we have to treat as simple. Russell's reasoning
at this point closely follows Hume's. For Hume too thought
it self-evident that the process of definition which breaks up
complex ideas must come to a halt with simple ideas which
are replicas of simple impressions,[80] and this thesis of his is not
affected by the possibility that impressions might not be
intrinsically simple. For, like Russell, he was only concerned
to show that the intellectual apparatus through which we
understand the world must contain general elements which
are, at least for us, unanalysable. In his case the elements were
ideas, whereas in Russell's case they are symbols.

There is, of course, another similarity between Russell's
and Hume's views about our intellectual apparatus. They both
thought not only that it must contain simple general elements,
but also that they had succeeded in identifying them, and they
both made the same identifications. For, as was pointed out
earlier,[81] Russell's examples of simple general symbols are
exactly like Hume's. They include the names of colours and
the names of certain other sensory properties and relations.

This identification of general symbols denoting things which
we have to treat as simple obviously reinforces Russell's argument that there must be such general symbols. Similarly, his
argument that there must be logically proper names is reinforced when he identifies them with the names of sense-data.
But it is important to remember that his theory of meaning
contains nothing which compels him to say that particulars,
which are the denotations of logically proper names, are sense-
data, or that the properties and relations which we have to
treat as simple are those of sense-data. These identifications
are not produced by his theory of meaning. They are the
result of his acceptance of the traditional arguments of the

[80] *An Enquiry Concerning Human Understanding* § VII pt. i. (ed.
Selby-Bigge, p. 62).
[81] See p. 43.

sceptic against our ordinary belief in the external world.[32]

All that is needed in order to round off this account of Russellian complete analysis is a diagram which will show the effect of these identifications. Let us use a second horizontal line to divide things in the external world from sense-data. Things above this line will be in the external world, and things below it will be sense-data. Using this convention, let us illustrate the Russellian complete analysis of the proposition ' Avar is red ', asserted by a person who is actually looking at the tree, or remembers looking at it.[33]

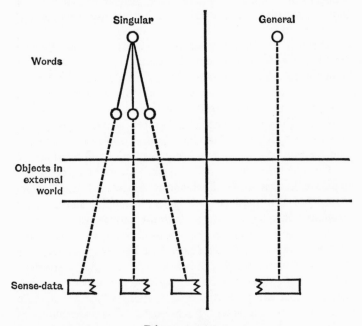

Diagram VIII

[32] See pp. 58-9.

[33] It is important that acquaintance with an individual can persist after perception of it has ceased. See p. 71, footnote 1.

This diagram is a development of Diagram I. It differs from it in two ways. First, it illustrates a case in which a complex individual emerges under analysis not as a single particular but as a group of related particulars. In this respect the pattern illustrated is like the pattern in Diagram VI, except that in Diagram VI the speaker only knew the particulars by description, whereas here he knows them by acquaintance. The second difference between this diagram and Diagram I is that the particulars are sense-data, and so the rectangles representing them appear below the new horizontal line. Naturally, the rectangle representing the property which is ascribed to them also appears below this dividing line. It is very important to notice that Russell assumes that this property of the sense-data is the colour red. As was pointed out earlier, that assumption could be questioned.[84]

It would be tedious to take all the other diagrams and adapt them to fit Russell's identification of particulars with sense-data. It is, for instance, hardly necessary to show what happens when we take a complex property instead of the simple property 'red'. For all that is needed in such a case is an adaptation of Diagram II. However, there is one very important point which must be made about the analysis illustrated in Diagram VIII; which is that, though that analysis is complete in the sense that it can not go any deeper, it could well expand laterally. For, in addition to the sense-data which the speaker is actually having, or remembers, there are also other people's sense-data, and there are *sensibilia*. These will only be known to him by description, and so, in order to include them in the diagram, we should have to add to it an adaptation of Diagram VI. Of course, if we took the case of a speaker who was not looking at the tree and did not remember it, the complete analysis of his proposition would be illustrated *entirely* by an adaptation of Diagram VI: there would be no sense-data with which he was acquainted, and so the pattern on

[84] See p. 36.

the left hand side of Diagram VIII would be no part of the complete analysis of his proposition.[85]

It has already been mentioned that Russell no longer holds the view about particulars which has just been outlined. When he wrote *The Philosophy of Logical Atomism*, his theory about complete analysis required the existence of simple individuals, or 'particulars'. But later he felt the nagging doubt which has coloured this exposition of his theory.[86] How can logically proper names avoid picking up the descriptions of their denotations? Perhaps it would be an exaggeration to say that all names incorporate the descriptions of their denotations in their connotations. But it is hard to see why the relationship between a logically proper name and the descriptions of its denotation should be any more distant than the relationship between an ordinary proper name and the descriptions of its denotation. It is especially hard to maintain the distance between a logically proper name of one of your sense-data and the basic description 'given to you now'.[87] For, when you have a sense-datum, although you can imagine that a *different kind* of sense-datum might have been given to you now, it does not make any sense to say that *this particular sense-datum* might not have been given to you now. The basic description is undetachable, because it gives the particular sense-datum its identity.[88]

When Russell abandoned his belief that there are singular

---

[85] This statement is based on the assumption that in the analysis of a proposition it is not legitimate to substitute logically proper names for definite descriptions. See pp. 77-81, 114-15, and p. 120, footnote 9.

[86] See pp. 46-7. [87] See pp. 93-4.

[88] This may be what lies behind Hume's thesis that one might expect that the impressions or ideas of a person would be necessarily connected (*T.H.N.* Appendix : vol. II, pp. 317-19). Evidently, it would be absurd to suppose that, when you had a sense-datum of a certain kind, it was necessary that the sequence of your sense-data should contain one of that kind at that moment. But it is not quite so absurd to say that that particular sense-datum could not have failed to occur at that moment. It is only a very misleading way of saying that, if it had failed to occur at that moment, it would not have existed. The basic description gives it its identity.

symbols denoting things which we have to treat as simple,[39] he faced a difficulty. For, quite apart from the logical argument for their existence, they seemed to provide the only adequate way of identifying individuals. Anyone who only uses descriptions in order to identify individuals has to admit the possibility that there might be two individuals which were exactly alike, and so could be described in exactly the same ways,[40] and that is tantamount to the admission that descriptions do not provide an absolutely adequate way of identifying individuals. So, when Russell changed his mind about logically proper names, he had to choose between finding another method of identifying individuals and admitting that there is no absolutely adequate method. He chose the second alternative, without much misgiving, because all individuals are identified through people, and it is enormously improbable that there should ever be two people exactly alike.[41]

The neatness of his earlier theory, that all identification of individuals depends on the use of logically proper names to identify sense-data, always was rather specious. It presents the

[39] See pp. 95-6. [40] Non-identical indiscernibles.
[41] See *M.PH.D.* pp. 160-64. The development of Russell's views on this subject is connected with the change in his attitude to Neutral Monism. See pp. 41-2 and p. 42, footnote 29. On p. 28 of *PH.L.A.* (*L.KN.* pp. 221-2) he uses against Neutral Monism the argument that the ego must be a particular, since, if it were not, no individuals could be adequately identified. (Cf. *R.U.P.* in *Proceedings of the Aristotelian Society*, 1911-1912.) When he argued in that way, he did not mean that you use the description ' given to me now ' in order to identify a sense-datum of yours. He meant that what makes it possible for you to identify it as the simple denotation of the word ' this ' is the fact that it is given to you now, and that this fact is intelligible only if the ego is a particular. See *O.N.A.* (*L.KN.* pp. 168-9). When he abandoned his belief that the ego is a particular, and accepted Neutral Monism, he had to admit that two people might conceivably have exactly similar psychological histories, and that is tantamount to the admission that descriptions do not provide an absolutely adequate way of identifying people; and, if the identification of people is not absolutely adequate, there will be the same minute defect in their identification of other individuals.

smooth surface of a scientific phenomenological language. The identification of sense-data never depends in any way on the context. Each sense-datum gets its tag, and there will be no cases of confusion. But, the moment that we look below the surface at the actual working of this language, problems appear. How do you make sure that you never use the same tag for two different sense-data? And how do you connect your filing system with the filing system of other people?[42] As we have seen,[43] exactly similar problems arise for general symbols. How do you know that you are using a general symbol consistently?[44] And how do you know that you are using it in the same way as other people?

[42] See P. F. Strawson, *Individuals*, p. 38ff.
[43] See p. 40 and pp. 78-82.   [44] See p. 40, footnote 21.

NOTE A

This is also Wittgenstein's fundamental idea in *T.L-PH*. If a singular symbol denotes a complex, it will not reveal the particulars, properties and relations which lie buried in its denotation. A proposition containing such a symbol is equivalent to a set of existential propositions about those particulars, properties and relations (plus, of course, whatever the original proposition said about the complex. See p. 52). Now existential propositions are, in a way, indeterminate: to say ' There is something which . . .' is less definite than naming it. So Wittgenstein says ' The requirement that simple signs be possible is the requirement that sense be determinate'. *T.L-P*. 3.23. He then goes on, in 3.24, to talk about the indeterminateness of propositions which mention complexes (see Note A, pp.115-17).

If it is true, as J. P. Griffin suggests, that Wittgenstein always analyses a macroscopic property or relation into a set of particulars arranged in a certain way, that would produce the effect that the number of particulars involved in the analysis of a proposition would be increased. Whether they are few or many, Wittgenstein's point is that the existential propositions which appear in its analysis gesture in their direction in an indeterminate way.

If Griffin's view is not correct, a Wittgensteinian complete analysis will mention macroscopic properties and relations. If it is correct, only certain ultimate relations will be mentioned. Either way, the question arises how someone who cannot specify these relations (and properties) will pick them out in his analysis. It seems that there is only one way in which he can pick them out, and that is to use definite descriptions of them. See Note A, pp. 115-17, and Note B, pp. 240-1.

These unavoidable definite descriptions of individuals, properties and relations introduce a very great element of indeterminacy into the analysis. Sometimes the speaker will not even know the logical form of the analysis of his proposition. For he will not know how many individuals, properties and relations he ought to pick out with definite descriptions. It is not clear how Wittgenstein thought that he could eliminate this indeterminacy, and advance from this stage in an analysis to the final stage which he describes in the preceding passage, 3.2—3.221.

Although Wittgenstein's fundamental idea is the same as Russell's, the use that he makes of it is not exactly the same. See Ch. IX.

CHAPTER IX

AN ALTERNATIVE DESTINATION

The alternative form of logical atomism, which Russell might have adopted, but did not in fact adopt, is, of course, the thesis that all the symbols that occur in the complete analysis of a proposition will be symbols whose denotations are intrinsically simple. This was Wittgenstein's destination in the *Tractatus*. The two philosophers' versions of logical atomism are very easy to confuse, because Wittgenstein's is a natural development of Russell's. So it is worth pausing to describe Wittgenstein's version. Even if he had never propounded it, a description of it would still have had to be included in the exposition of Russell's version. For it is necessary to see not only how far Russell goes, but also what lies beyond the point where he stops.

The difference between Russell's theory and the more extreme theory, which is now going to be described, is a formal difference, and not a difference of opinion about the kind of individuals which would be mentioned in a complete analysis. On that question, although there is no doubt that Russell thought that they would be sense-data, Wittgenstein's view is much less clear. Nevertheless, many commentators on the *Tractatus* are confident that he did not think that they would be sense-data.[1] They may be right, but it is a matter about which one would not expect to feel very confident.[2] However,

---

[1] e.g. G. E. M. Anscombe, *I.W.T.*, pp. 26-7; J. P. Griffin, *W.L.A.*, p. 5. See p. 59.

[2] In *N.B.* Wittgenstein discussed simple things, which he called 'objects', at very great length, and examined various suggestions about their nature, one of which was that they are phenomenological objects like sense-data, and another of which was that they are material particles (*N.B.*, p. 64, p. 67 and p. 81). He also explored Russell's idea that complex individuals may be treated as simple (but see p. 61, footnote 7), and his idea that properties and relations

there is no need to go into it here, because the point of difference which reveals the logical character of Russell's theory is formal, and does not depend on it.

The first thing that needs to be done is to recapitulate the distinction between Russell's thesis, that a complete analysis will only mention things which we have to treat as simple, and the more extreme thesis, that it will only mention things which are intrinsically simple. As usual, it is necessary to separate individuals from properties and relations. An individual which we have to treat as simple would be the sort of individual which could figure as the subject of a proposition in which everything that we can say about it is said about it.[3] An individual which is intrinsically simple would be the sort of individual that could figure as the subject of a proposition in which everything that is true of it is said about it. The distinction must be different for the denotations of general symbols, but it is not entirely clear how it should be drawn. Certainly a property which we have to treat as simple would

---

should be included among logical atoms (*N.B.*, pp. 60-1; but see Note A, pp. 115-17). In T.L-PH. most of this detailed argumentation was omitted, and what is left is a brief and obscure statement of the extreme version of logical atomism. There is no clear indication of the nature of intrinsically simple things. It is highly unlikely that Wittgenstein did not think it worth giving a clear indication. The obscurity and contraction of his views on this question in *T.L-PH.* is much more likely to have been caused by uncertainty how to answer it. In spite of this uncertainty he wrote very confidently about intrinsically simple things in *T.L-PH.*, because he thought that he had a logical argument which would prove that they must exist. His logical argument will be given later (see p. 147ff).

Of course, Russell's belief in his version of logical atomism was also founded on logic (*PH.L.A.* p. 14 [*L.KN.* p. 199]), but in his case it was reinforced by the belief that he knew what logical atoms were, namely sense-data, their properties and relations.

Those who say that at the time when Wittgenstein wrote *T.L-PH.* he did not think that sense-data are intrinsically simple things rest their case largely on *T.L-PH.* 6.3751. This passage will be discussed later (see pp. 152-3).

[3] See pp. 46-7.

be one which we could not define, or, if we could define it, at least the definition would not count as an analysis of it.[4] But what would an intrinsically simple property be like? Perhaps it would be one which could not be defined by anyone, however much he knew. For, if a property could be defined, the definition would always be there, waiting to be adopted as its analysis. If this is right, the colour red is not an intrinsically simple property, because the physical theory of colour provides us with a definition of it which could be, and in certain circumstances probably would be adopted as its analysis[5] However, it is a property which we have to treat as simple, because, so long as we continue to apply it in the way in which we do now, it will not be analysable.

It is important to observe that in the case of singular symbols the distinction between those that are intrinsically simple and those that are not intrinsically simple depends only on how many truths there are to be discovered about a given individual. But in the case of general symbols the same distinction depends on whether anything that is there to be discovered about a property or a relation would count as a definition of it. Moreover, in the case of singular symbols the distinction between those that we have to treat as simple and those that we do not have to treat as simple depends only on how many truths we know about a given individual. But in the case of general symbols the same distinction also depends on whether what we know about a property or relation counts as a definition of it, and, if so, whether it counts as an analysis of it. These differences between the ways in which the distinctions work in the two cases are further consequences of the fundamental difference between the singular and the general.[6]

The fact that Russell allows words like 'red' to occur in a complete analysis, and at the same time says that they are definable, is important. His allowing them to occur shows that he thought that the properties and relations which are mentioned in a complete analysis do not have to be indepen-

[4] See pp. 127-31.   [5] See pp. 128-9.   [6] See Ch. VI.

dent of one another. For it is obvious that the words 'red' and 'green' are not independent of one another. You cannot ascribe these two colours to one part of the surface of one object at the same time. Perhaps it is conceivable that a philosopher might refuse to classify this incompatibility as an *a priori* matter. But the fact that Russell says that such words are definable shows that he did regard it as an *a priori* matter. Now, though a Russellian complete analysis would be very elaborate, it would be composed entirely of atomic propositions. That is to say, it would consist of a number of propositions which only mention things which we have to treat as simple, strung together by logical connectives like 'and' and 'or'.[7] Since these atomic propositions may contain words like 'red' and 'green', they may be incompatible with one another, and, according to Russell, their incompatibilities would be an *a priori* matter. Hence he never says that atomic propositions are logically independent of one another. He only says that the individuals mentioned in atomic propositions, which he calls 'particulars', are self-subsistent, and he explains this by saying that the existence of each of them is logically independent of the existence of any other.[8] That does not mean that their properties and relations are logically independent of one another, and he makes it quite clear that he does not think that they are. It follows that atomic propositions are not logically independent of one another, and Russell never says that they are. This is the most conspicuous formal difference between Russell's version of logical atomism and Wittgenstein's. For Wittgenstein's elementary propositions, which are the counterpart of Russell's atomic propositions, are supposed to be logically independent of one another.[9]

It may seem strange that, though Russell and Wittgenstein had similar theories of meaning, based on similar considera-

[7] *PH.L.A.* p. 13 (*L.KN.* pp. 197-8).

[8] *PH.L.A.* p. 15 (*L.KN.* pp. 201-2), *PH L.A.* p. 17 (*L.KN.* pp. 203-4).

[9] *T.L-PH.* 4.211, 6.3751.

tions, they arrived in the end at different versions of logical atomism. The explanation is that Russell was very much concerned with the way in which people learn the meanings of words, whereas Wittgenstein, who developed his logic in an altogether more abstract and rarefied atmosphere, did not share this concern. Russell's account of knowledge by acquaintance may be read as part of a theory about the way in which people learn meanings, and so far in this book it has been taken exclusively in that way.[10] Its main point then is that there are certain symbols whose meanings can only be learned through acquaintance with their denotations. Those are Russell's simple symbols, and he was not worried by the fact that some of them are connected with one another through definitions. He thought that, so long as a definition does not enable people to learn the meaning of a symbol without acquaintance with its denotation, it does not detract from the simplicity of the symbol.[11] That is to say, according to him, a definition which does not provide a way of learning the meaning of a symbol does not count as an analysis. Wittgenstein shared neither this concern with learning nor this view about analysis. Not that the topic of learning and Russell's way of treating it has entirely dropped out of the *Tractatus*. But it is vestigial.

The passage in which Russell comes nearest to saying that atomic propositions are logically independent of one another occurs in *Our Knowledge of the External World* (1914). He says, ' Perhaps one atomic fact may sometimes be capable of being inferred from another, though this seems very doubtful; but in any case it cannot be inferred from premisses no one of which is an atomic fact.'[12] However, this is not very near to saying that atomic propositions are logically independent of one another, because, even if you could not infer one

[10] In Ch. XI it will be considered as a contribution to a theory about the way in which people learn truths.

[11] Hume, who thought that you could use a definition in order to acquire the idea of a specific shade of colour that you had never seen, ought to have been more worried by this supposed fact than he actually was. See *T.H.N.* I.i.1 (p. 15).

[12] *O.KN.E.W.* p. 62.

atomic fact from another, one atomic proposition might still imply the negation of another, and, as we have seen, Russell believed that such incompatibilities between atomic propositions exist, and that they are generated by definitions. This belief of his is one of the two things which prevented his version of logical atomism from developing into the extreme version. For, if a general symbol is definable, its denotation cannot be intrinsically simple.

The other thing which prevented Russell's version of logical atomism from developing into the extreme version is his attitude to the analysis of singular symbols. In *The Philosophy of Logical Atomism* there is a discussion at the end of the second lecture in which he says that ' it is possible to suppose that complex things are capable of analysis *ad infinitum*, and that you never reach the simple. I do not think it is true, but it is a thing that one might argue certainly '.[13] When he said this he was probably thinking primarily of individuals, as he so often did.[14] For, when he writes in a similar vein in *Logical Atomism*, he makes it clear that he has individuals in mind. He says:

When I speak of ' simples ' I ought to explain that I am speaking of something not experienced as such, but known only inferentially as the limit of analysis. It is quite possible that, by greater logical skill, the need for assuming them could be avoided. A logical language will not lead to error if its simple symbols (i.e. those not having any parts that are symbols, or any significant structure) all stand for objects of some one type, even if these objects are not simple. The only drawback to such a language is that it is incapable of dealing with anything simpler than the objects which it represents by simple symbols. But I confess it seems obvious to me (as it did to Leibniz) that what is complex must be composed of simples, though the number of constituents may be infinite.[15]

A little later he says:

If we take to be simple what is really complex, we may get into trouble by naming it, when what we ought to do is to assert it.[16] For

13 *PH.L.A.*, p. 16 (*L.KN.* p. 202).
14 See pp. 106-9.
15 *L.A.* p. 375 (*L.KN.* p. 337).
16 cf. *R.S-D.PH.* (*M. and L.* p. 147). This very important passage was discussed on pp. 121-2.

example, if Plato loves Socrates, there is not an entity 'Plato's love for Socrates', but only the fact that Plato loves Socrates.

Here he evidently has individuals in mind, and his point is that we might fall into a confusion if we used simple symbols for complex individuals. If the terminology that has been introduced in this book is adopted, his point is that, if we continue analysis only until we reach singular symbols denoting things which we have to treat as simple, we might be confused, if those things were not intrinsically simple. The confusion would arise because, if that were so, these singular symbols ought to expand under analysis into propositions, but we would be unable to take their analysis to that point.[17]

In *My Philosophical Development* Russell discusses Mr J. O. Urmson's criticism that his kind of analysis never succeeds in reaching symbols whose denotations are intrinsically simple.[18] He answers it by saying, 'I on occasion spoke of "atomic facts" as the final residue in analysis, but it was never an essential part of the analytical philosophy which Mr Urmson is criticising to suppose that such facts were attainable':[19] and he supports this by quoting his own earlier remarks in the discussion at the end of the second lecture in *The Philosophy of Logical Atomism*. He also quotes a passage from his later book *Human Knowledge, its Scope and Limits* (1948).[20] He might have added many earlier statements to the same effect.[21] Now many of these passages express doubt not only about the attainability of atomic facts, but also about the existence of intrinsically simple things.[22] But this creates

---

[17] We might conjecture that an individual which we had to treat as simple was intrinsically complex, but we could not name the particulars, properties or relations which would be mentioned in its analysis. Therefore, the most that we could do would be to gesture in their direction with existential propositions. This applies not only to particulars, but also to properties and relations. See Note A, pp. 115-17, Note A, pp. 136-7, and Note B, pp. 240-1.

[18] *Philosophical Analysis* p. 138ff.   [19] *M.PH.D.* pp. 221-3.
[20] *H.KN.S.L.* pp. 268-9.   [21] e.g. *I.M.PH.* p. 142.
[22] In fact the passage in *M.PH.D.* begins 'Wittgenstein in the *Tractatus* and I on occasion . . .', and then continues as it is presented above. Now it is very probably true that Wittgenstein did

a discrepancy. Why did he give a series of lectures entitled *The Philosophy of Logical Atomism* if he did not think that he could prove, or even think that it was important to prove that there really are logical atoms? The only plausible answer to this question is the answer which is being suggested in this book. He applied the phrase ' logical atomism ' to two distinct theories. First, he applied it to the theory that every proposition has a complete analysis which consists entirely of symbols denoting things which we have to treat as simple, and he believed that he had established this theory.[23] Secondly, he applied it to the theory that every proposition has a complete analysis which consists entirely of symbols denoting things which are intrinsically simple, and he regarded this theory as speculative, unlike Wittgenstein, who at the time when he wrote the *Tractatus* believed that he had established it. This double use of the phrase ' logical atomism ' is understandable, because the second theory to which it is applied develops naturally out of the first, but it is exceedingly confusing.

It is very interesting to see how the extreme version of logical atomism grew out of the moderate version. The process illustrates a common tendency in human thinking, whose aetiology was described by Kant.[24] We tend to project our requirements on to the world. That is to say, we tend to take the necessary conditions of human experience and impose them on everything, whether we experience it or not. In this particular case it may be necessary that the intellectual appar-

---

not suppose that atomic facts are attainable (see *N.B.* pp. 61-2). But the thesis that intrinsically simple things may not exist, which is what Russell says on p. 16 of *PH.L.A.* (*L.KN.* p. 202) and in many other passages, is certainly not one which Wittgenstein would have accepted at the time when he wrote *T.L-PH.*

[23] In *PH.L.A.* he never doubts that sense-data are particulars, and that some properties and relations of sense-data are simple; and particulars and simple properties and relations are the logical atoms mentioned in atomic propositions. See *PH.L.A.* p. 1 (*L.KN.* p. 178), and pp. 11-15 (*L.KN.* pp. 194-201).

[24] *Critique of Pure Reason, Transcendental Dialectic,* Bk. II, Appendix (Everyman edition, p. 373ff).

atus which we apply to our experience should consist of elements which are not infinitely divisible. Indeed, since intellectual equipment is supposed to be perspicuous, it may be fairly obvious when we have reached elements which we cannot subdivide further. But it would not follow that these elements correspond to things which are in reality not capable of being subdivided. Nor would it follow that there are in reality any elements not susceptible to further subdivision.

The logical argument for the extreme version of atomism is most easily understood in its application to individuals. The germ of the argument is contained in Russell's remark in *Logical Atomism*, which has just been quoted : ' If what we take to be simple is really complex, we may get into trouble by naming it, when what we ought to do is to assert it '. Let us see exactly what the trouble would be. When one of our analysable singular symbols is used as if it were a logically proper name, it will expand under analysis into a proposition.[25] But the situation is rather different when a singular symbol denotes an individual which we have to treat as simple, in spite of the fact that it is intrinsically complex. In such a case the symbol will have a meaning only if it has a denotation. For, because it is one of our unanalysable symbols, it cannot have acquired its meaning in the indirect way in which analysable symbols acquire their meanings. But, if it has a denotation, then, since *ex hypothesi* its denotation is complex, another proposition will be true, *viz.* the proposition into which the symbol would expand if only we could analyse it—but, of course, we cannot analyse it. The point of Russell's remark is that we ought to assert this proposition, but unfortunately we cannot assert it, because its constituents are beyond our ken. So what we do instead is to smother the complexity with a logically proper name, and that, he suggests, is a misleading thing to do, because it gives a false impression of intrinsic simplicity.

All this is rather abstract, and it is important to realise what it would amount to in a particular case. A singular

[25] See pp. 51-3.

symbol denoting something which we have to treat as simple is the kind of symbol that can occur as the grammatical subject of a proposition in which we say everything that we can say about the individual denoted by it. If that individual is intrinsically complex, there will be another proposition which is true of it, but its constituents will be beyond our ken.[26] So we cannot even formulate the description that would occur in that proposition, still less use it. Instead, we use a logically proper name, smothering the complexity which we cannot bring into the light of day.[27]

Now Russell does not offer this as a proof that there must be intrinsically simple individuals. He only says that, if we cannot continue analysis until we reach a point where our unanalysable symbols denote intrinsically simple individuals, what we say will be misleading. This contention of his is dubious. For why should the use of an unanalysable symbol be taken to imply that its denotation is intrinsically simple? But, if we may leave this doubt on one side, and concentrate on interpretation, his point is only that the use of unanalysable symbols for intrinsically complex things has an unfortunate consequence. The fact that it has an unfortunate consequence is not supposed to show that it does not happen, or that it is avoidable.

However, out of this material Wittgenstein constructed a logical argument which seemed to him to prove the existence of intrinsically simple individuals. Near the beginning of the *Tractatus*, where he is writing about ' objects ', which are the intrinsically simple things in his system, he says, ' Objects make up the substance of the world. That is why they cannot be composite. If the world had no substance, then whether a proposition had sense would depend on whether another

---

[26] This way of putting the point is too specific. It applies to the pattern illustrated in Diagram v, where a complex only has one particular in its analysis. But the point can readily be generalised so that it will also apply to the pattern illustrated in Diagram vi, where a complex is analysed into more than one particular. See p. 104 and p. 124.

[27] See pp. 45ff.   [28] *T.L-PH.* 2.021 and 2.0211.

proposition was true.'[28] He then goes on to suggest that it would be impossible to formulate any propositions if there were this infinite regress from the sense of one proposition to the truth, and so to the sense of a second proposition, and from the sense of this proposition to the truth, and so to the sense of a third proposition, and so on. Russell explains this argument in his introduction to the *Tractatus* :

The assertion that there is a certain complex reduces to the assertion that its constituents are related in a certain way, which is the assertion of a *fact*; thus, if we give a name to the complex, the name only has meaning in virtue of the truth of a certain proposition, namely the proposition asserting the relatedness of the constituents of the complex. Thus the naming of complexes presupposes propositions, while propositions presuppose the naming of simples.[29]

It might look as if Wittgenstein could not possibly have used this argument if he accepted Russell's Theory of Definite Descriptions. For, according to that theory, it is not the sense but the truth of a proposition containing a complex singular symbol which depends on the truth of the proposition into which that symbol expands under analysis. For example, if it is false that Hitler had one and only one daughter, a proposition mentioning the daughter of Hitler is not senseless, but false. Indeed, that is the whole point of Russell's theory, and Wittgenstein quite explicitly takes it over and re-affirms it in the *Tractatus*.[30] How then could he have used the argument which he appears to have used, and which Russell attributes to him? The answer is that the apparent incompatibility is an illusion. The argument starts from the hypothesis that the symbol which is applied to an intrinsically complex individual is, in spite of that application, a symbol which is for us unanalysable. Given that hypothesis, there is only one way in which it can get a meaning, and that is through the existence of its complex denotation. So the proposition which asserts the existence of the complex denotation must be true, if the symbol has a meaning, and the symbol must have a meaning if the original proposition, in which it occurs, has a sense.

There is, then, no reason to doubt Russell's interpretation of Wittgenstein's argument for the extreme version of logical atomism. However, the argument is not at all convincing. It depends on an illegitimate projection of our requirements on to the world. Perhaps certain singular symbols must remain unanalysable for us. But this necessity ought not to be projected on to the denotations of those symbols. Suppose that the denotation of such a symbol is not in fact intrinsically simple. What troublesome consequence follows from this? The idea is that there would be a vicious infinite regress, because the sense of a proposition containing the symbol would depend on the truth of another proposition asserting the existence of the complex, and so on. But is this regress really vicious? We, who have to learn the meaning of the symbol through acquaintance with its complex denotation, are not impeded by the regress. We do not have to traverse an infinite series of stages before we succeed in learning its meaning. As far as we are concerned the infinite regress has nothing to do with the meaning of the symbol, and so has nothing to do with our learning or understanding its meaning. If the regress exists, that is because individuals are infinitely divisible. Whether they are infinitely divisible or not is a question which has nothing to do with the meanings of the singular symbols which we apply to them. So it is illegitimate to draw the conclusion that there must be intrinsically simple individuals from the premiss that we can formulate propositions which have sense. If the conclusion follows from anything, it follows from premisses which have nothing to do with the theory of meaning. The extreme version of logical atomism is a sort of philosophical dream, in which language has become detached from human life and makes fantastic demands on reality.

Wittgenstein's argument is based on the assumption that, if we apply a singular symbol which we cannot analyse to an individual which is intrinsically complex, the description which would occur in the analysis of the individual will give part of the meaning of the symbol. But what is the justification of this assumption? The things that would be mentioned in that description are beyond our ken, so that we cannot even formulate it. Consequently the situation is not at all what it was when we were considering the relationship between descriptions and singular symbols which we may or may not treat as simple, like ordinary proper names.[31] In that situation the things that would be mentioned in the descriptions would not be beyond our ken, and we could formulate and assert the propositions applying the descriptions to the individuals. Now admittedly there are difficulties about the view that temporary *a priori* connections are formed between these descriptions and ordinary proper names. But in the situation which we are considering now there is a different, and much greater difficulty. For in the other situation the descriptions were known by the speaker, or, at least, could be known by him. But in this situation they cannot be known by him. So it really is extraordinary to regard them as giving part of the meaning of his singular symbol. Yet that is how they are regarded by anyone who says that in such a case analysis has not been carried sufficiently far, and that under further analysis the symbol would expand into a proposition. The very most that could be justifiably said about such a case is that the smothered proposition is *potentially* part of the meaning of the singular symbol. But, of course, the potentiality is unrealisable, because the symbol is one which we have to treat as simple.

When the extreme version of logical atomism is applied to individuals, the result is a very rarefied theory, which is exceedingly remote from human life. Russell's moderate version of logical atomism is much closer to reality. A philosopher who adopts it really need not be worried by the suggestion that his simple individuals possess properties, or stand in relations, which are not known to us. It is conceiv-

[31] See pp. 74-81.

able that such properties and relations might one day become incorporated in the meanings of our unanalysable singular symbols, but he can afford to neglect a possibility which cannot be realised before our knowledge is extended. Language does not reach so far into future possibilities. The meanings of words are founded on present actualities.

When the extreme version of logical atomism is applied to properties and relations, the situation is, as usual, very different. For analysis, according to Russell, stops at a point at which general symbols have admitted *a priori* connections with one another. We do not have to speculate that the word ' red ' might in certain circumstances acquire a meaning which would make it incompatible with certain other colour words, which, like it, are symbols that we cannot analyse. The fact is that it actually has such a meaning now, and this creates a very real problem for logical atomism, a problem which is quite unlike the rarefied speculation about singular symbols, denoting things which we have to treat as simple.

The problem arises because in logic we naturally demand that a single phenomenon should have a single explanation. Perhaps in other less tidy subjects one phenomenon may have a plurality of explanations, but it seems that in logic that ought not to happen. Now the moderate version of logical atomism succeeds in explaining those *a priori* connections which are not purely logical by saying that in most cases they depend upon the analyses of complex symbols. But when it reaches general symbols denoting things which we have to treat as simple, like the word ' red ', it admits the existence of further *a priori* connections which cannot depend on the analyses of these words because they have no analyses. They may depend on definitions of some kind, but at least they do not depend on the kind of definitions which show how we learn the meanings of the words and how we go about applying them, and which would, therefore, count as analyses of them. Is this not an anomaly? Does it not look as if the word ' red ' smothers some complexity which ought to be uncovered and analysed? If this is so, then further analysis might provide us with an explanation of these *a priori* connections which would be exactly the same as the explanation of all other *a priori* connections, and logic would have met our demand for unity.[32]

This is the most important line of thought leading from the moderate version of logical atomism to the extreme version. The idea is that all *a priori* truths should be explained in the same way. In all cases alike the explanation would consist in pointing to some feature of the structure of language. Of course, the structure of language matches the structure of things, and so we might say that this kind of explanation really makes an oblique reference to the structure of things. That would be admitted by a philosopher who hoped to explain all *a priori* truths in this way. But he would not admit that any *a priori* truths should be explained by appealing to hidden complexities in the structure of things which would not be matched by the structure of language, even if language were completely analysed. He would say that the analysis of language should be continued until its visible structure explained every *a priori* truth.

So Wittgenstein thought that colour-words like ' red ' are not, as they stand, completely analysed, and in an important passage which has already been mentioned[33] he contemplates the possibility that the physical theory of colour might enable us to analyse them further. This passage is usually taken to prove that his objects could not be phenomenological entities like sense-data.[34] However, it does nothing of the kind. Even if he accepted the thesis that the propagation of light

[32] This demand has two distinct parts. First, there must be no synthetic *a priori* propositions. Secondly, the definitions, on which *a priori* propositions depend, must give analyses. The thesis that all *a priori* propositions are analytic may be understood in either of two ways. It may be taken to mean that the first part of the demand can be met, or, alternatively, it may be taken to include the implication that the second part too can be met.

[33] *T.L-PH.* 6.3751, mentioned in Note A, pp. 115-17, and in footnote 2, p. 138.

[34] See p. 138, footnote 1.

with different wave-lengths, or the movements of particles with different velocities provide us with a logical analysis of the meanings of colour-words, it would not follow that his objects were not sense-data. All that would follow would be that, if his objects were sense-data, their properties, when they were completely analysed, would turn out to have a much more elaborate structure than they seem to have. A sense-datum can be a sense-datum of red, in spite of the fact that the word ' red ' applies to objects in the external world, and exactly the same is true if we replace the word ' red ' by its analysis. Of course it may well be wrong to say that Wittgenstein's objects were sense-data, but this passage in the *Tractatus* does not prove that it is wrong. Indeed, it is possible that he had not made up his mind what they were, but was nevertheless convinced that they must exist.

Anyway, Wittgenstein never committed himself to any particular complete analysis of colour-words, or of the other sensory properties and relations which Russell maintained that we have to treat as simple. He was only convinced that some further analysis of them must be possible. His conviction was based on the fact that they have *a priori* connections with one another. He thought that this is enough to prove that they are not completely analysed. For, if a word like ' red ' has an *a priori* incompatibility with another colour-word, its denotation is intrinsically complex. Indeed, the physical theory of colour shows us how we ought to begin to dissect the intrinsic complexity of the colour. We can start by saying that the word ' red ' would not have a denotation unless the proposition, that light has been propagated with a certain wave-length, or the proposition, that material particles have moved with a certain velocity, were true. Then the next stage would be to incorporate the scientific description of the colour into the analysis of the word ' red '.

Now, as we have already seen, there is a case for refusing to allow that this dissection of the denotation of the word ' red ' gives its analysis. But Wittgenstein seems to have dismissed this case, because he incautiously assumed that, if a

symbol denotes a thing which is intrinsically complex, the
dissection of the thing will give the meaning of the symbol.
His argument for the extreme version of logical atomism,
which has already been given,[35] depends on this assumption.
When it is applied to properties and relations, it takes the
following form : if a general symbol which we cannot analyse
has an intrinsically complex denotation, then that general
symbol will have a meaning only if another proposition is true,
viz. the proposition that the various general elements in the
denotation have been instantiated together, or, if there is only
one general element, that it has been instantiated. For example, the physical theory of colour tells us what the intrinsic
complexity of the denotation of the word ' red ' is. This word
has a denotation only if it is true that the properties and
relations mentioned in the theory have been instantiated together. But then the question arises whether *these* properties
and relations are intrinsically complex, and so on, supposedly
until we reach a point where all the properties and relations
mentioned in the analysis of the word ' red ' are intrinsically
simple.[36]

The interpretation of this argument is somewhat dubious,
because it is not entirely clear under what conditions the
denotation of a general symbol would be intrinsically complex. But at least there is no doubt that Wittgenstein believed
that the denotation of a general symbol which has an *a priori*
incompatibility with another general symbol of the same

[35] See pp. 147-50.
[36] If someone were unable to complete this analysis, it is probable
that Wittgenstein thought that he would use existential propositions
about the properties and relations which he could not name. If he
analysed all macroscopic properties and relations as arrangements of
particulars (see Note A, pp. 136-7), the only general entities which
would be mentioned in his complete analyses would be relations.
Now it may well be that he regarded those ultimate relations as
' forms ' rather than objects. But that is compatible with the interpretation of his logical argument for intrinsically simple relations
which is suggested above: someone who could not specify the relevant
arrangements of particulars would have to use existential propositions
in order to gesture in their direction.

level, is intrinsically complex. If we add that belief to his incautious assumption, that, if a symbol denotes a thing which is intrinsically complex, the dissection of the thing will give the meaning of the symbol, we can see why he drew the conclusion that such a symbol is not completely analysed.

Wittgenstein was so convinced that all *a priori* truths must be explained in the same way, that he does not seem to have reflected on the details of the kind of analysis of general symbols which he was proposing.[87] It is really very evident that propositions attributing positions and velocities to material particles will not be logically independent of one another.[88] More generally, whatever complete analysis he chose, its general symbols would almost certainly produce logical incompatibilities. There is only one kind of choice which would avoid this result. If a property mentioned in a complete analysis did not belong to a numerous family, like the family of colours, but was only contrasted with its opposite, as the word ' chromatic' is contrasted with the word ' non-chromatic', then a proposition ascribing this property to an individual would not be logically incompatible with any other proposition on the same level except its own negation. If all properties and relations mentioned in complete analyses were like this, and each field of possibilities were merely divided into two, there would be no embarrassing logical incompatibilities between elementary propositions. They really would be logically independent of one another, as Wittgenstein said that they are. All *a priori* connections would be visible in the structure of language, and the explanation of them would never depend on complexities in the structure of things, which had not been shown to be matched by complexities in the structure of language. However, it is evident that the positions and velocities of material particles do not meet this requirement. Indeed, any properties and relations which did meet it would almost certainly not have the multiplicity which would be needed in a complete analysis of ordinary propositions. Each field of possibilities would merely be divided into

[87] See *T.L-PH.* 6.3751.   [88] See J. P. Griffin *W.L.A.* p. 85.

two, instead of exhibiting the more numerous divisions that are required by our way of classifying things.

Russell never went so far in this direction as Wittgenstein did. As has already been stated, he never said that atomic propositions are logically independent of one another. He allowed them to mention properties and relations which are incompatible with one another, and he admitted that their incompatibilities are *a priori*, but denied the possibility of explaining them by further analysis of general symbols. He maintains this position in *The Inquiry into Meaning and Truth* (1940).[39] Wittgenstein adopted it in 1929 when he gave up the distinctive thesis of extreme logical atomism that elementary propositions are logically independent of one another.[40]

This chapter has been devoted to the exposition of a theory which Russell did not adopt, extreme logical atomism. One reason why this theory has been set out in detail is that many commentators have confused it with the version of logical atomism which he did adopt. Another reason is that the

[39] *I.M.T.* p. 82, p. 92 and p. 162. In these passages he connects tne question, whether there are unanalysable incompatibilities between propositions, with the question, whether there are negative singular propositions which are based directly on experience, and not reached by inference. He makes the same connection in *PH.L.A.* p. 23 (*L.KN.* pp. 213-14), when he is discussing negative facts. Mr Urmson's comment on this last passage is that Russell treats the question whether there are negative facts as if it were an empirical question (*Philosophical Analysis* p. 69). But he does nothing of the kind. He treats it as a question to be settled by philosophical analysis. According to him, the answer to it depends on whether or not the analysis of a negative singular proposition is that there is another proposition which is true and which is incompatible with the positive version of the original proposition. If this were the correct analysis, then the idea of incompatibility would be more fundamental than the idea of negation, and the negation of an atomic proposition would always depend on an unanalysable incompatibility. See *O.P.* (*L.KN.* pp. 287-9).

[40] See *L.F.* in *Proceedings of the Aristotelian Society*, 1929-30. This much neglected article is analysed very carefully by J. P. Griffin, *W.L.A.* pp. 80-6.

extreme version explains certain features of the moderate version. For the two versions have two things in common. First, they both seek an absolutely precise scientific language in which the words denoting individuals, properties and relations will be clear, unambiguous, and fully and finally explicable.[41] Each logically proper name will be used for one and only one individual, and successful reference to individuals will not depend upon the context as it does in everyday language. The same precision will be achieved by the general symbols of this language. For all ambiguity and doubt about the demarcation of properties and relations will be removed. Moreover, it will be possible to give a full and final explanation of the meanings of all the symbols in this language.

If we follow this line of thought, and ask why Russell stopped short of extreme logical atomism, the answer is that he did not think that the intrinsic complexity of the denotation of a singular symbol which we cannot analyse would introduce any vagueness into its reference. That is to say, he did not think that our use of logically proper names would be vague, if there were features of their denotations which we could not specify, because we were totally unaware of them. We can go on using logically proper names undeterred by the possible complexity of their denotations. We do not have to regard them as ' truncated or telescoped descriptions ', because the material out of which such descriptions would be constructed would be beyond our ken. Similarly, the material which might be used in an analysis of general symbols denot-

---

[41] Wittgenstein objected to Russell's Introduction to *T.L.-PH.* because Russell said that *T.L-PH.* described an ideally logical language, whereas in fact it describes a way of analysing every language. But of course these are not irreconcilable interpretations. Perhaps Wittgenstein meant that Russell was prepared to discard a considerable part of the meaning of everyday statements (see Ch. 1), whereas he was not prepared to discard any of it (see *T.L-PH.* 5.5563). This may well be a point of difference between Wittgenstein's version of logical atomism and Russell's version. But it is not incompatible with the similarity to which attention is being drawn here.

ing properties and relations which we have to treat as simple is not available to us. We cannot mean what is beyond us, and what we cannot mean cannot make what we do mean vague.[42]

The second thing which both versions of logical atomism have in common is that they both use the analysis of general symbols to explain those *a priori* truths which are not truths of logic. If we follow this line of thought, and ask why Russell stopped short of extreme logical atomism, the answer is that he did not think that this explanation of such *a priori* truths could succeed in all cases. He thought that it succeeded in most cases, but not in all, and that is why his atomic propositions, unlike Wittgenstein's elementary propositions, are not logically independent of one another.

[42] However, Russell had some misgivings about the use of logically proper names with intrinsically complex denotations. See pp. 143-4.

CHAPTER X

WHAT IS BEING DENIED?

Philosophical theories are usually developed polemically, so that in order to understand them it is necessary to ask not only what they are asserting, but also what rival theory they are denying. Russell's version of logical atomism is no exception. It was a theory of meaning designed to replace the Idealists' theory of meaning in which he had been instructed as an undergraduate at Cambridge.[1] The Idealists' theory was the direct descendant of Hegel's philosophy, which had been introduced into England in the first half of the nineteenth century. There is a strong element of Spinozism in its ancestry. It did not entirely dominate the philosophical scene at the turn of the century, but it was a more subtle and fully armed theory than the empiricism of John Stuart Mill's followers. What Russell did was to strengthen empiricism by giving it a theory of meaning which drew on the resources of the newly developed mathematical logic.

A rough way of describing the difference between Russell's theory of meaning and the Idealists' theory would be to say that, whereas Russell separates everything into its elements, his opponents encourage everything to coagulate. Russell thought that, before a philosopher can understand how people form propositions and say things, he must understand the elements which they put together. If this theory of propositions is pushed to its conclusion, we should have to take the analysis of the elements to the point where the symbols denoting them no longer smother propositions. For if we do not take it to this point, the order of priority would be reversed : there would be elements which we could not fully understand before we understood the propositions into which

---

[1] See *M.PH.D.* p. 37ff.

they would expand under analysis.[2] Now there are, as was shown in the last chapter, two possible views about the point to which analysis should be taken. Russell's view was the more moderate one, that it should be taken to the point where symbols do not smother propositions which we can formulate. This requirement is all that is necessary in order to secure the result that the elements of our propositions are understood first.

The theory against which he was arguing is more difficult to describe. What it asserts is fairly clear, and so too is the effect of what it asserts. But the arguments which it uses are less clear. What it asserts is that it is impossible to understand the elements of propositions separately in the atomic way. It claims that, when a philosopher tries to take meanings separately, he will find that they coagulate. Instead of the discernible elements of meaning which he hopes for, he will find that the meaning of one symbol always runs into, and fuses with, the meanings of an infinity of other symbols. According to the Logical Atomist the elements that are synthesised into propositions must first be separated out in analysis. According to the Idealist they cannot be.

The effect of this theory is the exact opposite of what Russell hoped to achieve by his theory of meaning. Russell hoped to reconstruct empirical knowledge in a way that would save what could be saved from the sceptic. The Idealists' theory leads to the abandonment of any such attempt because it regards empirical knowledge as a hopeless case. Not that it rejects our ordinary claims to such knowledge as false or ill founded. It seeks to undermine them in a more subtle way. Instead of attacking their truth or their grounds, as an ordinary sceptic would, it attacks their meaning, which is more unnerving. The attack is developed on a wide front. It does not concentrate on selected aspects of empirical knowledge, but spreads itself against the whole enterprise of recording the nature of things in propositions. It claims that there is something incurably wrong with all propositions. A proposi-

[2] See *PH.L.A.* p. 1 (*L.KN.* p. 178), and p. 17 (*L.KN.* pp. 203-4).

tion tries to achieve truth by synthesising elements which, as meanings, must first be understood in isolation. But it is impossible to understand them in isolation, and in any case, it would be impossible to restore by synthesis the original unity after it had been destroyed by analysis. Therefore truth can never be achieved by propositions.[3]

This is a very vague way of presenting the Idealists' case, and it will be made more exact in a moment. But it does serve to show that the first part of the argument used by Russell's opponents is very similar to the argument used by Russell himself. Russell insists that in the genesis of propositions, if it is set out in its right logical order, analysis must precede synthesis, and his opponents agree with him on this point. They part company with him at the next stage of the argument, when they maintain that what both sides agree to be necessary is in fact impossible.

If this pessimistic account of the function of propositions were correct, all empirical knowledge would be affected, because it all has to be expressed in propositions. It would not meet the fate which the ordinary sceptic predicts for it, but it would be down-graded to the more frustrating category of things whose expression is incurably faulty, so that they cannot even enter the competition for perfect truth.[4] When a philosopher like F. H. Bradley pronounces this sentence on empirical knowledge, a very natural reaction is to enquire what kind of thing would be assigned to the superior category of things which are at least admitted to the competition. But the answer to this question is far from clear. However, we are not concerned with the positive import of the doctrine, but only with its negative import. Its theory of meaning, in its negative aspect, condemns all propositional knowledge to the limbo of things whose expression is incurably faulty.

We now need a more exact account of the reasoning which led to this verdict. It would be beyond the scope of this book to survey all the arguments, and it is probably sufficient to

[3] See R. A. Wollheim, *F.H.B.* p. 120.
[4] See *F.H.B.* p. 182ff.

select the one to which Russell attached most importance, which is the contention that all relations must be internal. He attacked this contention in *The Principles of Mathematics*,[5] and he returned to the attack on several occasions, but not in *The Philosophy of Logical Atomism*. In the latter work he names his adversaries,[6] but he is more concerned with developing his own theory than with attacking the theory which it was designed to replace. In the later essay *Logical Atomism,* which is rather more of a manifesto, considerable space is devoted to his arguments against the internality of all relations.[7] Much later, when he is reviewing the development of his theory of meaning, he quotes at length from another of his earlier treatments of the same topic.[8]

What exactly does the contention that all relations must be internal mean? A relation is internal if the proposition attributing it to an individual is true *a priori.* For instance, the married state is a relation between two individuals, and the proposition that a particular husband is married, or a particular wife is married, is true *a priori,* because it is guaranteed by definition. So in these two cases we have an internal relation. On the other hand, if the husband or the wife is employed by someone, that is not guaranteed by any definition, but is only a contingent fact. So in this example employment is an external relation. When we draw this distinction between the two kinds of relation, it is essential either to specify the *kind* of individual to which a relation is internal, or external, or else to say that no such specification is presupposed. In our example, a particular *man* might or might not be married, but a particular *husband* must be married. So the question whether this relation is internal or external to an individual, cannot be answered as it stands. One way of making it answerable would be to mention a specific description which

[5] *P. of M.* ch. xxvi.
[6] *PH.L.A.* p. 1 (*L.KN.* p. 178) and p. 17 (*L.KN.* pp. 203-4).
[7] *L.A.* pp. 369-74 (*L.KN.* pp. 332-6).
[8] *M.PH.D.* ch. v, where Russell quotes from his essay *M.TH. of T.* (*PH.E.* pp. 160-69).

we suppose to apply to the individual, and then, given that description, it will be possible to answer the question : in our example, given the description 'husband', the first relation is internal, and the second is external. But if we do not start with any description of the individual, the question will be unanswerable, unless we explicitly say that no such description is presupposed. The reason for this is plain : the answer to the question depends on whether or not there is a definition at work, and a definition can get a grip on the individual only through some general symbol; in this example, the general symbol 'married' is connected by definition with the general symbol 'husband', but not with the man's name. If we make the question answerable in the other way, by saying that no general description of the individual is presupposed, the answer to it will be that the relation is external.

This is a straightforward way of drawing the distinction between internal and external relations. Russell's treatment of ordinary proper names introduces a certain complication into it, which makes it a little less straightforward, but it will still work smoothly, and separate the two kinds of relation very easily. The complication comes in because he thinks that ordinary proper names are often 'truncated or telescoped descriptions': that is to say, according to him, someone who uses an ordinary proper name will often form in his own mind a temporary *a priori* connection between it and some definite description of the named individual.[9] In the example that was being used just now he might think of the man as the husband of his secretary. If he did so think of him, there would be an *a priori* connection between the ordinary proper name of the man and the general symbol 'married' : for the latter would be connected by definition with the definite description in his mind, and the definite description would be connected not by definition, but in a temporary *a priori* way with the man's name. This complication does not make it difficult to use the distinction between the two kinds of relation. We still need a description, or alternatively an explicit

[9] See pp. 74-81.

statement that no description is presupposed, before we can answer the question whether a relation is internal or external in a given case. The only effect of the complication is that in some cases the singular symbol itself will provide us with a description. It will provide us with one when it is an ordinary proper name which is not being used as a logically proper name.

It might even be thought that the distinction works too easily. For how could there be any controversy about the question whether all relations are internal? Only too obviously, if the distinction is drawn in this way, some relations are external. Hence Wittgenstein in the *Tractatus* immediately dismisses doubts about the existence of external relations, and concentrates on what he clearly regards as the much more interesting question, what the status of so-called ' internal relations ' really is.[10] However, it often happens in this kind of philosophical controversy that a problem which is fairly easy to solve masks a more profound and difficult problem. In such cases one side may be thinking of the profound problem, but formulating it in words which are appropriate to the more superficial problem : and, when this happens, the other side will be apt to take the arguments at their face value and to dismiss them summarily. Not that Russell does dismiss Bradley's arguments summarily. In fact, he examines

[10] *T.L-PH.* 4.122—4.1252. Wittgenstein's criterion of an internal relation differs from the criterion which was introduced on pp. 162-3. That criterion allows that a relation is internal to an individual if it is connected by definition with a property which the individual, as a matter of contingent fact, possesses, provided that the individual is specified as possessing the property. In such a case Wittgenstein would not allow the relation to count as internal. According to his criterion, the property too would have to belong to the individual necessarily. This means that there will be fewer internal relations. For instance, it will be an internal relation of the number 2 that it is the successor of the number 1, but being married will not be an internal relation of a particular person, even if he is specified as a husband. Nor is it only Wittgenstein's criterion of an internal relation that differs from the criterion that has been introduced here. His treatment of the problem is also entirely different from Russell's.

them very carefully. But when both sides have presented their cases, the most important thing still seems to have been left unsaid.[11]

What is the profound problem? In order to isolate it, it is necessary to trace the development of Bradley's case, noting Russell's objections at each stage, and noting the surprising extent to which Bradley accepts them. Of course the extent to which he accepts them is surprising only if the controversy is taken at its face value. For it then looks as if the two philosophers ought to be disagreeing at every stage. Indeed, as has just been pointed out, it will look as if Bradley ought to be denying what is only too obviously true, that, when the distinction is drawn in the straightforward way, some relations are external. If, on the other hand, we are prepared for the possibility that something more profound may be at issue, we shall be less surprised by the extent to which the two philosophers agree, and we shall hurry past those stages in order to arrive more quickly at the point of fundamental disagreement.

The most striking thing about Bradley's case is that he always tries to reduce relations to properties.[12] For instance, he would argue that, if two people are married, the relation must make some difference to them. If this contention is interpreted in the ordinary way, nobody would deny it. But he means that the two people must each possess a property which makes the relationship intelligible. If this were interpreted to mean that they must possess traits of character which would explain the marriage, it would seldom be denied. But he means something very different. He means that the relation can be understood only if it is taken to be *identical with* certain properties of the individuals. If it were regarded in any other way, its connection with them would be unintel-

---

[11] Bradley's case is analysed very lucidly, in a way that separates the profound issue from the more superficial one, by R. A. Wollheim *F.H.B.* pp. 104-22.

[12] This word is here used in contrast with the word ' relation '. See p. 62, footnote 10.

ligible because it would make no difference to them. It would be as if it were attached to them without any points of attachment. This is a way of insisting that relations which are apparently external must really be internal. But the way in which Bradley is insisting on it is very peculiar. He is not saying that, whenever you examine an apparently external relation, you will always *discover* that the related individuals possess properties given which it follows *a priori* that the relation holds between them. He is saying that in such a case you must *invent* properties to the following specification : the fact that the individuals possess the properties will be *the very same fact* as the fact that the relation holds between them. However, in spite of this peculiarity, you might say that he is insisting that relations which are apparently external are really internal, because the connection between the relation and the invented properties is established by an *a priori* statement of identity.[13]

This explanation of the functioning of relations is of course malicious. It is going to end by representing as impossible what it began by appearing to want to explain. Russell objected that to say that a relation holds between two individuals cannot be the same thing as to say that each of them possesses a certain property. Let us use a less elaborate example in order to present his objection. His point is that to say that two lines are of equal length cannot be the same thing as to say that each is of a certain length : we still have to add that the two lengths are equal, since, if we do not make this addition, the explanation of the meaning of the original proposition will be incomplete; yet, if we do make the addition, the explanation will involve a relation, and, if we try to equate this relation with properties, we shall meet the same difficulty again, and so we shall be launched on a vicious infinite regress.[14] Perfectly ordinary properties have been

[13] See *A. and R.* p. 512ff. See also *A. and R.* cc. II and III.

[14] *P. of M.* p. 223. Russell applies this argument to the proposition ' A is greater than B '. In this case the relation is asymmetrical, since, if A is greater than B, it follows that B is not greater than A. But the

used to illustrate this argument, but it would work for any properties, even for Bradley's invented ones.

Bradley agrees that his explanation of the functioning of relations is not successful. His reasons for regarding it as unsuccessful are, in fact, not quite the same as Russell's. But the differences need not concern us here,[15] because we want to get to the fundamental point of disagreement as quickly as possible. At this stage the important thing is that Bradley was ready to attribute the failure of his explanation to the unintelligibility of relations rather than to the inadequacy of his particular way of explaining them. However, he was prepared to try another explanation, which, like the first one, reduces relations to properties, but does so in a different way.

He suggests that to say that two individuals are related is really the same thing as to attribute a property to the pair of them taken together.[16] For example, the married state is a property of couples, or, to take a larger number of individuals, a collection of five dots arranged as they are on the face of a die forms the pattern which the Romans called ' quincunx '. But, as the latter example shows very clearly, this way of reducing relations to properties cannot deal with asymmetrical relations.[17] If you merely describe the pattern as a whole, you will not say which dot is surrounded by the other four. Of course, you may not care whether the dot which is surrounded by the other four is the one that the craftsman en-

---

argument is quite general, and so it can be applied, as it is here, to a relation like equality of length which is symmetrical. The argument is not intended to show that equality is not an internal relation between the two lengths. Obviously, it is an internal relation between the two lengths. The argument is directed only against Bradley's attempt to reduce all relations to properties. The connection between that attempted reduction and Bradley's attitude to internal relations will be explained on pp. 168-9.

In *P. of M.* Russell goes on to develop another argument which only applies to asymmetrical relations. See p. 168, footnote 18.

[15] See *F.H.B.*, p. 113ff.   [16] See *A. and R.* Ch. II.
[17] See *F.H.B.* p. 119.

graved first, or the one that he engraved last. But the point is that this asymmetrical relation, encirclement, cannot be reduced to a property of the set of related individuals. This is a general point about asymmetrical relations, and as Russell says it demolishes Bradley's second explanation of relations.[18]

Bradley believed that his second explanation was a little better than his first, because it seemed to him that, in general, any move in the direction of unity was an improvement. Russell's objection to it certainly demolishes it, and, as far as such points can be judged, probably shows that it was not an improvement on the first explanation. However, their disagreement about the comparative evaluation of the two failures is of minor importance. For even if Bradley's second explanation had given a better account of the structure of the unified whole which is produced by an asymmetrical relation, he himself was going to argue that in the end it could not possibly succeed. At this stage too the important point of disagreement between the two philosophers is that, whereas Russell attributes the failure of the explanation to its inadequacy, Bradley is going to attribute it to the inexplicability of relations.

Bradley's reason for thinking that his second explanation is bound to fail in the end is an interesting one, and it points towards the deeper problem which underlies this rather baffling controversy. In order to appreciate his reason, it is necessary to keep the general strategy of his treatment of relations clearly in mind. If victory would have consisted in finding a rational explanation of them, he was not seeking victory, because he regarded it as unattainable. He was retreating slowly under the pressure of the logic of the situation as he saw it. His second explanation seemed to him to be a position which could be held for a short time. For at least it met the requirement that relations must be identical with properties of the related individuals, and so, in the peculiar way that was described just now, it met the requirement that apparently external relations must really be internal. But he did not think that the position could be held for long. He would

18 *P. of M.* p. 225.

abandon it as soon as someone asked how the property which belongs to the group of related individuals is attached to that group. For he thought that this attachment is just as inexplicable as the original attachment of the apparently external relation to the individuals. Indeed, all attachments seemed to him to be inexplicable. In the diagrams that were used earlier the broken ends of the rectangles represent something which he regarded as unintelligible.

This shows that he was not really defending the thesis that all relations are internal, even when apparently external relations are transformed into internal ones by the invention of new properties of the related individuals, or of the groups which they form. On the contrary, he thought that all relations are unintelligible because all predication is unintelligible, including the predication of properties. He treats internal relations with more respect only because they make a gesture which shows that they appreciate the general impossibility of the situation in which all relations find themselves.

Let us look more closely at Bradley's picture of the impossible situation of all relations. The business of relations is to relate,[19] but how are they going to carry on their business? If a relation is going to relate two individuals, it must make some difference to them. It cannot be nailed to them without nail-holes. That is to say, it cannot be attached to them in the purely external way that Russell suggested. According to Bradley, Russell is like a man who wants to fix a cross-piece to two upright posts, but does not want the method of fixing to depend on any property of the posts. But that is impossible. However, when Bradley takes over the task, he finds that he cannot do any better in the end. He knows how it would have to be carried out, if it were possible to carry it out : the method of fixing would have to depend on some property of the individuals. Now at first sight it looks as if an ordinary internal relation can be attached in the required way, because it has a straightforward *a priori* connection with ordinary properties of the related individuals. It also looks as if an

---

[19] See G. E. Moore, *Philosophical Studies* pp. 277-8.

ordinary external relation can be prepared for the same kind of attachment. For we can invent properties whose possession by the individuals, severally or as a group, will be equivalent to the holding of the relation. But all this only puts off the moment of inevitable failure. For in the end there will always be the question how the properties are attached to the individuals, and Bradley thinks that the only intelligible attachment would depend on further properties, either discovered or invented, and so we are launched on an infinite regress, and no rational explanation of relations can ever be given.

So the long running battle between Russell and Bradley about the nature of relations, although it is extremely interesting in itself, is only a prelude to the real clash. What they are really arguing about is the nature of facts. Russell's view is that a fact is formed when things of the right kind are combined: for instance, an individual and a property are combined in the way that leads us to say that the individual possesses the property. Bradley argues that this view makes facts unintelligible, but he has no better view to substitute for it. He only claims to see how it would be improved if it were possible to improve it. It would be improved if we could *explain* the attachment of the property to the individual. But we cannot do this, because the only available explanation would be to appeal to another property, which is useless.

It is interesting to see how much agreement there is between the two philosophers even at this level. They both think that the most perfect kind of singular symbol picks out its denotation without the intervention of any descriptions. Bradley expresses this ideal by saying that the denotations must be treated as 'existences' and not as 'characters';[20] Russell expresses it by saying that the singular symbols must be logically proper names, or at least must be used as logically proper names. The point of disagreement comes when they ask how properties and relations can be attached to individuals picked out in this way. Russell's answer is that they just are attached to them, and he treats this as something ultimate

[20] *A. and R.* p. 517.

which the philosopher has to accept without really being able to explain it. He can classify the various types of things according to the attachments that they are capable of forming, but he cannot explain the general phenomenon of attachment. Bradley's answer is that, since attachment cannot really be explained, it cannot really occur.

It does not take much experience of metaphysical controversies to make one realise that it is not much good asking which side is right. In this case Bradley is not absolutely rejecting the whole edifice of human knowledge on the ground that there is something incurably wrong with the propositions in which it is expressed. He is really comparing knowledge expressed in propositions unfavourably with certain forms of intuitive experience. So there would be some truth in the view that the real disagreement between the two philosophers is about the value of the scientific way of looking at the world. However, this will not do as a complete summing up of the controversy, because it omits two important points. First, when Bradley is trying to reduce relations to properties, ostensibly in order to improve their allegedly hopeless position, he makes a number of important logical mistakes which are pointed out by Russell. Secondly, on the other side, there really is something in Bradley's contention that the phenomenon of attachment should be explained.[21]

However, the kind of explanation that is needed is not at all the kind that Bradley demanded. He talked as if he knew what an explanation of the phenomenon as a whole would be like, and as if the only trouble was that it is impossible to find one. But in fact it is impossible to say what such an explanation would be like. The demand itself is unintelligible. What is needed is a theory about specific attachments, which will tell us what can be attached to what. This demand is intelligible, and in fact Russell attempts to meet it in his Theory of Types.

The Theory of Types belongs to Russell's work on logic

[21] See Wittgenstein *T.L-PH.* 4.221 : ' This raises the question how such combination into propositions comes about.'

and mathematics, and so it falls outside the scope of this book. However, in the connection in which it has just been introduced, there are two points which ought to be made about it. The first point takes us back to the doubt which has coloured this whole exposition of Russell's logical atomism. Is there really anything which we have to treat as simple? It now appears to be necessary to divide things into types, according to their possibilities of attachment, and this in itself seems to be enough to introduce some complexity into things which would otherwise be simple. It seems that nothing comes to us without being filtered through some description, even if it is only the sort of description which says in a very general way what kinds of attachments it is capable of forming. For instance, my acquaintance with a particular visual sense-datum is acquaintance with a thing which can possess properties belonging to a certain range, and cannot possess properties belonging to another range. Or is it possible to treat the propositions which state these elective affinities like ordinary propositions? Can they just be added to the list of all the things that can be said about the particular, in order that it may be extruded in the usual way as the unanalysable subject?[22]

The second point is that this kind of classification of things into types does not provide any support for Bradley's view of internal relations. For he was seeking, without any hope of success, for some way of establishing that an individual's external relations and properties really belong to it necessarily. But this kind of theory tries to show that what belongs to it necessarily is the *possibility* of having external relations and properties belonging to a certain range. However, the two enterprises have something in common: anything that belongs necessarily to an individual like a sense-datum or a material object belongs to it because it fits some other general

[22] Wittgenstein answered this question in the negative, because he took the more radical view that such elective affinities cannot be stated in propositions at all. There is no Theory of Types. See *T.L-PH.* 3.33—3.333.

description, and the question is, what is left when that description too is peeled off.

This confrontation of Russell's logic with Idealist logic helps to establish the interpretation of Russell's logical atomism that has been given in the preceding chapters. For he developed his theory as an answer to Idealism, and the effectiveness of the answer certainly does not depend on the existence of intrinsically simple things. At the very most it only requires that it should be possible to trace back the meanings of symbols to things that we have to treat as simple. If this could be done, it would be quite enough to show that the coagulation of meanings which is characteristic of his opponent's logic is a figment of their imaginations. So when Russell points out that he never adopted extreme atomism, he observes that the question whether it is true or not is unimportant.[23] Indeed, he sometimes seems to use the phrase 'logical atomism' to mean little more than 'pluralism', which is the thesis that meanings can be separated from one another. He says himself that he first used the phrase 'logical atomism' to describe his philosophy in 1918 when he incorporated it in the title *The Philosophy of Logical Atomism*.[24] But he later came to apply it retrospectively to the stage which his philosophy reached in the years 1899-1900, when he had not yet worked out all the distinctive ideas even of moderate atomism.[25] Perhaps it would have been better to call that stage 'pluralism'.[26] But we need not depend on labels, since the books can still be opened and read.

[23] *M.PH.D.* pp. 221-3. This passage was discussed on pp. 144-5.
[24] *M.PH.D.* p. 113.   [25] *M.PH.D.* p. 11.
[26] See *M.PH.D.* p. 54, where Russell calls this development in his philosophy 'the revolt into pluralism'.

CHAPTER XI

SENSE-DATA AND TRUTH

The veto on the discussion of acquaintance as a source of truth can now be suspended. It was imposed in Chapter VI, in order that acquaintance as a source of understanding meanings might be investigated first, and the natural order of exposition preserved. For meaning comes before truth, and it is especially important to respect its priority here, because Russell's system is an attempt to save our claims to factual knowledge from the sceptic by pruning their meaning in the way that was described in Chapter I.

Something has already been said about his views about sense-data,[1] but more must now be added. For the earlier discussion was mainly concerned with the question, what kind of thing Russell thought that a sense-datum is, and it hardly touched on the question what kind of factual knowledge a sense-datum yields about itself. It is this question about factual knowledge which must now be answered. But, before it is answered, it would be as well to recapitulate the results of the earlier discussion. There are really three things which need to be mentioned here. First, Russell thought that sense-data are events in people's nervous systems, and this is very important, because it puts them outside their minds. Secondly, in the period which led up to the writing of *The Philosophy of Logical Atomism* he regarded sensation as a relation between ego and sense-datum. Thirdly, in 1919 he abandoned the thesis that the ego is a detached particular to which sense-data are given, and consequently he had to revise his ideas about sense-data : he continued to regard them as events in people's nervous systems, but he ceased to regard them as data, because he thought that there was no detached receiver to whom they could be given; instead, he treated them

[1] See Ch. III.

as the neutral material out of which people as well as objects in the external world can be constructed logically.[2] This change in his view about the ego, which is essentially an acceptance of Hume's view,[3] then produced further developments which will be described at the end of this chapter.

Perhaps the best way to understand Russell's theory about sense-data is, as usual, to ask what exactly he was denying. What were the chief rival theories which his theory was designed to supplant? The answer is that he was denying the two main forms of Idealism, Berkeleian and Hegelian. The development of his theory away from Berkeleian Idealism has already been described:[4] convinced by the traditional arguments of the sceptic that the range of perception is restricted to sense-data, he nevertheless placed them outside, in fact only just outside the mind, and used them as the foundation for his reconstruction of the edifice of human knowledge. But emancipation from what he regarded as the stuffy Idealism of Berkeley was not enough. There was also a more subtle threat from Hegelian Idealism. Perhaps the intellectual apparatus which we try to apply to things outside the mind prevents us from really making contact with them. This is a more subtle suggestion, but its effect is very similar. If it were correct, Russell's refutation of Berkeley would be a useless victory. He would have succeeded in showing that the objects which we perceive lie outside the mind, only to find that, in any case, we cannot really make contact with them. Or, if that seems exaggeratedly pessimistic, the Hegelian Idealist's contention would be that, although we do make a sort of contact with them, it is no good, and the results that we bring back do not really count as knowledge, because they are spoilt by the intellectual apparatus which we have to use.

Russell's logical answer to this contention was discussed in

---

[2] See pp. 41-2 and p. 42, footnote 29. Of course, the material out of which people are constructed also includes thoughts.

[3] *T.H.N.* I.iv.6 (vol. I, p. 238ff). But see also *T.H.N.* Appendix (vol. II, pp. 317-19).

[4] See p. 33.

the last chapter. His epistemological answer was to treat sensation as an affair between ego and sense-datum with no intellectual go-betweens. The go-betweens, if there had been any, would have been ideas and thoughts. That is to say, a philosopher who took the view that Russell's account of sensation was incomplete, would say that he had left out ideas and thoughts. Now it would have been quite possible for Russell to admit that ideas and thoughts should be added to his account. He could have relied on his own arguments against the logic of Idealism to establish that our intellectual apparatus does not distort the nature of things, and that the results which the mind brings back from its contact with the world really do count as knowledge. For his defence of propositions and their constituents could easily be extended to thoughts and ideas. In any case, thoughts and ideas are not go-betweens which might possibly misrepresent sense-data. That way of looking at them is a mistake which comes from assuming that the only function of the mind is to produce replicas of things that it has experienced. Given this assumption, it looks as if an idea which butted in on sensation would just be in the way.[5] But the assumption is wrong, because an idea can be part of the thought in which a person describes his sense-datum. It is part of the record, and not part of the process through which what is recorded arrives.

However, when Russell first threw over Idealism, he did not feel that he could make this concession to ideas. His caution is very understandable. It is characteristic of a period immediately after a revolution that everyone who was a success under the old régime should be suspected of being reactionary. So Russell's theory of judgement makes no use of ideas, but relies instead entirely on propositions and their constituents. In *The Philosophy of Logical Atomism* he gives no reason for excluding ideas from his theory of judgement,[6] but in *Knowledge by Acquaintance and Knowledge by Description*

[5] See pp. 29-30 where this way of looking at the matter was attributed to Hume.
[6] *PH.L.A.* pp. 29-32 (*L.KN.* pp. 222-8).

he says that the theory that 'judgements consist of ideas' is fundamentally mistaken, because 'on this view ideas become a veil between us and outside things '.[7]

Although the question what part ideas play in judgement is important, it is not nearly so important as the question what part judgement plays in factual knowledge. Now Russell maintained that pure sensation does not involve judgement. Judgement is something which is added to sensation. Sensation gives you acquaintance with a particular sense-datum, but, in order to know a truth about it, you need 'observation of a complex fact which may suitably be called perception '.[8] This way of separating sensation from factual knowledge is, as far as it goes, undoubtedly correct. The point is roughly that, though you may acquire factual knowledge through sensation, your acquisition of it will not be complete until you have reacted in a discriminating way to what comes through the senses.[9] It would of course be a mistake to insist that your reaction must be expressed in words, because it could be an unexpressed thought. It may even be an exaggeration to say that in every case of factual knowledge about what is sensed there must actually be a reaction. Certainly there will be one in most cases, but sometimes it may be enough that you are able to react in a discriminating way. So the point would be more accurately expressed by saying that factual knowledge requires not only an input of material, but also a discriminating reaction, or the possibility of a discriminating reaction to it.

---

[7] *KN.A.KN.D.* (*M. and L.* pp. 221-2).

[8] *R.S.-D.PH.* (*M. and L.* p. 147).

[9] In *PH.L.A.* he does not keep to this version of the distinction. He says, 'I am inclined to think that perception, as opposed to belief, goes straight to the fact and not through the proposition ' (*PH.L.A.* p. 32 [*L.KN.* p. 228]). This, of course, is just a matter of terminology. When he uses the terminology of *PH.L.A.*, he treats judgement as something which is added to perception rather than as something which is added to sensation. Either way, he distinguishes the pure relation between ego and sense-datum from the total result, including the proposition, which is factual knowledge.

Although Russell made this point very clearly in the passage just quoted from *The Relation of Sense-data to Physics*, and in many other passages, it did sometimes get submerged during this period in the development of his philosophy, and it only emerged firmly and finally after 1919 when his view about the ego changed. There are two explanations of its intermittent submergence during the earlier period, or perhaps we should say one and a half explanations, because the second one really overlaps with the first. The first, which is given by Russell himself in *My Philosophical Development*,[10] is that, if sensation is regarded as a relation between ego and sense-datum, it is very easy to slip into thinking that sensation in itself amounts to factual knowledge. For is not sensation a cognitive relation? However, though the answer to this question certainly ought to be in the affirmative, all that this means is that factual knowledge *comes through* sensation. It does not mean that sensation *amounts* to factual knowledge. But it is very easy to slip into thinking that it does amount to it. It was all the easier because the whole history of the philosophy of perception which lay behind Russell was pushing him in that direction. The non-propositionality of Hume's philosophy, which was pointed out earlier,[11] was far from unique. It was in fact the general rule, to which the most conspicuous exceptions were Kant, and, among Russell's contemporaries, Frege. It would not be a great exaggeration to say that the marriage between logic and epistemology, which was arranged by Aristotle, only came about at the end of the nineteenth century, after logic had developed a relationship with mathematics.

Anyway, whatever the pressures of history, that is the main reason why Russell's point, that factual knowledge is essentially propositional, was sometimes submerged in his mind in the period which ended in 1919. He regarded sensation as a cognitive relation between ego and sense-datum, and that led him to think that in itself it might amount to factual knowledge. When he ceased to regard the ego as a particular, the

[10] *M.PH.D.* p. 135.   [11] See pp. 30-1.

situation completely changed. First, as has already been explained, he could no longer maintain that the material which comes by way of the senses was *given*, because there was no longer a detached receiver to whom it could be given. Secondly, he had to find another account of factual knowledge in this area. It could no longer be presented as a cognitive relation between ego and sense-datum, and yet it could not just consist in the mere occurrence of events in people's afferent nerves. It must involve something more, and propositions provide the most natural and obvious supplementation. So the point which he had already stated in *The Relation of Sense-data to Physics* (1910-11) was forced finally and permanently to the surface by the change in his view about the ego. This development, which is really the key to understanding twentieth-century empiricism, will be described in this chapter.

If we now bring in Russell's theory of knowledge by acquaintance, we shall find that this explanation of the intermittent submergence of his main point in the period before 1919 acquires a new dimension. Or perhaps, as has already been suggested, what we shall get is a second explanation which partly overlaps with the first. Anyway, the important thing is to see what the theory of knowledge by acquaintance does in this area, and that will require quite a lot of explanation.

When you are acquainted with a thing and are actually confronted by it, it would be natural to suppose that something happens between you and it. In fact, it looks as if one of two things will happen. It may be that the confrontation is the beginning of your acquaintance with the thing, and in that case you may learn the meaning of the word for the thing through whatever sense it may happen to be : for example, if you are looking at a colour for the first time, you may extract the meaning of the colour-word from what you see. That is one possibility. Alternatively, the movement may be from you to it : for you may already know the meaning of the word, so that you will be able to take the initiative and apply it to what you see with confidence gained from previous experience.

Now these two alternatives seem to be exhaustive and exclusive. That is to say, on any given occasion the movement ought to be in one of the two directions, and could hardly be in both at once. But it is very easy for this distinction between the two directions of movement to get lost in the theory of acquaintance. For the fact that confrontation can produce either of the two results might make the difference between them seem unimportant. It might look as if factual knowledge does not really require a proposition to which you assent either externally or internally. You might think that, in order to know a fact, you do not need to commit yourself in that way : you can be more cautious and let your words draw their meanings from the object with which you are confronted.

It is not being suggested that Russell slipped into thinking that on a given occasion of confrontation the movement might be in both directions at once. He did not. Certainly, he always held a denotational theory of meaning and a correspondence theory of truth.[12] But he never made the mistake of supposing that the denotation from which a person extracts the meaning of a word might simultaneously be the subject of his claim to factual knowledge. That is to say, he never made the mistake of supposing that one and the same thing on a single occasion of confrontation could both give a person understanding of the meaning of a word and give him factual knowledge expressed in a proposition containing that word.[13] What is being suggested here is only that in the area of sensation Russell's theory of acquaintance tends to conceal the importance of the logical movement from person to thing. When a person applies a word to a sense-datum we are apt not to notice the movement because Russell says that what then occurs is acquaintance, and, if we turn to his theory of acquaintance, we find that it makes so much of the flash of understanding that occurs on the other occasions when he extracts the meaning of a word from a sense-datum. This is

[12] See *M.PH.D.* pp. 240-1 and p. 175.
[13] This is probably the mistake which Wittgenstein calls a ' crucial superstition ', *PH.I.* p. 18, footnote.

at the moment a very vague suggestion, and no evidence has yet been produced for it. But later in this chapter it will be elaborated and supported by citation from Russell's works. The reason why the suggestion is first made in this vague and unsupported way is that that will make it easier to follow the general drift of this criticism of Russell's treatment of sensation before 1919. The point, in its general form, is that in this period Russell allowed theory of meaning and theory of truth to merge into one another. However, when this charge is elaborated, as it will be shortly, it will appear that the extent to which he allowed them to merge was much less than some of his critics have claimed.

Throughout this chapter and the next two it must be remembered that what is being described is a phase in the development of Russell's ideas which was not going to last. The phase was one of tension. On one side there was his general thesis that all factual knowledge is propositional : on the other side he felt the pull of the idea that in the area of sensation factual knowledge might be more immediate and intuitive. In 1919 the tension was resolved largely in favour of propositions. This chapter will describe the development of his views about sensation, and the next two will deal with a closely related topic, the development of his theory of judgement.

The first thing to be done now is to dissect Russell's theory of sensation in the period up to 1919. This is not an easy task because the theory is a piece of miniaturised mechanism. Therefore, let us choose a starting point where things are large and obvious. According to some students of Russell's philosophy he believed that, at least at the level of complete analysis, empirical propositions can only be used in the actual presence of the sense-data, properties and relations that their words denote. Conclusive evidence against this interpretation has already been given.[14] But we might now ask why anyone

[14] See p. 71, footnote 1, where J. O. Urmson's interpretation of Russell's theory of knowledge by acquaintance was given as an example. Max Black takes the same line in his essay on *Russell's Philosophy of Language in PH.B.R.* p. 252. Russell rightly repudiates

was ever convinced by it. The answer to this question seems
to be that Russell's theory, that the understanding of meanings
comes through acquaintance, was taken to imply that acquaintance, and therefore understanding, lapsed when the person's
confrontation with the relevant sense-data came to an end;
as if cars had no batteries of their own, and so could not move
without disconnecting the wires which gave them the electricity
which would enable them to move. If Russell had held this
absurd view, there would have been no room in his system
for the distinction that was drawn just now, between the confrontation with a sense-datum through which a person learns
the meaning of a word and subsequent confrontations which
allow him to use the word to express factual knowledge about
other sense-data. For that distinction depends on the assumption that people's minds are retentive, and that the occasions
for applying lessons that they have learned do not necessarily
turn into occasions for re-learning the same lessons. If the
distinction is abandoned, the consequence is extremely bizarre.
There would be no truth or falsity for propositions about
sense-data, because there would be no standard by which their
truth or falsity could be judged. To put the point in a slightly
different way, although it might look as if a proposition about
a sense-datum could be true, it could not be false, because the
sense-datum from which a speaker extracted the meaning of a
word would automatically make his proposition containing
that word true: but truth which could not fail would be a
degenerate kind of truth, which might satisfy Humpty
Dumpty, but could not express factual knowledge, because, in
order to do so, it would have to violate the principle which
was stated just now, that on any given occasion of confrontation the logical movement cannot be in both directions at once.

If Russell did not merge the meaning and the truth of propositions about sense-data in this extreme way, is there any
case for saying that he merged them to some lesser extent? In

---

the view that Black ascribes to him on p. 695 of the same volume.

order to answer this question, it is necessary to recall a point
which has often been made in previous chapters; which is
that, according to him, though you need not learn the meaning
of a complex symbol through acquaintance with its denotation,
you can learn it in this way. Now a complex symbol is one
which it is humanly possible to analyse. So it is very likely
that you can analyse such a symbol, or at least that you can
learn to analyse it so as to be able to pick out the different
elements in its denotation with the symbols which occur in its
analysis. But this has a curious effect. You extract the meaning of the complex symbol from its denotation in a flash of
understanding, in much the same way that a bird which has
just laid a fifth egg is said to learn immediately what the
pattern of five eggs looks like without actually being able to
count. But it may be that you are also able to perform the
operation which would be the equivalent of the bird's actually
counting the eggs with its foot : that is to say, it may be that
you can already analyse the denotation of the complex symbol
into its elements, so that you not only did not need acquaintance with the complex, but also do not have to rely on the
Gestalt when you do have acquaintance with the complex. If
in such a case you can perform the analysis, it looks as if you
will not only extract the meaning of the complex symbol from
its denotation, but also simultaneously acquire a piece of
factual knowledge about its denotation. For example, when
you learn the meaning of the name ' Avar ' by finding the tree
which it denotes, you might acquire the factual knowledge
that it is deciduous. In that case it seems that this fact would
be drawn into your mind along with the meaning of the name.
One and the same confrontation would give you both. If the
piece of factual knowledge were actually included in the
meaning of the name, if, for instance, the girth of the trunk
were mentioned in a definite description giving its analysis,
and if you could carry out the analysis, it would be quite
likely that, when you extracted the meaning of the name
from the thing, you would acquire the factual knowledge too.
Of course, even in this example it would not be impossible to

extract the meaning alone, because you might look at the tree without seeing what its girth was. But suppose that the analysis of the ordinary proper name were taken down to the level of sense-data. It then looks as if it would be impossible to extract the meaning of a complex symbol which you could analyse without acquiring factual knowledge. For the properties and relations of sense-data are so very obvious at the moment when you are having them.

This can be illustrated by an adaptation of Diagram VIII. Diagram VIII showed how the proposition ' Avar is red ' might partly be analysed into propositions about your present sense-data. Let us adapt it to illustrate the slightly different situation with which we are here concerned. Suppose that you do not know the meaning of the ordinary proper name ' Avar ', and that you learn it through confrontation with sense-data which are, as a matter of fact, red. Then the point is that it is difficult to see how the meaning of the ordinary proper name can possibly be conveyed along the dotted lines in Diagram IX which represent your acquaintance with the sense-data, without bringing with it the fact that the sense-data are red. How can acquaintance convey meanings without conveying facts?

It is important to observe that the question how acquaintance can extract meanings from sense-data without extracting facts is not the same as either of the two questions about the unanalysability of logically proper names which were discussed earlier. One of the earlier difficulties about the unanalysability of logically proper names was that, if you take a particular and pare away all the facts about it, it is not clear that there is anything left for acquaintance to convey : or, in other words, the result of this subtraction sum seems to be zero.[15] But the difficulty with which we are concerned now is the difficulty of doing the subtraction sum at all, whatever its result is going to be. Suppose that we do understand what pure acquaintance with a particular would be like. Then the problem is to see what filter could possibly exclude all facts

[15] See p. 126.

about the particular, only letting the pure meaning pass into the mind. The other question about the unanalysability of logically proper names which was discussed earlier was the question how they can avoid picking up descriptions of their denotations in whatever way ordinary proper names pick up descriptions of theirs.[16] That is a problem about what happens to facts after they have passed into the mind, and so it is quite distinct from our present problem, which is about the way in which facts pass into, or are excluded from, the mind.

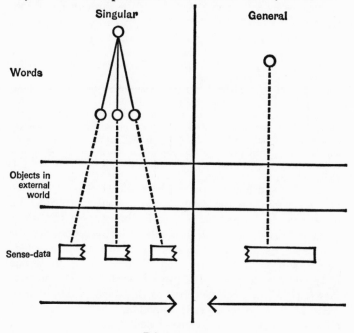

Diagram ix

There is no doubt that this diagram represents Russell's way of looking at the matter. His thesis that we may be acquainted with a complex thing suggests that we may be acquainted with

[16] See pp. 46-7.

a fact, because, if the complex thing is an individual, the analysis of the symbol which is applied to it will expand into a proposition which, if it is true, will correspond to a fact. Nor does he repudiate the suggestion. In *The Problems of Philosophy* he says that one of the ways in which a complex fact may be known is 'by means of acquaintance with the complex fact itself, which may (in a large sense) be called perception, though it is by no means confined to objects of the senses'.[17] When this thesis is applied to sensation, acquaintance with the complex fact will be through direct confrontation. Russell describes what happens in such a case in the Introduction to *Principia Mathematica*:

Let us consider a complex object composed of two parts a and b standing to each other in the relation R. The complex object 'a-in-the-relation-R-to-b' may be capable of being *perceived*; when perceived it is perceived as one object. Attention may show that it is complex; we then *judge* that a and b stand in the relation R. Such a judgement, being derived from perception by mere attention, may be called 'a judgement of perception'. This judgement of perception, considered as an actual occurrence, is a relation of four terms, namely a and b and R and the percipient.[18] The perception, on the other hand, is a relation of two terms, namely 'a-in-the-relation-R-to-b' and the percipient.[19]

It is true that Russell does not here call the relation between the percipient and the complex object 'acquaintance'. But there is no doubt that that is what he thinks it is. The whole passage reveals the tension in his theory of sensation. On the one hand, the percipient is directly related to the complex object by acquaintance, while on the other hand his factual knowledge has to be expressed in a proposition. The proposition is obviously important even at this stage in the development of the theory, and its importance became still more obvious in 1919, when he abandoned the ego and its direct relationship with the complex object. But in the period before that development occurred he certainly allowed acquaintance with facts at least in the area of sensation, because it is dif-

[17] *P. of PH*. p. 136.
[18] This statement will be explained in the next chapter.
[19] *P.M.* 2nd edition, p. 43.

ficult to see how acquaintance with a sense-datum could occur without acquaintance with a fact. His general view about acquaintance with complex objects, which has just been illustrated from *Principia Mathematica*, is also given in *Philosophical Essays*.[20] Its special application to sense-data is made very clear in *Knowledge by Acquaintance and Knowledge by Description*, where he includes 'the-yellowness-of-this' among complex individuals with which we are acquainted,[21] and in a passage in *The Problems of Philosophy*, in which he says, 'in the presence of my table I am acquainted with the sense-data that make up the appearance of my table—its colour, shape, hardness, smoothness, etc.'.[22] These two passages show that he was prepared to allow pure acquaintance with a sense-datum to spread so as to include its properties and relations, and that means that he was prepared to allow acquaintance with the complex object, and so, by analysis, acquaintance with the fact.

Whatever the merits or demerits of this view, it clearly does not expose Russell to the charge of merging the truth of propositions about sense-data with their meaning in the extreme way that was discussed earlier. For on this view the source of a proposition's truth will never be the same as the source of its meaning. Consider, for instance, the proposition that you are having a yellow sense-datum, which is about a simple individual. What makes this proposition true is the complex object 'the-yellowness-of-this': but it is given its meaning by the two parts of this complex taken separately, the sense-datum denoted by the word 'this', and the property denoted by the word 'yellow'. Similarly, a proposition about a complex individual will maintain this separation between the source of its truth and the source of its meaning. If you say that Avar is deciduous, the complex object which gives the name 'Avar' its meaning in the way that was illustrated in Diagram IX is different from, and contained within, the com-

[20] *O.N.T. and F.* (*PH.E.* pp. 181-3).
[21] *KN.A.KN.D.* (*M. and L.* p. 213).
[22] *P. of PH.* p. 46.

plex object which makes the whole proposition true. Nor is this surprising. The complex object which makes a proposition true is certainly a fact, but, if the proposition mentions a complex individual, that individual will expand under analysis into *another* fact. It follows that, if the person who asserts the proposition happens to be acquainted with the complex individual, *that* acquaintance will not yield the fact which makes the proposition true.

However, this part of Russell's theory of knowledge by acquaintance does merge the learning of truths with the learning of meanings to some extent. Consider again the fact which according to this theory may be learned when someone learns the meaning of a complex singular symbol by acquaintance with its denotation. There seems to be no doubt that it is possible for him to learn the meaning of the symbol in a flash, the moment that he is confronted with the thing. But does he learn the fact in the same complete and self-contained way? That might well be doubted. For, if we go back to the example illustrated in Diagram IX, we might enquire what exactly is meant by the suggestion that he might be able to perform the operation which would be the equivalent of the bird's actually counting the eggs with its foot. What does it mean to suggest that he might already be able to analyse the meaning of the complex symbol into its elements, so that he not only did not need acquaintance with the complex, but also does not have to rely on the Gestalt when he does have acquaintance with the complex? The idea is that, when he finds the tree, he has a red sense-datum,[23] and analyses this complex object into two parts, the sense-datum itself and the colour red. Of course, the proposition that this sense-datum is red is only a minute part of the analysis of the original proposition ' Avar is deciduous '.[24] But that does not affect the present question, whether his ability to analyse the complex object into its two parts is sufficient to give him the

[23] Russell believes that adjectives like ' red ' are appropriate to sense-data. This might be challenged. See p. 36.
[24] See p. 133.

factual knowledge which he would express in the proposition about his sense-datum, 'This is red'. The answer to this question is that it is not sufficient. He also needs the ability to apply the correct symbols to the two parts of the complex object.

Now the sense-datum itself will not present him with a problem : all that he has to do is to use a logically proper name which has not been used before. But how will he know what to call the colour? This will be a problem for him, unless he is encountering the colour for the first time and learning the meaning of the word ' red' from it. But if that is what he is doing, his proposition about the sense-datum will not express factual knowledge : the logical movement will be in the reverse direction. If, on the other hand, the logical movement is in the right direction for factual knowledge, he must already know the meaning of the word ' red ', and so he must have learned it from some earlier sense-datum. But in that case his proposition will not be based entirely on the sense-datum with which he is now confronted. Therefore, his piece of factual knowledge will not be extracted entirely from the sense-datum with which he is now confronted, in the way in which his understanding of the meaning of the complex symbol ' Avar ' might be. So it is a mistake to maintain that factual knowledge can ever be acquired through acquaintance in the same complete and self-contained way in which meanings can sometimes be learned through acquaintance.

The dilemma is really inescapable. Either the proposition ' This is red ' does not express a piece of factual knowledge, or, if it does, it is not based entirely on the complex object ' the-redness-of-this ', but is partly based on a comparison with something else. It is easy to overlook this dilemma if perception is treated as the ego's acquaintance with the sense-datum. For that same acquaintance, when it is construed as a source of meaning, with the logical movement in the reverse direction, really can sometimes be a complete and self-contained affair : and so it is easy to forget that, if it is construed as a source of factual knowledge, it cannot be a complete and

self-contained affair. As Wittgenstein says in criticism of the
logical analysis of perception which Russell gives in *Principia Mathematica* and *Philosophical Essays*,[25] ' To perceive a
complex means to perceive that its constituents are related to
one another in such and such a way ' :[26] and if anyone tries to
say how they are related, his proposition will not be based
entirely on the perceived complex.[27]

Russell did not exactly overlook this dilemma about factual
knowledge. But he certainly failed to feel its full force, largely
because he thought that he could rely on the ego's acquaintance
with the complex object. So the passage already quoted from
Principia Mathematica continues :

Since an object of perception cannot be nothing, we cannot perceive ' a-in-the-relation-R-to-b ' unless a is in the relation R to b.
Hence a judgement of perception, according to the above definition,
must be true. This does not mean that in a judgement which
appears to us to be one of perception we are sure of not being in
error, since we may err in thinking that our judgement has really been
derived merely by analysis of what was perceived.[28]

This is an attempt to break one horn of the dilemma by
suggesting that a proposition derived merely by analysis of
the complex object might express factual knowledge. But it
cannot be broken in this, or in any other way. It is only an
ambiguity in the phrase ' analysis of the complex object '
which suggests that it might be. The discrimination of the
parts of the complex object is indeed a complete and self-
contained affair : but, if the word ' analysis ' also includes the
application of the correct symbols to those parts it is not a
complete and self-contained affair.

It is important to see exactly what is dubious in Russell's
account of perception. A very concise version of it appears in
The Philosophy of Logical Atomism :

I am inclined to think that perception, as opposed to belief, does go
straight to the fact, and not through the proposition. When you

[25] *P.M.* 2nd edition, p. 43, and *PH.E.* pp. 181-3.
[26] *T.L-PH.* 5.5423.
[27] *N.L.* (*N.B.* App. 1, p. 98), *T.L-PH.* 4.027—4.03.
[28] *P.M.* 2nd edition, p. 43.

perceive the fact, you do not, of course, have error coming in, because, the moment that it is a fact that is your object, error is excluded.[29]

No doubt is being cast on the second sentence in this passage, which is, of course, a tautology. Russell's substantial point is contained in the first sentence: it emerges when we ask how you know that your judgement is a pure judgement of perception. His answer to this question is that it will be a pure judgement of perception if you confine yourself to analysing the complex object. It is this point that is being doubted, because, if you are going to end with a proposition expressing factual knowledge, your analysis of the complex object must include a description of its parts, and that description must bring in a comparison with something in your past experience. It is interesting to see that Russell seems to have felt this doubt when he wrote *The Problems of Philosophy* (1912). At one point in that book he gives the doctrine which is here being criticised,[30] but later on he seems to have misgivings about it:

Supposing we first perceive the sun shining, which is a complex fact, and then proceed to make the judgement 'The sun is shining'. In passing from the perception to the judgement, it is necessary to analyse the given complex fact: we have to separate out 'the sun' and 'shining' as constituents of the fact. In this process it is possible to commit an error; hence even where a *fact* has the first and absolute kind of self-evidence, a judgement believed to correspond to the fact is not absolutely infallible, because it may not really correspond to the fact.[31]

This passage clearly reveals the tension within Russell's account of perception. Contingent propositions must connect one thing with another, and that must bring in the possibility

---

[29] *PH.L.A.* p. 32 (*L.KN.* p. 228). Cf. *O.N.T. and F.* (*PH.E.* pp. 181-2): 'I shall take it as agreed that perception, as opposed to judgement, is never in error, i.e. that, whenever we perceive anything, what we perceive exists, at least as long as we are perceiving it.'

[30] *P. of PH.* pp. 113-14.

[31] *P. of PH.* p. 137. Russell here uses an example taken from the external world. The point is a general one, and can be illustrated at this level just as well as at the level of sense-data.

of error.[82] They are denied this essential function by the theory that some perceptual knowledge is based entirely on the ego's acquaintance with a sense-datum, which is construed as a complete and self-contained relationship. In this theory propositions and acquaintance have to part company. On the one side we have a relationship which cannot amount to factual knowledge, because it is non-propositional; and on the other side we have propositions which cannot meet the high standard of self-evidence which that relationship demands.

The ultimate source of this tension is Russell's failure to maintain a strict distinction between a sense-datum treated as a bare particular in abstraction from whatever properties and relations it may possess and a sense-datum treated as a complex object which includes its properties and relations. Not that he does not draw this distinction. But his dividing line falters. Even in the passage part of which has already been quoted from *The Relation of Sense-data to Physics*,[33] where he draws the distinction very clearly, he only applies it to sense-data which are particulars standing in certain relations to one another, and does not apply it to sense-data which are particulars possessing properties. For after saying that, when he speaks of sense-data, he means ' particular patches of colour, particular noises and so on ', he continues:

There is some difficulty in deciding what is to be considered *one* sense-datum: often attention causes divisions to appear where, so far as can be discovered, there were no divisions before. An observed complex fact, such as that this patch of red is to the left of that patch of blue, is also to be regarded as a datum from our point of view: epistemologically it does not differ greatly from a simple[34] sense-datum as regards its function in giving knowledge. Its *logical*

---

[82] The further controversy about the kind of error which is possible for propositions about sense-data will not be pursued here. Is it always purely verbal error? Or is it sometimes substantial error? And how should the distinction between these two kinds of error be drawn? See Austin, ' *Other Minds* ', *Proceedings of the Aristotelian Society*, supplementary vol. xx (reprinted in Flew, *Logic and Language*, [*Second Series*], and Austin, *Philosophical Papers*).

[33] *R.S.D.PH.* (*M. and L.* p. 147).

[34] i.e. a sense-datum with a property, e.g. a patch of colour (*D.F.P.*).

structure is very different, however, from that of sense: *sense* gives acquaintance with particulars, and is thus a two term relation in which the object can be *named* but not *asserted*, and is inherently incapable of truth or falsehood, whereas the observation of a complex fact, which may be suitably called ' perception ', is not a two term relation, but involves the propositional form on the object side, and gives knowledge of a truth, not mere acquaintance with a particular.

But why not apply the same treatment to sense-data which are particulars possessing properties? Even a patch of colour is a patch possessing a certain colour, and so even it has a complex logical structure. Here again we must maintain the same distinction between sense-data treated as bare particulars and sense-data treated as complex objects. Only in this way can Russell's theory of meaning be kept absolutely apart from his theory of truth. If the distinction between simple and complex individuals, which is the foundation of his system, is not maintained, it will appear to be possible that a contingent truth might be learned from one sense-datum in the way in which a meaning sometimes can be.

In the development of this criticism it has been assumed that the meaning of a word can sometimes be learned in a flash from one sense-datum, or from the observation of one thing in the external world, and that this is a complete and self-contained affair between the learner and the thing. Of course, the meaning of a word is not always learned in this way, but it has been assumed that it sometimes is. However, this assumption might be challenged on two grounds. First, it might be objected that, although the meaning of a word may sometimes be learned in a flash, the question whether it has or has not been learned is a question which can be settled only by watching the subsequent performance of the learner, so that the extraction of the meaning from the thing is not really a complete and self-contained affair. Secondly, if we look at what happens before someone learns the meaning of a word in a flash, we may find that the beginning of the affair is not really so clear-cut either. For it is plausible to maintain that such an achievement cannot come out of a clear sky: if a person has never come across this specific kind of thing before, at least he must have learned reactions to things belonging to the same general family; for example, he may never have seen the colour red, but at least he must have learned to discriminate other colours, or, if not that, then, even more minimally, he must have learned to discriminate between some sensory qualities. These two contentions are developed by Wittgenstein in *Philosophical Investigations*,[35] not specifically against Russell, but against his own earlier theory of meaning, which was, of course, similar to Russell's.

If truth is not a matter of pinpoint contact, then it is reasonable to suppose that meaning will not be a matter of pinpoint contact either. That is to say, if truth needs another point of contact between word and thing in the past in order to get a comparison, then meaning too will need more than one point of contact. For both truth and meaning depend on consistency of reaction, and consistency of reaction requires repetition. However, the first of the two objections does not really make any difference to the way in which the criticism of Russell's theory has been presented. For, though it may be necessary to observe the learner's performance on other occasions in the future, in order to discover whether he *has* learned the meaning of the word in a flash, that would not show that his actual learning of it was not a complete and self-contained affair. But the second objection does make some difference to what has been said. For the apparently instantaneous learning of a meaning through acquaintance with a thing is something of an illusion. The acquaintance of the moment does not completely explain it, and some general background of acquired aptitudes is presupposed. However, there is still this much difference between the learning of a meaning through acquaintance and the establishing of a truth through acquaintance : the former does not require any previous knowledge of *another example of the same kind*, whereas the latter does. This is enough to justify the way in which this criticism of Russell's account of acquaintance with sense-data has been presented.

[35] *PH.I.* § 143ff and §§ 31-2.

The point which has been criticised is not Russell's main theme. His main theme is the propositionality of factual knowledge, and, as was explained earlier,[36] it was his realisation of the importance of propositions that enabled him to advance beyond the point which Hume had reached in the development of his empiricism. But there are obstacles which impede the flow of his ideas, and produce eddies and backward currents. The theory that perceptual knowledge is sometimes a complete and self-contained relation between ego and sense-datum is an obstacle of this kind. It does not belong to the main stream, but was produced by an idea which was left to him by his predecessors, the idea that the purest and most certain kind of knowledge depends entirely on contact with the thing that is known and does not involve any reaction to it. This idea naturally produces a static theory of knowledge : knowing becomes a sort of gazing, and the life and movement of propositions and all their connections are forgotten. Russell's realisation of the importance of propositions prevented his theory of knowledge from developing in that direction, but the idea remained embedded in his philosophy until after 1919. In that year he finally ceased to regard the ego as a particular. That made it even more obvious that the rôle played by propositions in perceptual knowledge is always indispensable, and that their rôle is always to reach beyond the experience of the moment. If there were no propositions, there would only be sensations, which by themselves obviously cannot amount to pieces of knowledge. If there were propositions, but they did not reach beyond the experience at the moment, there would still be no possibility of perceptual knowledge, although in this case it might appear, at first sight, to be possible.

Perceptual knowledge does not require that the percipient should actually express what he knows in words. So, when Russell ceased to regard the ego as a particular, he naturally began to investigate the rôle played by propositions which are not expressed in words. He thought that part of this

[36] See pp. 51-3.

problem, but only part of it, could be solved in the Behaviourists' way.[37] For there are other overt reactions besides the production of words, but even when these have been added, the list of rôles played by propositions will still not be complete, because there are also inward reactions and thoughts.

The further development of Russell's theory of perceptual knowledge will not be described here, because it lies outside the period to which this book is restricted. Something more will be said in the next two chapters about his general account of propositions. But his views about their specific contribution to perceptual knowledge will be left at this point. *My Philosophical Development*[38] contains a sketch of their development after 1919. The way in which he came to see the problem in the later period may be illustrated by the following passage :

' Perception ' as opposed to sensation involves habit based upon past experience. We may distinguish sensation as that part of our total experience which is due to the stimulus alone, independently of past history. This is a theoretical core in the total occurrence. The total occurrence is always an interpretation in which the sensational core has accretions embodying habits.[39]

[37] *M.PH.D.* p. 137ff.   [38] *M.PH.D.* pp. 134-44.
[39] *M.PH.D.* p. 143.

CHAPTER XII

JUDGEMENT

The theory of judgement which Russell developed in the period before 1919 was first published in 1910 in *Philosophical Essays*.[1] It is, as he says, a theory of belief,[2] and its scope is restricted to beliefs about things that are not being perceived at the moment. Hume had imposed the same restriction on his theory of belief.[3] Both philosophers made a sharp contrast between belief and perception : according to Hume, perception depends on impressions, whereas belief depends on ideas, and Russell maintained, at least during that period, that perception depends on direct contact with sense-data, so that the object of perception must exist, whereas the object of belief need not exist. It is, of course, tautological to say that you cannot perceive what does not exist, and, as was pointed out in the last chapter,[4] the important question is how you know that you really are perceiving what you think you are perceiving, and that question brings in propositions. Now it may be that you can always be more certain of the truth of a proposition about what you are perceiving at the moment than about the truth of a proposition about what you are not perceiving at the moment. If so, the word 'belief' might be too weak a description for your attitude to propositions about what you are perceiving at the moment. Nevertheless, everything else that Russell says in his theory of judgement applies to these propositions too. For if his equation of judgement with belief is omitted, his theory of judgement is a general account of the affirmative attitude to propositions. Its extension to propositions about what you are perceiving at the moment would not obliterate the distinction which he draws

[1] *O.N.T. and F.* (*PH.E.* p. 170ff). Cf. *P. of PH.* pp. 123-30.
[2] *O.N.T. and F.* (*PH.E.* p. 172, footnote).
[3] *T.H.N.* I.iii.7 (p. 96ff). See pp. 29-31.   [4] See pp. 190-1.

by saying that the object of perception, unlike the object of judgement, must exist. So after 1919, when he came to see the full importance of the rôle that propositions play in perceptual knowledge, he might well have extended his theory of judgement into this area. However, what actually happened was rather more complicated. For, as we shall soon see, the year 1919 also brought a change in his theory of judgement.

The best way to approach his theory of judgement is to identify the main problem which it was designed to solve. Of course, it was designed to explain what judging is. But that is a very general statement of purpose, and it does not really locate the problem for us. Perhaps the centre of the problem is the special difficulty of seeing how people can judge what is not the case. Now, it is only too easy to see some of the things which lead people to form mistaken beliefs. But that is not the kind of explanation that he wanted. He wanted to know what the objects of judgement are. The objects of perception are sense-data, but it is not so easy to see what the objects of judgement are. If you say that they are facts, you immediately run up against the difficulty that the object of a false judgement cannot be a fact. What is not the case is not a fact. But what is it? Is it anything? If it is not anything, it looks as if judgements have no objects. But that would be extraordinary. Surely when a person judges something, there must be something outside his mind that he judges?[5] Here it is important to remember that Russell developed his theory of judgement as an answer to the suggestion of the Hegelian Idealists, that we never really make contact with anything outside our own minds. The claustrophobia produced by this suggestion might well lead to an excessive reaction against it. Russell's theory of mind at this period was certainly designed to achieve maximum exposure to the external world. He even refused to allow that judgements might consist of ideas, because he thought that ' on this view ideas become a veil between us and outside things—we never really, in knowledge, attain to the things

[5] See *O.N.T. and F. (PH.E.* pp. 173-4).

that we are supposed to be knowing about but only to the ideas of those things.'[6]

Now the problem, how a person can possibly judge what is not the case, contains within itself another problem. It contains the problem, how a false proposition can have a meaning. For at least part of the solution of the first problem would consist in explaining the meaningfulness of false propositions. How do false propositions acquire a meaning? Naturally, they acquire their meanings in exactly the same way that true propositions acquire theirs. For a proposition must get its meaning in a way that leaves the question of its truth or falsity open. But false propositions present the problem in an especially clear way. The suggestion, that propositions get their meanings from facts, which anyway will not do, is a spectacular failure in their case.

At this point we might expect that Russell would simply use the same logical apparatus which he had used for the analysis of complex phrases. For the question how a false proposition can have acquired a meaning is quite like the question how a meaning can have been acquired by a complex phrase which lacks a denotation. It looks as if the same explanation might serve in both cases. A complex symbol like ' Avar ' has to be analysed into its elements, each of which taken separately will have a denotation: and it might be supposed that the analysis of a proposition, which is only a rather special kind of complex symbol, would proceed in the same way. Now it is perfectly true that there is an analogy between the two problems, and Russell's treatment of false propositions does begin by running parallel to his treatment of complex phrases which lack a denotation. But he soon reaches a point where the two subjects diverge, because a proposition is a very peculiar kind of complex symbol. Indeed, it is easy to see that the divergence is inevitable long before

---

[6] *KN.A.KN.D.* (*M. and L.* pp. 221-2). This passage was quoted on p. 177. When Russell rejected the Idealists' theory of judgement, he had an ally, G. E. Moore. Moore's influential article, ' *The Nature of Judgement* ', appeared in *Mind*, 1899.

we reach the point where it occurs. For it is obvious from far off that propositions are very peculiar. Yet, as so often happens in philosophy, when we look more closely at them, it is not at all easy to say exactly what their peculiarity is.

Let us take first the part of Russell's theory of propositions which does run parallel to his theory of complex phrases. Even if there were nothing to stop true propositions deriving their meanings from the facts that make them true, it is very obviously impossible for false propositions to acquire their meanings in this way. How then did the proposition that Charles I died in his bed acquire its meaning? Evidently its meaning is built up out of the separate meanings of its elements, just like the meaning of a complex symbol which is not a proposition. It could hardly be derived all in one piece from the fact that Charles I died in his bed, because there is no such fact. However, it is still open to us to say that the proposition corresponds to a possibility, provided that we do not offer this as an explanation of the way in which it acquired its meaning. The acquisition of its meaning cannot be explained in this way. Indeed, the suggestion that it might be is as absurd as the suggestion that the meaning of the phrase ' the daughter of Hitler ' is derived from an entity existing in the so-called Platonic world.[7] Meanings are derived from actualities, and are then used to construct possibilities, and it is absurd to suggest that this order of things might be reversed. But, if we avoid this implication, what is wrong with the view that all propositions, including false ones, correspond to possibilities, and that what makes a proposition true is the realisation of the possibility to which it corresponds?

Wittgenstein was to adopt this view later in the *Tractatus*. Russell does not really consider it when he is developing his theory of judgement in *Philosophical Essays*. He considers the closely related view of Meinong,[8] that every judgement, true or false, has an objective, and he rejects it on three

[7] See p. 50.

[8] Meinong: *Uber Annahmen* c. vii. See Russell: *M.TH.C.A. II, Mind*, 1904, p. 349ff.

grounds : because in general it is difficult to believe in the existence of objectives; because false judgements would correspond to false objectives, and it is especially difficult to believe in false objectives; and because, anyway, on this view the difference between the truth and falsity of judgements is not explained, but, if anything, made more difficult to understand, because we are merely referred to the more obscure difference between true and false objectives.[9] These criticisms do not really apply to the view which Wittgenstein was later to adopt, and it was probably Russell's ' vivid sense of reality ' which led him to overlook that view, or at least not to look at it squarely. His theory of meaning is the theory of a philosopher who prefers actualities, and looks at possibilities obliquely and reluctantly. In any case, even a philosopher who liked possibilities would hardly maintain that propositions derive their meanings from them.

So far we have been tracing the parallelism between Russell's account of propositions and his account of complex phrases. If a proposition is false, it obviously must have acquired its meaning through its separate elements, and in a parallel way, if a complex phrase lacks a denotation, it too must have acquired its meaning through its separate elements. The point of divergence comes when we ask whether true propositions acquire their meaning in the same way as complex phrases when they have a denotation. The answer to this question is negative. For, as we have seen, a person can learn the meaning of a complex symbol like ' Avar ' entirely through acquaintance with its denotation, without being able to analyse it, and so without being able to open up the alternative way of learning its meaning. But nobody could learn the meaning of a proposition entirely through confrontation with the fact which verifies it, without being able to divide it up into its separate words, and so without being able to understand what each word contributes to the whole. If you are now confronted with a fact, and if you now understand the proposition which it verifies, you must now know how to take

[9] *O.N.T. and F.* (*PH.E.* pp. 175-6).

the proposition to pieces and what the pieces mean, and that knowledge would have enabled you to understand the proposition even if you had not been confronted with the fact. The complexity of a proposition is part of its very nature, whereas the complexity of a symbol like an ordinary proper name is not so essential to it. That is why ordinary proper names can be used as logically proper names.

This identifies the peculiarity of propositions, but it does not really explain it. However, before we complain about the mysteriousness of propositions, we ought to ask ourselves what would count as an explanation. Now it is exceedingly likely that in this kind of subject the only possible explanation would be a thorough description of the phenomenon.[10] It is not to be expected that the distinction between propositions and symbols which denote things will turn out to depend on another distinction which we already understand. That kind of explanation, which connects the unfamiliar with the familiar, is often possible in science, but it is seldom possible in philosophy, and it is very unlikely to be possible with this kind of philosophical problem. The trouble is that propositions are already perfectly familiar, and yet we do not really understand their peculiarities. If we try to understand them through the peculiarities of facts, we shall make no progress, because the distinction between facts and things is too closely related to the distinction between propositions and phrases. But a thorough description of the way in which propositions function might help, particularly if it succeeded in showing how their peculiarities are connected with one another.

Why is it that the meaning of a proposition cannot be understood all in one piece? The reason is that a proposition puts things together in thought, and that operation can only be understood by someone who knows where the join comes, and so knows how to dismantle the proposition.[11] It might look as if this is not enough to explain why the meaning of a

[10] Cf. Wittgenstein, *PH.I.* § 93.

[11] This was the principle on which the diagrams used earlier in this book were constructed.

proposition cannot be understood all in one piece. For, although it does put things together in thought, it might seem possible for the hearer to accept the finished product as a whole, like an ordinary proper name. However, a closer look at the kind of construction that a proposition is will show that this is not possible. The hearer must be able to do it himself. For a proposition conveys a message, that something is so, and nobody could understand the message unless he knew how to divide it up. For instance, if it were a singular proposition, containing a subject and a predicate, he would have to be able to separate the subject from what was being said about it. This is particularly clear if we consider negation. If affirmation is putting things together, negation is pushing them apart. Now, if the hearer did not know where the join between the two things came, how could he understand the operation of pushing them apart? But, if he did not understand this operation, he would not understand the possibility that the message might be false, and so he would not understand the opposite possibility that it might be true : and if he did not understand what it would be like for the message to be true, he would not understand the proposition.

This peculiarity of propositions is never explicitly stated by Russell when he is developing his theory of judgement in *Philosophical Essays*. It is just below the surface of his discussion, on the point of formulation, but it never actually emerges. When it does emerge in *The Philosophy of Logical Atomism*, Russell attributes it to Wittgenstein :

A man believes that Socrates is dead. What he believes is a proposition on the face of it, and for formal purposes it is convenient to take the proposition as the essential thing having the duality of truth and falsehood. It is very important to realise such things, for instance, as that propositions are not names for facts. It is quite obvious as soon as it is pointed out to you, but as a matter of fact I never had realised it until it was pointed out to me by a former pupil of mine, Wittgenstein. It is perfectly evident as soon as you think of it, that a proposition is not a name for a fact, from the mere circumstance that there are *two* propositions corresponding to each fact. Suppose it is a fact that Socrates is dead. You have two propositions : ' Socrates is dead ' and ' Socrates is not dead '. And those two propositions corresponding to the same fact, there is one fact in the world which makes one true and one false. That is not accidental, and illustrates how the relation of proposition to fact is a totally different one from the relation of name to the thing named.[12]

Wittgenstein in *Notes on Logic* (1913) called this phenomenon ' the bi-polarity of propositions '.[13] It may look rather obvious and unimportant, but the theory of meaning which he presented in the *Tractatus* really grew out of it. Of course, other ideas went into the making of that theory. There was the idea that a proposition is a kind of picture,[14] and there was also the idea that all connections between propositions can be exhibited in truth-tables.[15] But bi-polarity was the starting point.

The sharp contrast between propositions and names is of course blurred by the use of complex singular symbols. For a complex singular symbol looks like a name, and yet under analysis it expands into a proposition. Does it then have the duality of truth and falsehood like a proposition, or is it like a name with a single filament reaching out for a denotation? The answer to this question depends on how the symbol is being used. If it is being used as a logically proper name, it will not have the dual connection with reality which is characteristic of propositions : but if it is not being used as a logically proper name, its connection with reality will, in the end, be dual. This complication vanishes at the level of complete analysis. For when all symbols are completely analysed the contrast between propositions and names is absolutely sharp.

The essential duality of propositions is very closely connected with the fact that they have to be complete messages. Hume's theory of thinking can be used to illustrate the connection. His theory was criticised because he always reduces a thought to an isolated idea, which would really only be a fragment of a thought.[16] This criticism could be put by saying

---

[12] *PH.L.A.* p. 6 (*L.KN.* p. 187). Cf. p. 20 (*L.KN.* pp. 208-9).
[13] *N.L.* (*N.B.* App. I, pp. 93-7).   [14] *T.L-PH.* 2.1ff.
[15] *T.L-PH.* 4.25—5.   [16] See pp. 29-31.

that in his system thoughts are always incomplete. Of course, if he had translated thoughts into words, their incompleteness, when they are treated in his way, would have been very evident. Their verbal expression would have been obviously inarticulate, and there would have been no message. But Hume confined his attention to the inner workings of the mind and what goes on there is much less fully developed, so that its inarticulateness, if it is inarticulate, can easily be missed. You have only got to try to write something in order to realise that this is so.

There was also something else which caused him to overlook the incompleteness of isolated ideas : he maintained that ' To reflect on anything simple and to reflect on it as existent are nothing different from one another ',[17] and on this view an idea will always be part of the thought that something corresponding to it exists. This view was criticised in Chapter v on the ground that it cannot allow for negative existential propositions. The criticism might now be reinforced in various ways. For instance, the reason why the view cannot allow for negative existential propositions is that it treats the combination of the two ideas, the idea of existence and the other idea, say the idea of the Loch Ness Monster, as an indivisible unit, a sort of solid block without a join. In any case, it cannot possibly be right to treat existential propositions as the basic type of proposition. They cannot be the basic type, because, as was pointed out in Chapter v, the formulation of existential propositions is a rather sophisticated achievement which is derivative from the formulation of ordinary singular propositions. The derivation uses the operation of generalisation, and it involves propositional functions. Ordinary singular propositions must come first.

But the criticism of Hume's view need not be taken any further here. The point of mentioning his view was only to connect the essential duality of propositions with the incompleteness of thoughts in his system. The connection is this : Hume was criticised earlier for reducing thoughts to isolated

[17] *T.H.N. I.ii.6* (p. 70ff). This passage was quoted on p. 54.

ideas, a reduction which results in the same kind of incompleteness as the reduction of propositions to isolated phrases; but his treatment of the idea of existence seems to provide him with a way of avoiding this criticism; however, if he avoids it in this way, he only falls into the error of treating complex thoughts as indivisible units, and that error leads inevitably to the denial of the essential duality of propositions.

It is important to observe that the completeness of a thought or of a proposition is entirely different from the completeness of a symbol which is not a proposition. A proposition is complete when it conveys a definite message. But the standard of completeness for a symbol which is not a proposition is roughly the opposite. Such a symbol is complete if it denotes something which we have to treat as simple. For in that case its meaning cannot be learned through the meanings of other symbols, but only through acquaintance with its own denotation, and that acquaintance is a complete and self-contained affair. Incomplete symbols deviate from this ideal in various ways which were discussed in Chapter VI. The extreme contrast between the two standards of completeness is only to be expected, because they set up the axis on which Russell's whole theory of meaning turns.

There is another connection which might be made at this point. It was stated earlier[18] that propositions have life and movement, whereas symbols which are not propositions are static. The point of this metaphor was that, when someone asserts a proposition, he moves in thought from one thing to another, perhaps from an individual to the property which he is ascribing to it. Later, in Chapter XI, something was said about the nature of this movement. It is not contained within the moment of speaking, but involves a comparison which starts from some earlier point in the speaker's experience. For the general word which denotes the property draws its meaning not from the property of this individual with which he is now confronted, but from the earlier experience, and it carries that meaning with it when it is applied to the property

18 See p. 52.

of this individual, and then the property of this individual determines whether the proposition is true or false. This point can now be connected with the fact that a proposition cannot be understood all in one piece, and so with the essential duality of propositions. The connection is this : any contingent proposition which ascribes a property or a relation to anything necessarily involves a comparison, because, if there were no comparison, its meaning and its truth would both come from one and the same source; but a comparison obviously requires two things, one in the past from which the general symbol draws its meaning, and one in the present to which it is being applied; it also requires, perhaps less obviously but no less necessarily, that the thing in the present should be identified in a way that is independent of the fact that the general symbol is correctly applied to it; and this requirement can be met only if the proposition contains another symbol, and so is not understood all in one piece.

The connection between the impossibility of understanding a proposition all in one piece and the essential duality of propositions has already been explained. We are, of course, moving in a circle. But what is wrong with a circle? Maybe it is impossible to do more than describe the peculiarities of propositions and show how they are connected with one another. Not that this task has been completed in this small compass. But it is unlikely that its completion would involve anything of an entirely different kind. Why should we expect to be able to connect the distinction between propositions and names with some other more familiar distinction? Perhaps such an expectation is no more reasonable than the hope that the general phenomenon of the attachment of properties and relations to individuals should be explained.[19] The two problems are, of course, closely connected, and they have that peculiar kind of philosophical depth which suggests that they will never be solved by the dramatic discovery of some hitherto unsuspected explanation.

The life and movement of a proposition is the life and

[19] See pp. 171-3.

movement of thought. It is inside the mind of the person who thinks that something is so, although of course it may be externalised in the words which express his proposition. So a theory of judgement cannot confine itself to studying the nature of propositions apart from their connection with people. Certainly Russell's theory is concerned with propositions, and particularly with the problem how false propositions can have a meaning, but the investigation of this problem inevitably leads back to people, and the part which they play. When someone judges that something is so, in what relationship does he stand to the proposition? This is the wider question which Russell's theory of judgement was designed to answer, and the question about the nature of propositions, important though it is, was contained within it.

Now we already have part of Russell's answer to the question how a person who judges that something is so is related to the proposition. He must be acquainted with its constituents, and in the period before 1919 Russell understood this acquaintance to be a relationship between ego and things. Not that the person who makes the judgement has to be actually perceiving the things at the time of judging. If Russell's theory had to be interpreted in that way, it would be absurd, and evidence against that interpretation has already been given.[20] In any case, as we saw in the last chapter, even when the person is making a judgement about something which he is now perceiving, the meaning of his proposition cannot come entirely from the things with which he is confronted at that moment. But the theory of acquaintance provides only part of Russell's answer to the question about the relationship between person and proposition. For, as we have just seen, the proposition is not lying there in his mind like a complex symbol which is not a proposition. He is not just meditating on its meaning, or considering it as a possibility. He is actually judging that it is so. How does he do that?

Let us use an example in order to illustrate Russell's answer to this question. Suppose you say that the knife was on the

[20] See p. 71, footnote 1.

right of the fork. Then, according to him, your proposition has three constituents, the two individuals and the relation *on-the-right-of*.[21] How is your actual judging to be explained? Russell says that the judging is a relation between your ego and the three constituents.[22] It is important to observe that this relation is an additional one, quite distinct from your acquaintance with the three constituents. You are already acquainted with them, and then, when you make the judgement, you set up a new relationship with them. This new relationship is not only distinct from the relationship of acquaintance, but also has a different kind of pattern. You are acquainted with each of the constituents separately, but your judging takes all three of them together.

This point, that your judging takes all the constituents of the proposition together, is crucial, and deserves close scrutiny. Russell puts it by saying that *judging* is a multiple relation.[23] A straightforward example of a multiple relation would be *giving* : giving requires a donor, a recipient and a gift, and, if one of these three is lacking, the relation will be out of work. Acquaintance is only a dual relation, requiring an ego and an object. Hence your lack of acquaintance with one of the constituents of your proposition would not affect your acquaintance with the others. That is what is meant by saying that you are acquainted with each of the constituents of your proposition separately, whereas your *judging* takes them together. Or rather, it is *part* of what is meant by saying that your *judging* takes the constituents together. For though

[21] The analysis of the past tense in this proposition will here be ignored, because, though the question how it should be analysed is interesting, it does not affect the present discussion.

The two individuals are only constituents of the proposition according to Russell's looser use of the phrase (see pp. 88-90 and p. 90, footnote 26). This too is irrelevant to the present discussion. If we used a completely analysed proposition to illustrate Russell's theory, that would merely complicate the exposition without improving it.

[22] *O.N.T. and F. (PH.E.* p. 177ff).

[23] *O.N.T. and F. (PH.E.* pp. 178-80).

judging is a multiple relation like *giving*, it is not at all a straightforward multiple relation, and the peculiarity which it does not share with *giving* is of the utmost importance. The peculiarity will be described in the next chapter. First, we need the remainder of Russell's theory of judgement as it is given in *Philosophical Essays*. That will set the stage for the peculiarity.

Russell's next task in constructing his theory is to explain the difference between a true judgement and a false one. His explanation may be illustrated by the same proposition, that the knife was on the right of the fork. Now one of the constituents of this proposition is the spatial relation. If the two individuals are in fact related by it as they are in the proposition, the judgement will be true, and if they are not so related, it will be false. Since this particular spatial relation is asymmetrical,[24] there has to be a distinction between judging that the knife was on the right of the fork and judging that the fork was on the right of the knife. When these two propositions are expressed, the distinction is marked by the order of the words. But Russell's theory requires that the distinction should be preserved in the mind. So the multiple relation *judging* ought to group the three constituents in two different ways in the two cases. The last point that he makes in developing his theory in *Philosophical Essays* is that that is just what it does do: 'The relation must not be abstractly before the mind, but must be before it as proceeding from A to B rather than from B to A'.[25]

This theory looks deceptively smooth and free from difficulty. But that is only because the peculiarity which *judging* does not share with a relation like *giving* has not emerged in *Philosophical Essays*. It begins to appear when we notice that *judging* seems to be superfluous in a way in which a relation like *giving* is not superfluous. For if you took the complex formed by the *giving*, the donor, the recipient and the gift, and removed the *giving*, there would be no relation

[24] See p. 166, footnote 4.
[25] *O.N.T. and F.* (*PH.E.* p. 183). His example is ' A loves B '.

left to relate the three individuals; but, when we consider the judgement about the arrangement of the things on the table, we find that one of the three things that are related by the *judging* is itself a relation, *on-the-right-of*, and so, if the *judging* were removed, there would still be a relation to relate the two individuals, the knife and the fork. Now presumably the relation *judging* is not really superfluous. It appears to be superfluous only when we assume that it performs the same function as a relation like *giving*, or *on-the-right-of*. But it could not possibly perform that function. For if the relation *on-the-right-of* were removed, how could the relation *judging* conceivably relate the knife and fork? Evidently, it is a peculiarity of *judging* that it needs another relation, or, alternatively, a property. Now Russell recognises this need in *Philosophical Essays*,[26] but he does not realise what a very odd effect it has. He writes as if the fact that *judging* needs a relation or a property among the things which it relates does not make very much difference. Naturally, he realised that it makes some difference, but he still presents *judging* as a multiple relation like *giving*.

[26] *O.N.T. and F.* (*PH.E.* p. 181).

CHAPTER XIII

WITTGENSTEIN'S CRITICISM, AND THE CONSTRUCTION OF RUSSELL'S NEW THEORY OF JUDGEMENT

The peculiarity of judging first emerges clearly in a passage in *The Philosophy of Logical Atomism*, in which Russell gives Wittgenstein the credit for noticing it.[1] What Russell there says is rather difficult to understand, because it takes for granted certain points which presumably came up in conversation with Wittgenstein, or at least in some kind of exchange of ideas with him. So we shall approach it obliquely by asking a question about the point that was made at the end of the last chapter. Why does judging need another relation or property? It is easy to answer this question in a general way. The difficulties lie in the details. The general answer must be that a judgement needs a proposition, and a proposition needs a relation or a property among its constituents. When a person judges that something is so, he moves in thought from one end of his proposition to the other, touching each of its constituents one by one in the right order. This sequence of contacts is the judging, just as a sequence of movements is a dance. The order in which they are made must be intentional, and the principle governing it must be understood. If there were no relation or property among the constituents, the contacts could not produce the right total effect. They could not present a proposition. So the judging performs an entirely different function from the relation which is a constituent of the proposition. The latter makes it possible for the person to make a propositional movement in his mind, but the judging actually is the movement.

[1] *PH.L.A.* p. 30 (*L.KN.* pp. 224-6).

This general answer to the question about the nature of judgement is easy to understand if the constituents of propositions are ideas. For if the constituents of propositions are the psychological things out of which thoughts are composed, it is natural to interpret a judgement as a series of contacts with those things. Judging would be like touching the keys of a typewriter which did not take advantage of spelling, but used a separate key for each word. However, in the period before 1919 Russell did *not* consider that the constituents of propositions are ideas. According to him, they are things outside the mind, namely sense-data, their properties and relations. He believed that, if the constituents of propositions were ideas, they would act as a kind of veil interposed between the ego and things outside the mind, and so making any knowledge of those things unattainable.[2] His theory of judgement was designed to achieve the maximum exposure of the ego to the external world. Of course, given his views about perception, the ego could never be exposed to whatever things lie behind our sense-data and cause them, but it could be exposed to sense-data, which are at least just outside the mind. When we are interpreting his theory of judgement, we must never forget that, for him, the constituents of propositions are things outside the mind. It follows that, if the general answer to the question about judgement that has just been given is going to be any help in the interpretation of his theory, it cannot be taken in the easy way. The things that are touched must not be ideas. They must be sense-data, and the properties and relations of sense-data.

But how can the things that are touched possibly be sense-data? Would that not mean that the touching was perceiving, and would that not produce the absurd result that the constituents of propositions could only be things that were actually being perceived at the moment?[3] It may look as if

[2] See pp. 176-7, and the passage from *KN.A.KN.D.* quoted there.

[3] The absurdity of this theory, and the reasons why it should not be attributed to Russell were explained on pp. 181-2. Cf. p. 71, footnote 1.

this is the way that the interpretation of Russell's theory has
to go, but in fact there is another route which it can take. For
there is another way in which things can be touched. Mentioning a subject is touching it, and there is no necessity that the
thing that you mention should actually be perceived by you
at the moment of speaking. Russell's views about the contact
between the ego and the constituents of the proposition
should be interpreted in this way. His idea is that, when a
person judges that something is so, he touches each of the
constituents of the proposition in something like this other
sense of the verb ' to touch '. Perhaps this metaphor makes
the interpretation of his theory seem rather far fetched. If so,
we can drop the metaphor, and look at two of the things that
he says in the development of his theory of judgement. First,
he says that judging is not the same relation as acquaintance,
although it requires acquaintance with the constituents of the
proposition.[4] This shows that, if judging is a kind of contact,
at least it is not the same kind of contact as acquaintance.
Secondly, he allows that you can be acquainted with things
that you are not actually perceiving at the moment.[5] This
shows that acquaintance can continue after the kind of contact
in which it originates, namely actual perception, has ceased.
These two points, taken together, are enough to prove that,
when Russell said that judging relates the ego to the constituents of a proposition, he did not mean that the constituents had to be perceived at the moment of judging, still
less that the constituents of the proposition are actually
imported into the mind of the person who makes the judgement.[6]

However, Russell's theory does not contain an explicit
positive account of what judging is. It is certainly important
that it is *not* identical with acquaintance, and that acquaintance
is *not* identical with perception. But what is the positive
characterisation of judging? It must be admitted that even the

[4] *KN.A.KN.D.* (*M. and L.* pp. 219-21). [5] See p. 71, footnote 1.
[6] See Note A at the end of this chapter.

interpretation so far given goes beyond what Russell actually says. Not that it is an incorrect explanation of what he says. But it is more explicit. If we omitted Russell's negative points, we should only be left with the thesis that judging is a multiple relation which relates things one of which must itself be a relation,[7] and that this related relation 'must not be abstractly before the mind, but must be before it as proceeding from A to B rather than from B to A'.[8]

Why is the theory so bare? Or perhaps the right question to ask is why it looks so bare. It looks bare because Russell has swept away all the clutter of ideas which, in other theories, fill the space between the ego and the things that the ego either is perceiving or remembers having perceived. According to this theory of Russell's, memory actually maintains contact with what was perceived in the past, and does not merely preserve traces laid down in the mind by the earlier experience. Consequently, when a person judges that the knife was on the right of the fork, his relationship with the relation *on-the-right-of* cannot be interpreted as the reactivation of a trace laid down in his mind on some other occasion when he perceived one thing on the right of another. It must be interpreted as a contact made in thought with the relation itself. Our reaction to this theory is likely to be that this cannot be the whole story. The mind of someone who is thinking cannot be so empty. How could he think without manipulating tokens of some sort in his mind? Surely thinking must be something like internalised typewriting.

Russell's reason for rejecting any such suggestion before 1919 has already been given. It was suspicion of ideas, which in this period he regarded as go-betweens rather than as part of the record.[9] But the rejection of these very natural suggestions produces a consequence which has not yet been mentioned, and which is really rather difficult to put into words.

[7] Or a property. Russell omits this alternative in *O.N.T. and F.* (*PH.E.* p. 178), but it can readily be included in his theory.

[8] See *O.N.T. and F.* (*PH.E.* p. 183). [9] See pp. 176-7 and p. 198.

It makes judging into a very strange operation. When a person judges that something is so, he formulates a proposition in his mind. But, according to Russell, the formulation is not done with any kind of psychological tokens. It is done by arranging the actual things themselves in thought. Of course, this does not mean that the things which the thinker arranges are in his own mind. That would be an absurd suggestion, because they are not mental.[10] But the arranging *is* mental. It is not a matter of his pushing around the things outside his mind. If Russell had not been so averse from possibilities, he could have said that what the person who makes the judgement does is to construct a possibility and judge that it is realised. We might use a remark of Wittgenstein's to explain the kind of construction that is meant : ' In a proposition a situation is, as it were, constructed by way of experiment '.[11] This does not mean that the situation is actually set up in reality. Similarly, Russell's theory does not mean that the arranging of the things is actual.[12]

So far we have been examining the function which Russell's theory assigns to the relation *judging*. Let us now look at the other relation, which, in the example used, is the spatial relation *on-the-right-of*. This is a perfectly ordinary relation, unlike *judging*, but it has been placed by *judging* in a rather extraordinary position. Its function is not to relate the knife and fork, although it may happen to do so, and, if it does,

---

[10] See p. 214, footnote 6. (Note A at the end of this chapter).

[11] *T.L-PH.* 4.031.

[12] It may seem to be a mistake to use Wittgenstein's remark to illustrate a point in Russell's theory. For the theory of propositions which Wittgenstein published in *T.L.-PH.* was, in part, an attempt to fill the vacuum in Russell's theory which has just been described. According to Wittgenstein, a proposition is always a complex of tokens, either external and physical, or internal and psychological. But, in spite of this great difference, their views about what is judged are, as might be expected, similar : except that Russell preferred not to talk about possibilities. See p. 201.

the proposition will be true. Its function is to be *thought of as relating them*. But this produces a difficulty. If it does not have to relate the two things, but only has to be thought of as relating them, it does not have to *do* anything. It is, as it were, a dormant relation. The difficulty about this is that, if it is dormant, it might quite well be the wrong type of relation without making any difference to the mechanism of judgement as it is described in Russell's theory. For instance, it might be the relation *the-square-root-of*, which could hardly relate the knife and fork. There is nothing in the pattern of analysis suggested by Russell to prevent such a mésalliance. This is the point of Wittgenstein's criticism of Russell's theory : ' The correct explanation of the form of the proposition, " A makes the judgement p ", must show that it is impossible for a judgement to be a piece of nonsense. (Russell's theory does not satisfy this requirement.)'[13]

It is not easy to gauge the force of this criticism. Russell could have replied[14] that, though the relation *on-the-right-of* is

[13] *T.L-PH.* 5.5422. *Cf. N.L. (N.B.* App. 1, p. 96). P. T. Geach in his criticism of Russell's theory makes a rather different use of the fact that, according to it, the relation is dormant : ' Yet if the relation R is before the mind, not as relating a and b, but only as a term of a judging relation that holds between the mind, a, the relation R, and b, how can there be any talk of the relation R's " proceeding from a to b rather than from b to a "?' *(Mental Acts,* p. 51).

[14] He evidently did not make this reply. Wittgenstein in a letter to him dated 22 July 1913 says, ' I am very sorry to hear that my objection to your theory of judgement paralyses you. I think it can only be removed by a correct theory of propositions.' *(N.B.* App. III, p. 121.) The objection, conveyed in an earlier letter, is substantially the same as the objection stated in *T.L-PH.* In *PH.L.A.* Russell admits that the theory of judgement which he published in *PH.E.* ought to be modified in order to deal with this difficulty. He talks about ' the impossibility of putting the subordinate verb on a level with its terms as an object term in the belief. That is a point in which I think that the theory of judgement which I set forth once in print some years ago was a little unduly simple, because I did then take the object verb as if one could put it as just an object like the terms.' *PH.L.A.* p. 31 *(L.KN.* p. 226).

dormant, it must have the requisite potentialities; it must be capable of relating the knife and fork. Otherwise, the person who makes the judgement will be thinking of it as doing something which it cannot do, and so his judgement will be a piece of nonsense. If this barrier to nonsense seems too flimsy and contrived, how could it be improved? Perhaps any device for excluding the judging of pieces of nonsense will have to rely in the end on the impossibility of certain combinations of things. Wittgenstein's own theory of propositions is founded on the distinction between possible and impossible combinations of things. It is a very different theory from the one that Russell maintained until 1919. For Wittgenstein thought that a proposition is always a complex of tokens. If the proposition is expressed, the tokens will be symbols, and if it is not expressed, they will be psychological entities of some kind.[15] Now these tokens draw their meanings from the things which they denote. Consequently, if they are combined in a way in which the things cannot be combined, they will snap the lines which connect them with the things and lose their meanings, and the result will be not a proposition but a piece of nonsense. A full examination of this theory is beyond the scope of this book.[16] But one of its advantages does emerge in the brief description of it which has just been given. It meets the very natural demand that thinking should be interpreted as some kind of internalised behaviour. But does it produce a more profound explanation of the impossibility of judging a piece of nonsense?

If it is difficult to produce an adequate theory of judgement,

[15] See letter to Russell, dated 19 August 1919 (*N.B.* App. III, p. 129): ' I don't know *what* the constituents of a thought are but I know *that* it must have such constituents which correspond to the words of language.' (sic).

[16] But the exposition of the theory will be taken one stage further in this chapter. What has just been said only gives a rough and preliminary indication of it. The analogy between propositions and pictures, around which the theory is built, has scarcely been mentioned.

at least it ought to be easier to say why it is difficult. The reason why it is so difficult is that *judging* is a peculiar relation which not only requires another relation, but also changes its function. This peculiarity does not really come to the surface in Russell's essay on *The Nature of Truth*. His first explicit description of it, which he says is due to Wittgenstein, appears in the passage in *The Philosophy of Logical Atomism*, which was mentioned earlier, and which will now be quoted.

I want to try to get an account of the way that a belief is made up. That is not an easy question at all. You cannot make what I should call a-map-in-space of a belief. You can make a map of an atomic fact but not of a belief, for the simple reason that space-relations always are of the atomic sort or complications of the atomic sort. I will try to illustrate what I mean. The point is in connection with there being two verbs in the judgement and with the fact that both verbs have got to occur as verbs, because if a thing is a verb it cannot occur otherwise than as a verb. Suppose I take 'A believes that B loves C'. 'Othello believes that Desdemona loves Cassio'. There you have a false belief. You have this odd state of affairs that the verb 'loves' occurs in that proposition and seems to occur as relating Desdemona to Cassio whereas in fact it does not do so, but yet it does occur as a verb, it does occur in the sort of way that a verb should do. I mean that when A believes that B loves C, you have to have a verb in the place where 'loves' occurs. You cannot put a substantive in its place. Therefore it is clear that the subordinate verb (i.e. the verb other than believing) is functioning as a verb, and seems to be relating two terms, but as a matter of fact does not when a judgement happens to be false. That is what constitutes the puzzle about the nature of belief. You will notice that wherever one gets to really close quarters with the theory of error one has the puzzle of how to deal with error without assuming the existence of the non-existent. I mean that every theory of error sooner or later wrecks itself by assuming the existence of the non-existent. As when I say 'Desdemona loves Cassio', it seems as if you have a non-existent love between Desdemona and Cassio, but that is just as wrong as a non-existent unicorn. So you have to explain the whole theory of judgement in some other way. I come now to this question of a map. Suppose you try such a map as this:

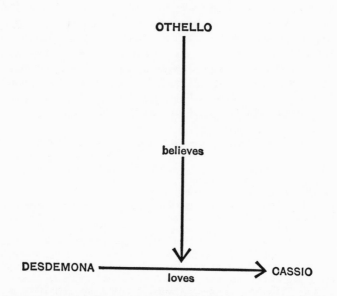

This question of making a map is not so strange as you might suppose because it is part of the whole theory of symbolism. It is important to realise where and how a symbolism of that sort would be wrong: where and how it is wrong is that in the symbol you have this relationship relating these two things and in the fact it does not really relate them. You cannot get in space any occurrence which is logically of the same form as belief. When I say ' logically of the same form ' I mean that one can be obtained from the other by replacing the constituents of the one by the new terms. If I say ' Desdemona loves Cassio ' that is of the same form as ' A is to the right of B '. Those are of the same form, and I say that nothing that occurs in space is of the same form as belief. I have got on here to a new sort of thing, a new beast for our Zoo, not another member of our former species but a new species. The discovery of this fact is due to Mr Wittgenstein.[17]

In this passage Russell is not offering a new theory of judgement. He admits on the following page that his earlier theory needs to be modified, because of ' the impossibility of putting the subordinate verb on a level with its terms as an object

[17] *PH.L.A.* p. 30 (*L.KN.* pp. 224-6).

term in the belief '.[18] But he is not yet prepared to offer a new theory, and he observes that ' one has to be content on many points at present with pointing out difficulties rather than laying down quite clear solutions '.

Let us look more closely at the difficulty about the two verbs. This is, of course, the problem that we have just been examining. How can the relation *judging* work together with the relation which is mentioned in the judgement? What exactly are the functions of the two relations, and how do they interlock? Russell does not actually answer these questions, but he makes some contributions towards their answers. He makes some of the points which we have already examined, and he adds two points which were not introduced in our earlier discussion. He says that the proposition that ' A believes that B loves C ' is constructed in an unusual way, and he says you cannot draw a diagram of the corresponding fact. Both these points deserve scrutiny.

In order to understand the first point, we need to know what Russell regarded as the usual way of constructing propositions. His theory of analysis provides us with the answer to this question. When a proposition is analysed, its truth depends entirely on the truth of the propositions into which it is analysed. For instance, the truth of a proposition containing a definite description depends entirely on the truth of three propositions : the first says that there is something which fits the description, the second says that there is only one thing which fits it, and the third says about that thing whatever the original proposition said about it. All three must be true if the original proposition is true, because in the analysis they are joined together by the word ' and '. If the word ' or ' had appeared in the analysis, the mechanism would have been different. For, although the truth of the proposition ' It is a primary colour ' depends entirely on the truth of the three propositions, ' It is red ', ' It is yellow ', and ' It is blue ', it only requires the truth of one of these three propositions.[19]

[18] i.e. he concedes Wittgenstein's point. See p. 217, footnote 14.
[19] See *PH.L.A.* p. 20 (*L.KN.* p. 209).

However, in both cases alike the mechanism is truth-functional: that is to say, the truth of the original proposition depends entirely on the truth of the propositions which appear in its analysis. This form of dependence would still be preserved if the analysis of the two propositions were taken down to the level of sense-data. For the sense-datum propositions in the final analyses give the meanings of the propositions in the preliminary analyses, just as those propositions gave the meanings of the original propositions. This, according to Russell, is the usual way in which propositions are constructed.

But the proposition ' A believes that B loves C ' does not appear to be constructed in this way. As our earlier examination of such propositions has shown, it certainly cannot be analysed into two propositions, joined together by a logical connective like ' and ' or ' or ', and each using one of the two verbs. For the believing must not be deprived of its content, and, since the loving is only believed, the truth of the main proposition does not depend in any way on the truth of the subordinate proposition. Nor is it at all easy to see into what other propositions it could be analysed. Yet it certainly is not an atomic proposition, because it contains two general symbols, *viz.* the two verbs. So Russell hails it as a new beast for his zoo.[20]

It is worth observing that what makes it difficult, indeed perhaps impossible, to analyse this proposition in Russell's usual way is not just the occurrence of the two relations without a logical connective. For consider the proposition ' The distance from Edinburgh to Cambridge is greater than the distance from Oxford to London '. Here the pattern of relations is more complicated, and there is no logical connective. Yet the analysis of this proposition does not present the same difficulty. We could find even more complicated networks of relations without logical connectives which still would not present the same difficulty. For example, you might

20 Russell's later treatment of this species of proposition is to be found in *I.M.T.* pp. 267-73. See *M.PH.D.* pp. 117-19.

say that the acceleration of your car is greater than the acceleration of mine. But let us ask why the less intricate proposition about the four cities is not so recalcitrant as the proposition 'A believes that B loves C'. Its analysis certainly requires a new logical device, because it is an existential proposition about relations which cannot be replaced by a proposition mentioning specific relations. For it says, in effect, that there are two distances, one of which is the distance between Edinburgh and Cambridge, and the other of which is the distance between Oxford and London, and that the first is greater than the second, and it does not specify the two distances. So the existential proposition about the two distances could not have the same meaning as any proposition which specified the two distances, and that is an obstacle to Russell's usual analysis of propositions, which does not contain existential propositions about properties and relations.[21] But this is not the obstacle which prevents him from analysing the proposition 'A believes that B loves C' in his usual way. For in the proposition about the four cities all the relations actually relate their terms. They are not held in suspense like a relation that occurs in a substantival clause giving the content of a belief. So the proposition about the belief really is radically different.

The fact that it is radically different can even be discerned in Hume's much more rudimentary system, which was sketched in Chapter II. The problem of belief for Hume is the problem of explaining the difference between ideas of belief and other ideas. For his system is non-propositional, and his theory of thinking reduces every complete thought to an idea. According to him, an idea of belief is distinguished by its strength, and his considered view is that this strength is not a pictorial property of the idea but a relation between it and the person who has it. An idea of belief imposes itself upon the mind in a masterful, and perhaps irresistible way. It is something like the way in which pictures are sometimes hung. The reason

[21] See Note B at the end of this chapter.

why strength cannot be a pictorial property of an idea of belief is that, if it were true, the *content* of the belief would depend on its presence or absence.[22] It has to relate the believer to the belief without altering the content of the belief. But this leads straight into Russell's problem about the radical difference between belief and other relations. The connection becomes clear if we make Hume's theory propositional by giving the belief the internal complexity that it obviously needs. Then, since the believing must not alter the belief, it must not contribute to its internal complexity, but must relate it, *taken as a whole*, to the believer. Russell's problem is about the nature of this relation, and about the way in which the belief is taken as a whole.

Russell's second point was that you cannot draw a diagram of the fact that A believes that B loves C. Of course, the reason why you cannot draw a diagram of this fact is not that love is not a spatial relation. For spatial representation can easily be used for non-spatial relations, and in this case you could perfectly well draw a diagram of the fact that B loves C. But you cannot draw a diagram of the fact that A believes that B loves C, because, as Russell implies, the convention governing diagrams is that a relation between two things in a diagram shows that those things are related in reality. Naturally, it does not follow that they really are related, since the person who drew the diagram might be mistaken. But the message which he conveys, whether it be true or false, is that they are related. This convention allows us to represent a very intricate network of relations diagrammatically. For instance, it would be quite possible to produce a diagram which would illustrate the fact about the comparative accelerations of the two cars. Such a diagram would need an elaboration of the kind of pattern with which Russell tries to illustrate the situation between Othello, Desdemona and Cassio, but it would succeed, whereas Russell's point is that his diagram is not successful.

It might be objected that Russell takes too narrow a view of the possibilities of spatial representation. Why should not a

[22] See pp. 30-1.

cautious cartographer distinguish between the parts of his map about which he felt unsure, and the parts which he filled in with confidence, and to whose accuracy he really committed himself? He certainly could do this. But, if we ask what exactly he would be doing and how he would do it, it will be apparent that this sort of possibility does not tell against Russell's view of the limitations of spatial representation. For someone who put his doubt into his map, for instance by using dotted lines, would really be doing more than drawing the object. The reason why he would be doing more is not that coastlines and rivers are not in fact discontinuous. For maps can contain conventional signs, and there are various conventional ways of projecting the surface of the globe on to a flat sheet. But his use of these dotted lines could not be explained by saying that he was drawing the object according to some convention. They would be an expression of his attitude to what he was drawing, and that is something entirely different. If he wished to represent his attitude spatially, he really ought to represent it in another dimension. He would need a diagram in two different planes, one for the drawing of the object, and the other for his attitude to the drawing. But then there would be the question how the relationship between the two parts of the diagram, one at ninety degrees to the other, should be interpreted. This question easily passes unnoticed when he uses his pencil performatively, not only in order to draw the object, but also in order to express his attitude to what he is drawing. But if he used a more discriminating method of spatial representation, it would immediately come out into the open. How should we understand what happens at the hinge of the diagram? The moment that this question is asked it becomes clear that the objection has no force against Russell's point. Either spatial representation leaves out the attitude of the person who makes use of it, or, if it includes it, it contains within itself a difficulty which we cannot resolve by appealing to the familiar conventions.

The impossibility of representing belief spatially is even clearer when the belief is another person's. For in that case it is not possible to represent the believing by a device like dotted lines, because the belief is someone else's. It is not your attitude to the believed proposition that has to be represented diagrammatically, but the other person's attitude. This task even more evidently would require a diagram in two different planes, which would transcend the usual conventions.

Although Russell credits Wittgenstein with the discovery of these two points, Wittgenstein certainly did not share his pessimism about the possibility of finding a truth-functional analysis of propositions like ' A believes that B loves C ', and probably did not share his pessimism about the possibility of drawing a diagram of the corresponding facts. Russell presumably means that Wittgenstein first made the extreme difficulty of these two undertakings clear to him. There is a passage in the *Tractatus* which shows that Wittgenstein did not regard them as impossible. He thought that a truth-functional analysis is unattainable only if the proposition is construed as saying that the believer is related to the believed proposition. As a matter of fact, in the theory which he published in 1910 in *Philosophical Essays* Russell never said that the believed proposition is one of the terms in a dual relation, and in *The Philosophy of Logical Atomism*,[23] when he denies that it is, his denial is not a recantation of any part of that theory, but, rather, refers to the view which he held before the great change in his theory of meaning in 1905, which was described at the beginning of Chapter I. However, the theory of 1910 does treat the believer, or his ego, as one of the terms in a multiple relation, and the passage in the *Tractatus* is worth quoting in full for the sake of its comment on this point :

5.54. In the general propositional form propositions occur in other propositions only as bases of truth-operations.[24]

5.541. At first sight it looks as if it were also possible for one proposition to occur in another in a different way.

Particularly with certain forms of proposition in psychology, such as ' A believes that p is the case; and ' A has the thought p ', etc.

---

[23] *PH.L.A.* p. 31 (*L.KN.* p. 226).
[24] i.e. truth-functionally (D.F.P.)

For if these are considered superficially, it looks as if the proposition p stood in some kind of relation to an object A.

(And in modern theory of knowledge [Russell, Moore, etc.] these propositions have actually been construed in this way.)

5.542. It is clear, however, that ' A believes that p ', ' A has the thought p ', and ' A says p ' are of the form ' " p " says p ': and this does not involve a correlation of a fact with an object, but rather the correlation of facts by means of the correlation of their objects.

5.5421. This shows too that there is no such thing as the soul—the subject, etc.—as it is conceived in the superficial psychology of the present day.

Indeed a composite soul would no longer be a soul.[25]

It is clear that Wittgenstein thought that the apparent uniqueness of such propositions is something of an illusion, but less clear why he thought this. His main thesis is that it is a mistake to suppose that a proposition of this kind is neither an elementary proposition[26] nor constructed truth-functionally out of elementary propositions : and, since he thought that both elementary propositions and propositions constructed truth-functionally out of them are, in a way, pictures, he probably saw no obstacle to drawing a diagram of the corresponding fact. So here is a second area in which he adopted a view which was a more extreme version of Russell's view.[27] Russell thought that these propositions are the only ones which are neither atomic propositions nor constructed truth-functionally out of atomic propositions.[28] Wittgenstein thought that he could show that their apparently exceptional character is an illusion. This is not a peripheral controversy for Wittgenstein. For it is the central thesis of the *Tractatus*

[25] Here follows 5.5422, which was quoted on p. 217 and then 5.5423, the first sentence of which was quoted on p. 190.

[26] Wittgenstein's elementary propositions are not the same as Russell's atomic propositions, but they do play the same rôle in his system. See Ch. IX.

[27] The first area was the analysis of complex symbols into simple symbols. See Ch. IX.

[28] See *O.KN.E.W.* p. 63, footnote, where he says that propositions about wishes are also an exception to the general rule. So are propositions about hopes, fears, etc. Of course, the controversial question is not only about propositions about beliefs, but about all propositions belonging to that category.

that all propositions are either elementary propositions or constructed truth-functionally out of elementary propositions.

But, though the thesis is clear, the arguments which Wittgenstein uses in order to support it are less clear. According
to the analysis which he is rejecting, the believing subject or
ego would be what he calls ' the object A '. The first stage in
his analysis is to replace this subject by a complex. This is to
adopt the view which William James supported, and which
Russell resisted for so long.[29] But it is also more than this. In
fact, it includes two more ideas. First, it depends on the usual
treatment which both Russell and Wittgenstein always apply
to a complex individual; which is to analyse the symbol denoting it so that it expands into a proposition. But, though the
treatment is the usual one, its application to the complex which
has been substituted for the ego produces unusual results. For
this complex is composed of things in the believer's mind.
So, when someone mentions it, the singular symbol which he
uses to denote it will be replaced in the complete analysis by
the proposition that certain named psychological entities are
arranged in a particular way in the believer's mind. The
unusual feature of this analysis is that both the complex and
the fact which is elicited in its place by analysis are psychological.

The second idea which appears, or rather is embedded, in the
passage quoted from the *Tractatus* is Wittgenstein's new
contribution to the subject. It emerges when we ask what
sort of psychological fact he meant. Now the original complex was " p ", which is a proposition. But, as has already
been pointed out, Wittgenstein, unlike Russell before 1919,
regarded a proposition as a complex of tokens. So the fact
which in the complete analysis is elicited to replace the
complex " p " will be the fact that certain tokens are arranged
in a certain way in the believer's mind.[30] These tokens do not
have to be internalised words. They might be the internalisa-

[29] See pp. 41-2 and p. 42, footnote 29.
[30] If the tokens were words, the letter inside the quotation marks
would be a standard abbreviation of those words.

tion of any kind of expressive behaviour. Wittgenstein, as we have seen, was not sure about their exact nature.[31] His confidence that they must be there was based on his general theory of propositions. The first axiom of that theory is that propositions are complexes in their own right. When the usual treatment is applied to these complexes, they come out as facts. If a proposition is expressed in words or in some perceptible substitute for words, the fact will be a propositional sign:[32] if it is not expressed, it will be a psychological fact, in which the part played by words has been taken over by tokens in the believer's mind. Either way, the words or tokens will be attached to their denotations, and this alone gives the proposition its meaning, or, to put the same point more obscurely, makes it possible for " p " to say p.

But what has happened to the believing? It may be correct to regard the believer, or rather his momentary state, as a psychological fact. But does his believing that something is so amount to no more than that this fact carries the meaning that it is so? Does the verb ' to say ' only mean ' to mean ' in the impersonal sense of that verb? It can hardly mean ' to say aloud ', since not all beliefs are expressed aloud, and Wittgenstein is trying to give, or at least to sketch, a general analysis of all propositions about beliefs. Does it then also mean ' to think '? Moreover, there is some obscurity about the way in which the believer who does this thinking is going to be specified in such an analysis. Nor is it entirely clear how the analogy between propositions and pictures is supposed to work here. It is easy to draw a diagram of the fact which corresponds to the proposition which A believes, and it may be correct to maintain that the proposition which he believes is very like the diagram. But what happens when you try to draw another diagram to show that that diagram was correlated with that fact?

There is not enough space here for an adequate answer to this question, or to the preceding questions. Wittgenstein

[31] See the letter to Russell quoted on p. 218, footnote 15.
[32] *T.L-PH.* 3.14.

seems to imply that, when you drew this second diagram, you would not encounter the difficulty which Russell describes in *The Philosophy of Logical Atomism*.[33] But why not? His idea seems to be that the second diagram would not be about the first diagram *taken as a whole*, but would deal with it bit by bit. That point, or rather the parallel point about the proposition is made in *Tractatus* 5.542. However, it is arguable that the diagram seems to evade the difficulty described by Russell only because it has not been completed. It is not enough to make the move suggested in 5.542; which is to draw lines connecting the words or psychological tokens with the objects. For that is only the first move towards producing a complete diagram. The next move would be one which is not suggested in 5.542; you would need to find some way of representing the further fact that combining the words is a way of saying that the objects are correspondingly combined. For the attachment of words to objects is only a preparation for the production of a proposition,[34] so that a diagram of these attachments would not be a complete diagram of the functioning of a proposition. But this further piece of draughtsmanship would immediately run up against the difficulty described by Russell. For the objects need not be combined in the way in which the believed proposition says that they are : but their being so combined will be illustrated in the diagram. Moreover, there is a special difficulty for Wittgenstein. For he maintained that you cannot have a proposition about the meaning of a symbol. This must mean at least that you cannot have an ordinary proposition about the meaning of a symbol.[35] Yet the proposition ' A believes that p is the case '

---

[33] *PH.L.A.* p. 30 (*L.KN.* pp. 224-6), quoted on pp. 219-20.
[34] See *PH.I.* § 26.
[35] *T.L-PH.* 4.12ff. It is really not clear how Wittgenstein proposed to solve these problems. 5.542 only gives an incomplete sketch of his analysis of the proposition ' A believes that p '. The conjunction of 5.541 and 5.542 shows that he thought that this sketch could be completed in a way that would demonstrate that the proposition is, after all, constructed truth-functionally. But the very real difficulties that are involved in completing the sketch are not overcome in

is a perfectly ordinary proposition, and, according to him, its analysis reveals that it is about the meaning of a symbol.

However, this last difficulty is peculiar to Wittgenstein's theory of propositions and does not affect a theory like Russell's which takes a less narrow view of their subject matter.[36] So it will be left on one side at this point, in order that we may return to the exposition of Russell's theory. The other questions which have been raised about the observations which Wittgenstein makes about belief in the *Tractatus* will also be left unanswered. Whatever its faults, 5.542 is a profound remark, in which it is possible to see the transition from Russell's early theory of mind to an entirely different kind of theory, which contains the germ of most of the subsequent developments in this field. Russell's early theory required some kind of immediate contact between the thinker and the objects of his thought. It was a Realist's answer to the Idealist's suggestion that the immediate objects of thought are all within the mind of the thinker, and that thought never penetrates beyond these objects.[37] The new theory, like Russell's early theory, rejects this suggestion, but it rejects it in a less drastic way. It allows that the thinker operates with things in his mind, thus conceding the plausible part of the

---

T.L.-PH. In *N.B.* (p. 52), Wittgenstein toys with the idea that there might be a meta-language about language. But the proposition ' A believes that p ' is an ordinary one, and, in any case, the idea of a meta-language is completely rejected in *T.L.-PH.* Even if this difficulty could be overcome, there is still the difficulty described by Russell, that the proposition cannot be regarded as a picture, and this obstacle seems to be insuperable.

Some of the other difficulties, which are involved in completing the analysis, do not seem to be quite so serious. A proposition stating that a name is correlated with an object, if it were not elementary, could be further analysed : and perhaps the identification of the believer does not present an insuperable obstacle. But the difference between ' meaning ' and ' believing ' seems to involve more than a theory about the nature of propositions.

[36] See *I.T.* (*T.L-PH.* p. xxii).
[37] See pp. 198-9. Cf. *O.P.* (*L.KN.* p. 305).

Idealist's suggestion. But it denies that those things are the objects of his thought. They are tokens, and so part of the record rather than go-betweens shuttling somewhere between the thinker and the objects which he can never encounter.

This examination of Wittgenstein's views about belief has not really been a digression. In the period before 1919 Russell's views on this topic are part of a dialogue with Wittgenstein, and can only be understood in that way. The same is true, though not quite to the same extent, of his views about logical atoms. Conversely, Wittgenstein's views on these two topics in the *Tractatus* must be understood as the other part of the dialogue. This does not mean that the two philosophers were not independent originators. Nor, on the other hand, does it imply that, when their ideas were not independent, each was only influenced by the other. In this particular area the development of Russell's ideas was influenced by William James, and Frege's works made a very great impact on Wittgenstein.[88]

It is not surprising that in his next contribution to this subject Russell[89] has moved in the general direction indicated in *Tractatus* 5.542. Not that his new theory is the same as Wittgenstein's. Nor of course is it entirely the result of Wittgenstein's influence. In fact, the main impulse which produced the change came from William James' essay *Does ' Consciousness ' Exist?* and so ultimately from Hume's theory of personal identity.[40] The turning point was Russell's abandonment of the thesis that the ego is a particular. The changes in his theory of perception which were produced by his new view of persons have already been described. The roughly parallel changes in his theory of judgement will be described now. Unfortunately, the parallelism between the two developments, in so far as it does exist, is very confusing. So in the description of Russell's new theory of judgement which now follows

[88] *T.L-PH.* Author's Preface, p. 3.
[89] *O.P.* (1919) (*L.KN.* p. 285ff).
[40] See p. 42, footnote 29, and p. 135, footnote 41.

no reference will be made to the parallelism. It will be illustrated in a series of diagrams at the end of this chapter.

When Russell ceased to believe that the ego is a particular, he could no longer treat judgement as a multiple relation between the thinking subject and the constituents of the proposition judged to be true. His theory had to develop in the general direction sketched by Wittgenstein in the *Tractatus*. He describes the change in his article *On Propositions*:

The theory of belief which I formerly advocated, namely, that it consisted in a multiple relation of the subject to the objects constituting the ' objective ', i.e. the fact that makes the belief true or false, is rendered impossible by the rejection of the subject.[41] The constituents of the belief cannot, when the subject is rejected, be the same as the constituents of its ' objective '. This has both advantages and disadvantages. The disadvantages are those resulting from the gulf between the content and the objective, which seem to make it doubtful in what sense we can be said to ' know ' the objective.* The advantages are those derived from the rehabilitation of the content, making it possible to admit propositions as actual complex occurrences, and doing away with the difficulty of answering the question: what do we believe when we believe falsely? The theory I wish to advocate, however, is not to be recommended by these advantages, or rejected on account of these disadvantages: it is presented for acceptance on the ground that it accords with what can be empirically observed, and that it rejects everything mythological or merely schematic. Whether it is epistemologically convenient or inconvenient is a question which has no bearing upon its truth or falsehood, and which I do not propose to consider further.

* An important part of ' knowing ' will consist in the fact that, by means of ' ideas ', we are able to act in a way which is appropriate to an absent object, and are not dependent upon the stimulus of present sensation. I have not developed this order of ideas in the present paper, but I do not wish to minimise its importance.[42]

Russell's cardinal point in this passage is that ' the con-

---

[41] Notice what a small verbal change is needed in order to transform Russell's earlier theory into a theory about possibilities. It would merely have had to have been the theory that belief consists in a multiple relation of the subject to the objects that constitute the possibility, which, if it were realized as a fact, would make the belief true (D.F.P.).

[42] *O.P.* (*L.KN.* pp. 306-7).

stituents of the belief cannot, when the subject is rejected, be the same as the constituents of its " objective " '.[48] Why does he say this? His reasoning starts from the indisputable fact that the constituents of the proposition ' A believes that the knife is on the right of the fork ' must differ from the constituents of the proposition ' The knife is on the right of the fork ', because these are two different propositions. This fact has the following consequence : when his earlier theory that the ego is a constituent of the first proposition has been abandoned, an entirely new analysis of that proposition is required. For it is no longer possible to explain the difference between the two propositions by saying that the ego is a constituent of the first proposition, but not of the second one.

His first step towards producing a new analysis of it is to change the meaning of the phrase ' constituent of a proposition '. The change which he makes is a radical one. He now uses the phrase to denote the tokens which are used in the actual formulation of a proposition. Here, of course, he is following Wittgenstein. Although this change in the meaning of the phrase ' constituent of a proposition ' is radical, it is a very natural one. As Russell puts it, ' the rehabilitation of the content [makes] it possible to admit propositions as actual complex occurrences '. Propositions are now facts in their own right, and, as such, they actually contain their own constituents. For example, if the proposition ' The knife is on the right of the fork ' is not expressed in words, its constituents will be psychological tokens. Why did he think it necessary to take this step? The answer is that he thought that only in this way could he achieve a satisfactory analysis of the proposition about A's belief. For he could no longer use the ego in his analysis of it, and it was very natural for him to suppose that the only alternative was to make his analysis of it refer to the tokens that would occur in A's mind.

The details of his new analysis of the proposition about A's

---

[48] See Note A at the end of this chapter.

belief will be given in a moment. Meanwhile, it is worth observing a very curious fact about the new theory: the moment that it is formulated, it becomes very difficult to understand what his earlier theory could possibly have been. For if the new constituents of the proposition' The knife is on the right of the fork' may be in a person's mind, it looks as if all the things which, according to the earlier theory, were constituents of that proposition, might have been in his mind. This is one source of the mistaken view that Russell's earlier theory in some ludicrous way imports objects into the mind.[44] The source of this mistake is neutralised the moment that we realise that the new constituents of the proposition 'The knife is on the right of the fork' are tokens which, if they are in anybody's mind, will be the psychological embodiment of that proposition.

But Russell's new theory is only like Wittgenstein's in its general outline. One difference between them is that, whereas Wittgenstein leaves the nature of the psychological tokens undetermined, in Russell's theory they are images. Some of these images mean particulars, while others mean properties and relations.[45] This is really a revival of Hume's account of thinking. The resemblance is particularly striking in Russell's next major work *The Analysis of Mind* (1921). But it is a revival of Hume's theory in a new form. The old form of the theory was non-propositional, but the images in the new version combine to form propositions, and this is a very great improvement. But in spite of this difference it is really remarkable how close Russell has come to Hume. He entirely shares Hume's belief that the theory of meaning is primarily concerned with images. He says, for instance,

This is really the most essential function of words: that, primarily through their connection with images, they bring us into touch with what is remote in time or space. When they operate without the medium of images, this seems to be a telescoped process. Thus the problem of the meaning of words is reduced to the problem of the meaning of images.[46]

[44] See Note A at the end of this chapter.
[45] *O.P.* (*L.KN.* p. 303).　　　[46] *O.P.* (*L.KN.* p. 303).

This passage raises an interesting question: In Russell's new theory is thinking treated as internalised behaviour? In a way it is, because the thinker arranges the images to form propositions, whereas in Hume's theory he merely contemplated them. But the genesis of the individual images is often like seeing an object rather than drawing a picture of an object, and in such cases it is internalised perception rather than internalised behaviour. Whatever the answer to this question, Russell clearly regarded the phenomenon of thinking in images as conclusive evidence against the extreme Behaviourist's thesis that belief is action.[47] He admitted that this thesis contained an important truth: for in the analysis of belief the actions which the believer is ready to perform or able to perform are very important;[48] but he regarded these manifestations as consequences of the belief rather than as the belief itself.[49]

But we still have not formulated the whole of Russell's new theory of judgement. We know his new view about the constituents of the proposition ' The knife is on the right of the fork '. But we do not yet know his new view about the constituents of the proposition ' A believes that the knife is on the right of the fork '. Obviously, it cannot have the same constituents as the believed proposition. Equally obviously, he cannot now say that it contains an ego as an extra constituent, because, according to his new theory, a person is merely a sequence of thoughts and experiences. Nor does his new theory even allow him to say that it contains the idea of an ego as a constituent. So what he does is to make belief consist in a feeling of assent to the proposition,[50] and, naturally, since he has abandoned the ego, this feeling is not to be understood as a relation between the ego and the proposition. Here again he is following Hume fairly closely.

He now has the material that he needs for his new theory

[47] See *PH.L.A.* p. 26 (*L.KN.* p. 219). Cf. *O.P.* (*L.KN.* p. 310).
[48] See *O.P.* (L.KN. p. 307, footnote [quoted on p. 233]). Cf. *M.PH.D.* p. 137ff.
[49] *O.P.* (*L.KN.* p. 310).   [50] *O.P.* (*L.KN.* p. 311).

of judgement. According to the new theory, the proposition
'A believes that the knife is on the right of the fork' says
that the believed proposition occurs with a feeling of assent
in A's psychological history. So, presumably, it has at least
the following constituents: an idea of the feeling of assent,
and ideas of all the ideas that are constituents of the believed
proposition. This still does not deal with the identification
of the particular psychological history that is meant. Whose
is it? But perhaps the problem of analysing the answer to
that question can be left on one side, because it would take us
too far from the present topic.

It is worth observing that there is another way in which
Russell's new analysis differs from the analysis which Wittgenstein sketches for the proposition 'A believes that p is the
case'. For Wittgenstein's analysis includes the statement that
certain tokens are combined to form a proposition with a
particular meaning: the proposition has this meaning because
its tokens are connected with certain objects. But there is
nothing like this in Russell's new theory. He assumes that the
images which, according to him, are the constituents of the
believed proposition have their meanings, and he does not
make his analysis of the proposition about A's belief include
the statement that they have those meanings: nor does he
allude to the facts on which their possession of those meanings
depends.

It was pointed out earlier that the effect which Russell's
abandonment of the thesis that the ego is a particular has on
his theory of judgement is, to some extent, parallel to its
effect on his theory of perception, and that this parallelism is
very confusing. There are really two things which might
cause confusion. The first is that the constituents of a proposition which is judged to be true do not have to be perceived, so that it is a little hard to see why something which
forced Russell to change his theory of perception should also
force him to change his theory of judgement. The second
source of confusion is that, even if the two effects really are
produced by the same thing, it is hard to keep them distinct

because perception often, if not always, involves judgement. Perhaps the following diagrams of Russell's two theories before 1919 will serve to put all these things in their places.

Diagram x

Here the dotted line represents the ego's acquaintance with a sense-datum which is actually being perceived at the moment. If a judgement is made about a sense-datum which is not being perceived at the moment, the situation will be different.

Diagram xi

Here again the dotted lines represent acquaintance, but they are different from the dotted lines in Diagram x, because the acquaintance which they represent is not contemporary perception, but memory. If the two diagrams are combined, as they have to be in order to illustrate a judgement about a sense-datum which is being perceived at the moment, we get the following result.

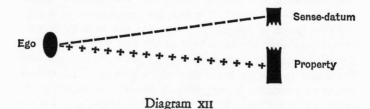

Diagram xii

In this diagram the sense-datum is being perceived at the moment, and the connection between it and the ego is represented accordingly. It might be expected that the connection between the property and the ego ought also to be shown as a case of contemporary perception. But, though the person *claims* to perceive that the sense-datum has the property, he must remember the property from some previous occasion,[51] and so this connection is represented as one of memory.

This gets rid of the two sources of possible confusion. The first one goes when we see that, although the ego is needed in Diagrams x and xi, it is needed in two different ways, which are distinguished by the two different kinds of connecting line. The second one goes when we see how these two diagrams can be combined to form Diagram xii.

[51] See Ch. xi for the argument for this assertion.

NOTE A

Mr. P. T. Geach seems to think that Russell believed in some such importation. In his book *Mental Acts* there is a passage in which he is trying to explain why Russell restricts our acquaintance to sense-data (p. 46). After mentioning sceptical arguments about perception, he says: ' Another reason for the restriction is that Russell regards the judgement as a complex, of which the things *really* judged about (*sc.* the objects of acquaintance) are actually constituents. Now if I judged that the present King of France is fat and bald, it would be hard to suppose that a bald fat man was bodily a constituent of my judgment, even if my judgment were true and even if I had the honour to be acquainted (in the ordinary sense) with the King. Sense-data, on the other hand, are sufficiently private, fleeting, and unsubstantial to be plausibly taken as constituents of a private mental act.' This betrays a complete misunderstanding of Russell's earlier theory of judgement (1910). One of the main points of that theory is that the constituents of propositions are outside the mind, and, according to Russell, this remains true even when he identifies them with sense-data.

However, there is some reason for the misunderstanding. It is very natural to interpret the phrase ' constituents of a proposition' to mean 'things in which a proposition is embodied', and, when someone believes the proposition, it might naturally be taken to be embodied in ideas in his mind. It would then follow that the constituents of the proposition would have to be mental (see pp. 233-5).

Not only is it natural to follow this line of thought, but also Russell himself followed it, *but only after he changed his theory of judgement in 1919*. In his article *O.P.* (1919) he says that his new view is that ' the constituents of the belief cannot . . . be the same as the constituents of its " objective " ' (*L.KN.* p. 307) [i.e. they cannot be the same as the things which he *used* to call ' the constituents of the proposition'].

Most of the preceding chapter has been concerned with the difficulty of understanding Russell's earlier theory of judgement, and with the reasons why he changed it in 1919. Mr Geach is quite wrong to import elements from the later theory into the earlier theory. Indeed, he does not seem to be aware that there were two theories.

NOTE B

The proposition 'The distance from Edinburgh to Cambridge is greater than the distance from Oxford to London' cannot be analysed in the way that was illustrated in Diagrams I-IX. For in those diagrams all the existential propositions were about individuals, and this proposition entails an existential proposition about two relations, and this existential proposition about the two relations cannot be eliminated by further analysis. The reason why it cannot be eliminated is that the speaker has not specified the two distances, and so the specification of them would alter his meaning.

It will be noticed that this reason is connected with a point that was made earlier about Russellian complete analyses (see pp. 77-81 and pp. 112-15). It was pointed out that Russell thought that, when you are carrying out the analysis of a complex singular symbol, you cannot substitute a logically proper name for a definite description. His reason for thinking this is identical with the reason that has just been given for thinking that the existential proposition about the two distances cannot be eliminated by further analysis: in both cases the specification would alter the speaker's meaning.

This point about the Russellian complete analysis of complex singular symbols produces the following consequence. If you are not acquainted with the relevant particulars, you must embark on an analysis which uses definite descriptions. But once you start in this way, you can never get back to the logically proper names of particulars. Even if you later became acquainted with the relevant particulars, you still could not substitute their logically proper names for the definite descriptions. For such a substitution would involve a change of meaning.

The same reasoning leads Russell to admit that a complete analysis would sometimes have to include existential propositions about properties and relations which cannot be eliminated. Of course, this will not always be necessary. For Diagrams I-IX illustrate Russell's usual way of analysing singular propositions: i.e. he usually assumes that, when you mention a complex property or relation, you will be acquainted with the properties and relations which would be mentioned in its complete analysis (or, at least, in that part of its complete analysis which you are able to produce. See pp. 88-90.) However, he is aware that you will not always be acquainted with those ultimate properties and relations (see Note A, pp. 136-7, and p. 144, footnote 17). When you lack that acquaintance, he allows your complete analysis to contain existential propositions about those properties and relations, and these existential propositions cannot be eliminated.

CHAPTER XIV

GENERALITY

Generality has already been touched twice in the course of this rather winding investigation of Russell's philosophy, once in Chapter v,[1] and again in Chapter VII.[2] But the discussion of it was incomplete. It dealt fairly fully with the kind of general proposition which begins with the word ' some ', but very sketchily with the kind that begins with the word ' all ', which are known as ' universal propositions '. Definitions, which are a kind of *a priori* universal proposition, were discussed, but contingent universal propositions were not mentioned. Something will now be done to fill this gap, but only enough to introduce the topic of contingent universal propositions in a systematic way, and to put Russell's ideas about them in their historical place. The discussion will not be taken nearly as far as the discussion of singular propositions. Since universal propositions are enormously important in science, this reticence needs some defence, or at least some explanation. Why should they not be discussed at equally great length? Russell's logical apparatus was going to be examined at every point where it plays an essential part in his reconstruction of empirical knowledge.[3] So, even if this book does not include any examination of the actual development of his logical apparatus, it ought to include an examination of all its applications to empirical knowledge. Therefore, contingent universal propositions, which obviously come into its application to empirical knowledge, ought to be examined. Why then is the discussion of them not going to be on anything like the same scale?

There are really two reasons for this comparative reticence about contingent universal propositions. First, the obvious way in which they might be expected to come within the scope of this book is through scientific generalisations about things in the external world, but in the period before 1919 Russell spent little time on such generalisations. Most of his detailed work on this part of the Philosophy of Science came later. Before 1919 he was on the whole working closer to the foundations of empirical knowledge, and trying to discover the correct analysis of singular propositions about things in the external world.

However, it might be objected that this is not an adequate reason for curtailing the discussion of contingent universal propositions. For they also come into the analysis of singular propositions about things in the external world, and this ought to put them back in a place of equal honour. In fact, there are two distinct ways in which they come into Russell's analysis of singular propositions about things in the external world. First, if, as he says, a singular proposition of this kind is analysable into propositions about sense-data, it will be bound to involve contingent universal propositions. For the majority of the relevant sense-data will not be received by the speaker at the moment of speaking, if indeed he is receiving any of them, and he will have to infer those that he is not receiving,[4] and the inference will have to be based on contingent universal propositions. Secondly, Russell's analysis of definite descriptions like ' the daughter of Hitler ' also involves contingent universal propositions. For part of his analysis of a proposition containing that definite description is given in the proposition ' There is one and only one thing which is female and was begotten by Hitler ' : and this proposition really contains a contingent universal proposition, because it means not only that there is at least one thing which has that property and that relation, but also that anything which has that property and that relation is identical with that thing.[5] So here is a second way in which Russell's analysis of singular propositions

[4] See pp. 39-40 and p. 133.
[5] See *O.D.* (*L.KN.* p. 44) and *PH.L.A.* p. 45 (*L.KN.* p. 249). This is the final stage in the exposition of Russell's analysis of definite descriptions, which was alluded to on p. 68.

about objects in the external world brings in contingent universal propositions. Why then should the discussion of them not be on the same scale as the discussion of singular propositions? A second reason is needed.

The second reason will serve as an introduction to the rest of this chapter. It is that Russell's analysis of singular propositions about objects in the external world, although it brings in contingent universal propositions, is not equally affected by all the features of their analysis. Some of the questions about the analysis of contingent universal propositions, however important they may be in their own right, do not make much difference to his reconstruction of empirical knowledge. This is such a vague statement that it may very well receive an interpretation which makes it false. So it will be made more specific immediately.

Russell uses propositional functions in his analysis of universal propositions. The way in which he uses them will be explained in a moment. But something can be said about it straightaway. It provides him with an analysis which has two striking features, both of which have brought down criticism on it. First, his analysis deprives universal propositions of existential import : that is to say, the proposition ' All A's are B ', as interpreted by him, does not imply that there are some A's. This feature of his analysis has been criticised on the ground that the word ' all ', as it is ordinarily used, especially in contingent universal propositions, does carry this implication. The other feature of his analysis of contingent universal propositions which has incurred criticism, is that, according to him, they merely say that things always happen in a certain way : they do not say that things must happen in a certain way, unless saying that they always do happen in that way counts as saying that they must happen in that way. This has exposed him to the criticism that his analysis leaves out the element of necessity which is present in many contingent universal propositions.

Now both these controversies about the analysis of contingent universal propositions are important. But Russell's analysis of singular propositions about objects in the external world is not much affected by them. It is, of course, very much affected by the use of propositional functions in the analysis of existential propositions. For, as we have seen, it is this use of propositional functions that enables him to explain the fact that existential propositions can be meaningful but false. But when he uses propositional functions in the analysis of universal propositions, and has to face the question whether the word ' all ' has existential import, his answer does not make much difference to his analysis of singular propositions about objects in the external world. Nor does the answer to the question whether his analysis of contingent universal propositions is sufficiently comprehensive, in spite of the fact that it appears to leave out the necessity. He could have left this question open, merely observing that the comprehensive analysis of contingent universal propositions, whatever it might be, would be needed at the two points in his system which were mentioned just now.

However, generality is an extremely important subject in its own right, and Russell's analysis of universal propositions ought to be examined in some detail, even if it does not much affect his analysis of singular propositions about objects in the external world. It is probably easiest to start with propositional functions, and first it might be useful to recapitulate what was said about them in Chapter v.[6] There were three main points. First, there was the explanation of what a propositional function is : it is what you get when you create a vacancy in a proposition; for example you take the proposition ' This is mobile ', and you strike out the word ' this ', leaving its place empty, and the result is the propositional function '— is mobile '. The second move was to introduce the concept of ' satisfying a propositional function ' : a thing satisfies a propositional function if the insertion of its name in the vacancy in the propositional function produces a true proposition. Thirdly, it was pointed out that there are various ways in which a propositional function might be satisfied, and

[6] pp. 62-4.

so various ways in which it might be said to be satisfied. You might say that the propositional function '— is mobile' is satisfied by one or more instances, or, to put this in a more familiar way, that at least one thing is mobile. Or you might say that it is satisfied by one and only one instance, which would be an analysis of the proposition 'Only one thing is mobile'; or by no instances, which would be an analysis of the proposition 'Nothing is mobile'.

These are, of course, different ways of carrying out the logical operation of generalising. There are also other ways of carrying out that operation which were not mentioned in Chapter v. You might say that all things are mobile, or you might say this about most things, or about some specified proportion of things. It is obvious that these propositions too can be derived from the same propositional function : they make various assertions about the extent to which it is satisfied. The most important of these propositions is the one that concerns us here, 'All things are mobile'. According to Russell, what this proposition means is that the propositional function is satisfied by all things.

It is, however, very unusual to assert contingent universal propositions like 'All things are mobile'. We nearly always cast our net less widely, and talk about some limited class of things. For instance, in the contingent universal proposition 'All animals require oxygen' the word 'animal' does not cover the entire contents of the universe. It is a word which applies only to a limited class of things, and in this proposition, since it follows the word 'all', it picks out everything that belongs to that class.

This limitation of scope makes the analysis of this proposition more elaborate than the analysis of the proposition 'All things are mobile'. According to Russell, it means 'If anything is an animal, it requires oxygen', and that means that the propositional function 'If — is an animal, — requires oxygen' is satisfied by everything.[7] This propositional function is more elaborate than the propositional function '— is

[7] *PH.L.A.* p. 33 (*L.KN.* p. 230).

mobile': it has two vacancies instead of one. The two vacancies are linked to one another in the way in which the corresponding words, 'anything' and 'it', are linked to one another. That is to say, if a particular name fills the first vacancy, it must also fill the second vacancy.

It is obviously the occurrence of the word 'animal' after the word 'all' that makes it necessary to have two vacancies in this propositional function. For when the word 'all' is followed by a word which picks out a limited class of things, the universal proposition states a relationship between two limited classes. It uses two nets, one to catch each class, and it states that the two classes are related to one another in a certain way. The relationship is, of course, inclusion, and, in this example, the universal proposition states that the class of animals is entirely included in the class of things requiring oxygen.

It would be natural to describe the mechanism of the propositional function by saying that the first vacancy in it catches individuals of the kind that we are talking about, and that the second vacancy catches individuals possessing the property which we are ascribing to individuals of the kind that we are talking about. If we interpret the universal proposition in this way, we shall say that it is true if and only if all names of animals are also names of things that require oxygen. Or, to put the same point in a slightly different way, we shall say that the propositional function is satisfied only by individuals which are animals and do require oxygen. Now the propositional function is satisfied by an individual if the insertion of the name of the individual in its vacancies produces a true proposition, which, in this case, would be the singular hypothetical proposition 'If this is an animal, it requires oxygen'. So, if we adopt this interpretation of the universal proposition, we shall say that a singular hypothetical proposition is true if and only if the stated condition is fulfilled and the stated consequence actually follows. That would be the natural view to take.

However, Russell does not take it. According to him, a

singular hypothetical proposition is true not only if the stated condition is fulfilled and the stated consequence actually follows, but also if the stated condition is not fulfilled. On this interpretation of singular hypotheticals the propositional function is satisfied by absolutely anything that avoids being an animal which does not require oxygen. For instance, it would be satisfied by a stone. The universal proposition only means that there exists nothing which is an animal and does not require oxygen.[8]

This interpretation of universal propositions is not so paradoxical when they begin with the words 'If anything'. But it must be remembered that Russell uses propositions beginning with the words 'If anything' as paraphrases of propositions beginning with the word 'All', so that his analysis is also meant to fit propositions like 'All animals require oxygen'. In such a case his interpretation really is paradoxical. It deprives the proposition of existential import. That is to say, it allows that it would be true that all animals require oxygen even if no animals existed. His reason for eliminating existential import from the meaning of universal propositions is that it leads to confusion to include it.[9] This might be disputed. Certainly, there are two distinguishable propositions here, 'There is nothing which is an animal and does not require oxygen', and 'There are some animals'. But it might be claimed that both are included in one way or another in the meaning of the proposition 'All animals require oxygen', and that this need not lead to any confusion.[10] However, this controversy belongs to logic, and it will not be pursued here.[11]

[8] *PH.L.A.* p. 32 (*L.KN.* p. 229). [9] *PH.L.A.* p. 32 (*L.KN.* p. 229).
[10] cf. P. F. Strawson, *Introduction to Logical Theory* pp. 163-84.

[11] If the correctness of an analysis is judged by its conformity to ordinary usage, Russell attaches no importance to the question whether his analyses are correct or not (see p. 15, footnote 5). What he demands of an analysis is that it should say absolutely clearly what can be legitimately said. In this case he thinks that his demand can be satisfied only if the meanings of the various types of general proposition are parcelled out in a new way.

If we now look back at the various ways in which the operation of generalising may be performed on a propositional function, we can see how they are connected with one another. Russell's version of the proposition ' Something is mobile ' is ' At least one thing is mobile ', and this means that the propositional function '—is mobile ' is satisfied by one or more things. If you negate this, you get the general proposition ' Nothing is mobile ', which means that the propositional function is not satisfied by anything. If you negate the predicate in this, you get the proposition ' Nothing is not mobile ', which means that the propositional function is satisfied by all things, and that is Russell's version of the proposition ' All things are mobile '. Finally, in order to get the proposition ' Only one thing is mobile ', which means that the propositional function is satisfied by one and only one thing, you have to use both the first and the third of these general propositions : for what you want to say is that there is at least one thing that is mobile, and that anything that is mobile is identical with that thing.[12]

In the earlier discussion of propositional functions something was said about the rather strange predicates which Russell applies to them.[13] There were two such predicates, ' possible ', and ' impossible '. When a propositional function is not satisfied by anything, he calls it ' impossible ', because in that case a particular thing cannot satisfy it : and conversely, when it is satisfied by at least one thing, he calls it ' possible ', because in that case a particular thing can satisfy it. A third predicate must now be added to the family. When a propositional function is satisfied by all things, he calls it ' necessary ', because in that case any particular thing that you choose must satisfy it.[14] Perhaps his use of the word ' necessary ' will not seem so strange as his use of the words ' possible ' and ' impossible '. But that would be an illusion. If the words ' possible ' and ' impossible ' seem to be strange predicates for propositional functions, then the word ' necessary ' ought to seem

[12] See p. 243.   [13] See pp. 63-4.
[14] *PH.L.A.* p. 33 (*L.KN.* p. 231).

equally strange. For the three words are connected with one
another by definitions, and their connections simply reflect the
connections between the three words ' some ', ' none ' and
' all ', which were traced in the last paragraph : for instance, if
you say that it is necessary that a particular thing should be
mobile, you will mean that it is impossible that it should not be
mobile. Consequently, if Russell's application of any of the
three predicates to propositional functions seems strange, so
too should his application of the others. The explanation of
his usage is the same in all three cases.

Russell's application of these three predicates to propositional functions must now be related to another use which is
sometimes made of them. We sometimes say that a contingent
universal proposition is necessary, meaning that it is a law of
nature, or something of that kind. In such a case we can just
as well say that the negation of the proposition is impossible,
relying on the definition which equates the impossibility of
the negative with the necessity of the positive. Would these
assertions have the same meaning as Russell's assertion that
the associated propositional function is necessary? The answer
to this question depends on what would be meant by someone
who said that a contingent universal proposition was necessary.
We know the meaning of Russell's assertion about the propositional function, but this assertion about the proposition
itself has not yet been interpreted.

There are two possible interpretations of it, one of which is
parsimonious, while the other is more generous. According to
the parsimonious interpretation, the thesis that a contingent
universal proposition is ' necessary ' only means that, if it is
true, any particular thing which you choose must do what it
says. Not that things conform to the contingent universal
propositions that we assert. On the contrary, we try to make
our propositions conform to the behaviour of things, which
often can only be inferred. It is only in this sense that, if the
proposition is true, the things must do what it says, and,
when we assert the proposition, we mean, rightly or wrongly,

that it is true, and that they will do what it says. On this parsimonious interpretation the assertion that the proposition is necessary is intended to have exactly the same meaning as Russell's assertion that the associated propositional function is necessary. In both cases the word 'necessary' is a transferred epithet. It does not really belong in the place where it is put. Russell calls the propositional function 'necessary' because, if it is satisfied by all things, any particular thing that you choose must satisfy it. Similarly, if the thesis, that a contingent universal proposition is necessary, is interpreted parsimoniously, what is necessary will not be the proposition itself, but, rather, the behaviour of any particular thing that you choose. Of course, the necessity that a particular thing should behave in the stated way is only conditional, because it depends on the truth of the universal proposition, or, alternatively expressed, on the fact that the propositional function is satisfied by all things.

However, there is an important difference between this transference of the epithet 'necessary' to contingent universal propositions and Russell's transference of it to propositional functions. The difference is most easily brought out if we explain the transference of the epithet to contingent universal propositions in a slightly different way. What is necessary might be said to be the truth of any singular hypothetical proposition which can be deduced from the contingent universal proposition. Again, of course, this necessity would only be conditional, since it would depend on the truth of the universal proposition. It is true that in everyday life we quite often slur over this dependence, and talk as if the necessity of such a single hypothetical were unconditional: for instance, we say that the proposition 'If this is an animal it requires oxygen' must be true, which is a way of saying that, if it is an animal, it must require oxygen. However, though it is natural that we should slur over the dependence, it must exist. Or rather, so long as we stick to the parsimonious interpretation of the assertion that a contingent universal proposition is necessary, we must admit that it exists. For on this view how could such a singular hypothetical proposition conceivably be necessary in itself? It obviously could not be logically necessary. All that logical necessity does here is to guarantee the connection between it and the universal proposition from which it is deduced. What it gets through this connection is only truth. This truth that it gets is called ' necessary truth ' only because every other singular hypothetical proposition which can be generated from the same propositional function will be true provided that the universal proposition is true. There is, as it were, no loophole through which particular things might evade the force of the universal proposition, if it really is true. That is what universality does to things. But of course this is only a rhetorical way of presenting the point. All that a contingent universal proposition really does is to try to conform to the behaviour of things.

When the transference of the epithet to contingent universal propositions is explained in this way, it immediately becomes clear that it contains a misleading suggestion, which, as we shall see in a moment, is not present in Russell's account. For if we stick to the parsimonious interpretation of the assertion that a contingent universal proposition is necessary, we can only mean that it is true. But if we allow that singular hypotheticals derive necessary truth from it, this suggests that it is necessarily true, and that is a misleading suggestion. Admittedly, we do ascribe necessity to such singular hypotheticals. But their necessity should be interpreted as truth on condition that the universal proposition is true, and not as necessary truth which is derived from the universal proposition. If we do interpret it in the second of these two ways, we shall be trying to conjure an unconditional necessity out of a conditional necessity, and suggesting that the universal proposition itself is necessarily true. But that is a trick which cannot be performed.

This misleading suggestion is not present in Russell's version of the parsimonious analysis of contingent universal propositions. For he transfers the predicate 'necessary' not to universal propositions but to propositional functions. When it is applied to a propositional function, it simply means that the propositional function is satisfied by all things. It does not mean that it is necessarily satisfied by all things. So Russell's transference of the predicate is innocuous. As has already been explained, it is exactly parallel to his transference of the other two predicates, 'possible' and 'impossible'. For instance, the truth of the general proposition 'At least one thing is mobile' makes it possible for a particular thing to possess this property, and this possibility is then transferred to the propositional function '— is mobile'. The family to which these three concepts belong also includes the concept of probability. But probability is a more sophisticated member of it, and it will not be examined here.

However, there is a point about probability which ought to be made, in order to guard against a misinterpretation of Russell's treatment of these concepts. The statement, that most October days are wet, entails that a given October day will probably be wet. But it is easy to imagine circumstances in which someone, who admitted that most October days are wet, might nevertheless reasonably claim that a given October day would probably not be wet. For instance, during a steady October anticyclone, he might say 'It is practically certain that tomorrow will not be wet'. The apparent inconsistency disappears the moment that we reflect that there is another fact about that particular October day, *viz.* the fact that it will be a day of high barometric pressure, which militates against the general probability of rain in October, and, in this case, is supposed to prevail. Probability is relative to evidence, and, when someone makes a final, balanced judgement of probability about a particular case, he will use all the evidence that he possesses.

It is important to observe that exactly the same is true of possibility, but that impossibility and necessity are slightly different. First consider possibility. If some things are mobile, it is possible that a given thing is mobile, and this is what leads Russell to apply the epithet 'possible' to the propositional function '— is mobile'. But there may be other evidence which establishes that a particular thing cannot be mobile. For instance, it might be a volcano. So the concept of possibility is, in this respect, like the concept of probability. Both are relative to evidence, and, in a particular case, the final judgement may need to take account of more than one piece of evidence.

The concepts of impossibility and necessity, as they are analysed by Russell, are slightly different. Impossibility is certainly relative to evidence; it is impossible that a volcano should be mobile, given that no volcanoes are mobile. The difference comes when we ask if someone who knows that no volcanoes are mobile needs to consider any *other* evidence before concluding that a particular volcano cannot be mobile. The answer to this question is that he need not consider any other evidence, because the evidence which he already possesses is conclusive. The same is true of necessity, as it is analysed by Russell. There is something absolute about impossibility and necessity, and in this respect they differ from probability and possibility. Of course, you might not *know* that a propositional function was satisfied by everything, or that it was satisfied by nothing, but that does not affect the present point, which is not concerned with induction. The point is that, *if* you knew that the propositional function was satisfied by everything, or that it was satisfied by nothing, you would not need to consider any more evidence before asserting the necessity, or the impossibility of a particular case of the relevant kind.

So far, the assertion that a contingent universal proposition is necessary has been interpreted parsimoniously, and then it is a misleading way of making the point that Russell makes by saying that the associated propositional function is necessary. It is misleading because, though it is perfectly right that the universal proposition should wear a badge, the one that is awarded to it should not be borrowed from the singular pro-

positions, given that their right to wear it is derived from its right to wear another badge, the badge of truth. On the parsimonious interpretation the necessity of contingent universal propositions can only be truth, but the word 'necessity' contains the misleading suggestion of necessary truth.

The second interpretation of the thesis that a contingent universal proposition is necessary, is more generous than the first. It is also a simpler interpretation. But, paradoxically, it is more difficult to understand. It is simpler, because it does not treat the word 'necessary' as a transferred epithet, but says that the necessity which belongs to some contingent universal propositions belongs to them in their own right. It is more difficult to understand, because usually there is no positive characterisation of this necessity. Most philosophers who believe in it tell us what it is not, but not what it is. It is not logical necessity, and it is not universal truth wearing a borrowed badge. But that is all that we usually learn about it. No doubt it is possible to make further progress in understanding this concept.[15] But no attempt to do so will be made here. This theory about contingent universal propositions is mentioned only because, in one form or another, it has nearly always been adopted by those who are opposed to Russell's parsimonious kind of theory. When Russell says that the necessity of propositional functions is only satisfaction by everything, and implies that the word 'necessity' is really borrowed, his adversaries will reply that their necessity must be something more which belongs to them in their own right. It is not that they just happen to be satisfied by everything, but, rather, that they are necessarily satisfied by everything. Similarly, when a parsimonious analyst interprets the necessity of contingent universal propositions as mere truth, his adversaries will protest that it is more than truth. According to them, it is a kind of necessary truth, which belongs to them in their own right. Of course, they do not maintain this thesis about all contingent universal propositions, but only about

[15] See W. C. and M. Kneale, *The Development of Logic*, pp. 648-51.

those which are laws of nature, or are, at least, like laws of nature.

This controversy goes back a long way. The most famous defence of the parsimonious kind of theory is to be found in Hume's Treatise,[16] and, as usual, the comparison between his version and Russell's is worth making. The scope of Hume's version is more restricted than Russell's, because Hume does not deal with all contingent universal propositions, but only with those that are about causal connections. So he presents it as a theory about causal necessity. He must have regarded it as the most important thing in the first book of his Treatise, if not in the whole Treatise. For it is the centrepiece in his Abstract of the Treatise.[17]

The question out of which Hume's theory grew is a question about verification. What is the evidence on which a proposition like ' A caused B ' is based? He gives his answer in the psychological terminology of his system, which was introduced in Chapter II. It is that the proposition is based on the sense-impressions of the two events A and B : whenever a sense-impression of an event like A occurs, it is immediately followed by a sense-impression of an event like B in roughly the same place.[18] According to Hume, that is all the evidence that is ever available. He then goes on to describe what happens to this material after it has been received, but he never allows any addition to it. What happens is that an association is formed between the derived ideas of A and B in the mind of the recipient, and thereafter, when he receives another impression of an event like A, he will follow the line of the association and infer that another event like B will ensue.[19] Indeed, he will feel that he must follow it, and Hume identifies this feeling with the impression of causal necessity, which is, therefore, not a sense-impression, but an impression pro-

[16] *T.H.N.* I.iii.14 (p. 153).

[17] *An Abstract of a Treatise of Human Nature*, which is included in *H.TH.KN.*

[18] *T.H.N.* I.iii.14 (p. 167).   [19] *T.H.N.* I.iii.14 (p. 167).

duced inside the mind by the association of ideas.[20] However, Hume's account of the psychological mechanism of causal inference, though it is extremely interesting, does not really concern us. The point that is important here is that a singular causal proposition always depends on a universal causal proposition, whose evidence, according to Hume, will never amount to more than a repetition of the sequence of the two sense-impressions, occurring in the way that he specifies. So, if the meaning of a proposition never goes beyond the method of its verification, the universal proposition will only mean that this sequence is never broken.

This version of the parsimonious theory of contingent universal propositions is very like Russell's. It is true that Hume only develops it for causal propositions, but its scope can easily be extended. A more important difference is that Hume, in effect, allows that these propositions have existential import: for according to him what they say is not only that there are no sense-impressions of A without sense-impressions of B, but also that there are sense-impressions of A. Another difference between the two versions is that Hume usually refuses to apply the epithet ' necessary ' to the connection between cause and effect. In itself this is not a very important point, since Russell's use of it is only a sort of courtesy. However, in Hume's case the refusal is associated with an element of scepticism. That is to say, he often suggests that his failure to find any evidence which would justify the use of the epithet leaves our ordinary belief in causation undefended, and this suggestion is important.[21] Russell's summing up is different. He thinks that the part of the popular idea of necessity which Hume fails to defend is illegitimate, and so, using Ockham's razor in his usual way, he removes it. But he keeps the epithet itself. Wittgenstein adopted a parsimonious theory about contingent universal proposition, which, like Russell's, is free from

[20] *T.H.N.* I.iii.14 (p. 163).
[21] See *An Abstract of a Treatise of Human Nature* (*H.TH.KN.* pp. 259-60).

scepticism, but, unlike Russell, he refused to allow that there is any necessity but logical necessity.[22] These variations on the parsimonious theme show how unimportant the question about the use of the word ' necessary ' really is.

But behind this question about usage there are two other questions which really are important. One is the question what contingent universal propositions mean. Does the parsimonious theory give a complete account of their meaning, or does it leave out something? The other question is about the evidence on which such propositions are based. Is this evidence ever really adequate, or does it always leave an opening for the sceptic? These two questions are, of course, connected in the way that was explained in Chapter 1. The word ' existence ' does not occur in their phrasing, but that is only because the problem that was introduced in that chapter has now been extended from singular propositions about various types of individuals to universal propositions. We are no longer concerned with the question in what sense individuals of a certain type may be said to exist : whether they exist according to the full popular idea of that type of individual, or whether they exist only in so far as they are thought of in a more cautious and parsimonious way. The problem has been transferred from the meaning of singular propositions to the meaning of universal propositions, and the effect of the transference is that it can no longer be presented as a problem about existence. Necessity is not an individual.

Russell does not appear to have felt any doubts about his analysis of contingent universal propositions. This is one of the cases in which he is confident that his analysis is sufficiently comprehensive.[23] It is true that he admits in *The Philosophy of Logical Atomism* that he does not know what the right analysis of general facts is.[24] But he does not make this admission because he thinks that his analysis of contingent universal propositions may not be sufficiently comprehensive.

[22] *T.L-PH.* 6.37.   [23] See pp. 14-15.
[24] *PH.L.A.* p. 37 (*L.KN.* pp. 236-7).

His reason for making it is an entirely different one which will be explained in a moment. It does not mean that he feared that he might have done less than justice to the popular idea of physical necessity.[25]

On the contrary, the trouble was that he might have done more than justice to the popular idea. For, even if a necessary propositional function is only one that is always true, it is still problematical how we can ever know that it is always true. Perhaps such claims to knowledge can never be adequately supported by evidence. If this were so, Russell's analysis of contingent universal propositions would be too comprehensive; it ought to have been more parsimonious. The question whether it is so depends on the question whether induction is justifiable. There is a brief discussion of induction in *The Problems of Philosophy*.[26] But the greater part of Russell's work on the Philosophy of Science comes after 1919. So his treatment of inductive reasoning will not be discussed here.[27] His final verdict on it is favourable.

If Russell felt no doubt that his analysis of contingent universal propositions was sufficiently comprehensive, some

---

[25] However, it is arguable that parsimonious theories of physical necessity, like Russell's, cannot account for the fact that unfulfilled singular hypothetical propositions can be deduced from laws of nature and from other similar contingent universal propositions. See W. C. Kneale, *Probability and Induction* pp. 74-5.

[26] *P. of PH.* p. 6off.

[27] It is to be found in *H.KN.S.L.* part V and part VI. Cf. *M.PH.D.* ch. XVI.

The connection between the question, whether inductive reasoning can be justified, and the question, how contingent universal propositions should be analysed, is this: even if the necessity of contingent universal propositions is interpreted parsimoniously, it is still problematical whether the evidence and reasoning which we use to support them is really sufficient to support them. In Hume's system this connection would be expressed in the following way: even if we do not need a sense-impression of causal necessity, we still need evidence and reasoning which will adequately support the belief that a sequence of a pair of ordinary sense-impressions will in fact continue unbroken.

other explanation must be found for the uncertainty which
he expresses in *The Philosophy of Logical Atomism*. His
words leave no doubt about his perplexity:

I do not profess to know what the right analysis of general facts is.
It is an exceedingly difficult question and one which I should very
much like to see studied. I am sure that, although the convenient
technical treatment is by means of propositional functions, that is not
the whole of the right analysis. Beyond that I cannot go.[28]

In the argument that leads up to this admission he explains
that the difficulty about general facts is that they cannot be
reduced to sets of singular facts. For example, the fact that
all the people who used a library on a certain day borrowed
works of fiction cannot be reduced to a set of singular facts
about those people: for when you have listed all the singular
facts, each of which would be recorded on a slip signed by the
borrower, you still have to add the further fact that nobody
else borrowed a book that day. In this sort of example it is
easy to see what Russell means when he talks about listing all
the singular facts: he means something which a clerk might
do after the library had closed. But he also argues in exactly
the same way for the irreducibility of the general fact corresponding to a proposition like 'All animals require oxygen ',
and in this kind of case it is not so clear what the task of
listing all the singular facts would be like. There are other
stars to be investigated, and other ages, some of which are
still to come. If a propositional function can be satisfied in
any place at any time, the task of listing all the singular facts
is more than difficult. Anyone who claimed to have carried it
out would betray that he had not really understood the meaning of the universal proposition.

There is also something else which makes it rather hard to
understand Russell's point, and to see why he says that he
does not know the whole of the right analysis of general facts.
He has another way of expressing his point: which is to say
that ' you can never arrive at a general fact by inference from
particular facts, however numerous '.[29] From this he draws the

[28] *PH.L.A.* p. 37 (*L.KN.* pp. 236-7).
[29] *PH.L.A.* p. 36 (*L.KN.* p. 235).

conclusion that there must be *primitive* knowledge of contingent universal propositions : that is to say, some of them must be known without inference. Here, of course, he is assuming that we really do sometimes know that a contingent universal proposition is true, and his point is that, if in a particular case we know this through examining instances, there must be *another* contingent universal proposition which we know, or at least think that we know without inference, *viz.* the proposition that we have examined all the instances. In order to illustrate such claims to knowledge without inference, he uses examples which are like the case of the people using the library : for instance, you look round a room and observe that each person whom you see is reading *The New Yorker*; you then claim to know without inference that you have seen everybody in the room, and so, given your observation, that all the people in the room are reading *The New Yorker*. The trouble about such claims to knowledge without inference is, as Russell says, that they are often very shaky. But his point is that, rightly or wrongly, we have to assume that we know some contingent universal propositions without inference, because otherwise we could never know any in any way.

This is really a point about the meaning of contingent universal propositions. But the way in which he connects it with inference makes it rather difficult to see exactly what the point is. How is it connected with the problem of induction? Is the connection the usual one, that the analysis of contingent universal propositions must be sufficiently parsimonious to keep within the bounds of what we can reasonably claim to know? And, whatever its connection with induction, why does Russell's point lead him to say that he does not know the whole of the right analysis of general facts?

In order to answer these questions, let us first examine the easier kind of example, in which the task of listing all the singular facts is clearly intelligible. The reasoning of the clerk in the library is exactly like the reasoning of the man who says what all the people in a certain room are reading. It involves the propositional function ' If — used the library today, — borrowed a work of fiction '. Although this propositional function could be satisfied by anybody,[30] it could be dissatisfied only by individuals who did use the library that day. Now the propositional function '— used the library today' does not cast its net very widely either in space or in time. Consequently, the clerk can be reasonably sure when he has made a complete list of the individuals who satisfy it, who are, of course, that day's users of the library. Since these are the only people who might dissatisfy the first propositional function, he can be reasonably sure that his list includes all the people who might falsify the original universal proposition ' All the people who used the library today borrowed works of fiction '. But that proposition is true if it is not false.[31] Therefore, if he finds out what books each of them borrowed, he can be reasonably sure that he has a complete list of all the singular facts on which its truth depends.

It is important to see that, when the clerk uses this list in order to establish the universal proposition, he does not make an inductive inference. An inductive inference moves from examined cases to unexamined cases. But he makes no such move. For instance, he does not argue from his readers' overwhelming preference for fiction. He has an alternative method of establishing the universal proposition, which is to list all the singular facts on which its truth depends. So what Russell says about this kind of case has nothing directly to do with inductive inference, and was not intended by him to have anything directly to do with it. He is making a point about the meaning of the word ' all '. His point is that this word fastens on to the individuals who might falsify a universal proposition in an unlimited way, but that, in this kind of case, the words that immediately follow it put an ascertainable limit on the individuals who are caught. This is why the clerk can dispense with inductive inference, and rely instead on making

[30] It is even satisfied by someone who did not use the library that day. See p. 248.
[31] See p. 248.

a complete list of the individuals who are caught, and on noting what sort of book each one borrows.

So Russell is not concerned with inductive inference here, but with logical inference. If the clerk has made a complete list of the singular facts which might falsify the universal proposition, and if none of them do falsify it, it follows logically that it is true. Of course, the premisses from which this follows logically are both matters of contingent fact. But in this kind of case he can be reasonably sure of both of them. The logical inference itself depends on the semantic mechanism of the word ' all ', which is, in general, an insatiable word, but in this kind of case has an ascertainable limit put on its capacity by the words that follow it.

There is obviously an important truth in this point of Russell's, but the first thing that has to be done is to restrict its scope a little. He offers it as an entirely general thesis about all uses of the word ' all '. But there is one kind of use of that word to which it does not apply. Consider the universal proposition 'All the Seven Sages of antiquity were born within a thousand miles of Athens'. A historian who runs through the Seven Sages by name may wonder whether his list is correct. Perhaps one of the names that he has put on it does not really belong there. But that would not be a mistake about a contingent matter. Those seven men are simply *called* ' the Seven Sages ', and there is an *a priori* connection between their names and the title: or, to put the same point the other way round, the composition of the list, which is given by direct enumeration,[32] is guaranteed *a priori*. So in this case there is nothing like the clerk's contingent premiss, that his list of users of the library for that day is complete. The historian's premiss, that his list is correct, if it is true, is true *a priori*, and, if he is confident that all the seven names that he has put on it really do belong there, he can hardly doubt that it is complete.

Now it is true that in this kind of case, as in the kind of

[32] cf. Wittgenstein *T.L-PH.* 5.501.

case that Russell considers, the natural insatiability of the word 'all' is limited by the words that follow it. But the limitation which operates in this kind of case is of an entirely different kind from the limitation which operates in Russell's kind of case. Its mechanism is *a priori*, and so the word 'all' never even looks as if it were going to break out and range over the whole contents of the universe. At least it looked as if it were going to do that in the proposition about the people using the library. For in that case the mechanism of the limitation was not *a priori*. That propositional function was genuinely open, and the list of individuals that might dissatisfy it was not fixed in advance. The limitation came in only because the propositional function did not cast its net very widely in space or time.

Does this difference between the two methods of limitation affect Russell's conclusion, which is that general facts cannot be reduced to sets of singular facts? It seems to affect it in two different ways. First, his conclusion does not apply to the general fact about the Seven Sages. For in that case the general proposition can be reduced to a set of singular propositions, and from this it follows that the general fact can be reduced to a set of singular facts. However, this is a very rare kind of exception to his thesis, and the exception can be explained. The explanation is that the effect of the meaning of the word 'all' is mitigated by the meaning of the words that follow it.

The second way in which his thesis is affected is, perhaps, more important. It seems that, although it does apply to examples like the case of the people using the library, it might be better expressed in a slightly different way. It is really a thesis about the meaning of the word 'all'. He is insisting that this word really does mean *all*, and that its meaning is not changed by the fact that the propositional function '— used the library today' does not cast its net very widely in space or time. He puts this by saying that, if you try to verify the universal proposition 'All the people who used the library that day took out works of fiction' by verifying the set of singular propositions, you will only find that you have assumed that you have a complete list of the singular facts, and that is another universal proposition, and one which you cannot verify in the same way. This leads him to suggest that, if you try to analyse the universal proposition ' All the people who used the library that day borrowed works of fiction ' into a set of singular propositions, you will only find that you have to include in your analysis another universal proposition which you cannot analyse in the same way. But this suggestion is misleading.

It is certainly true that you cannot analyse the original universal proposition into a set of singular propositions. But the reason why you cannot do this is not that you have to add another universal proposition to the set of singular ones. It is simply that in this universal proposition the effect of the meaning of the word ' all ' is not mitigated as it is in the universal proposition about the Seven Sages. Consequently, someone who begins to analyse this universal proposition by writing out a list of singular propositions has not even *started* his analysis in the right way. He has failed to realise that the universality of the proposition does not depend on the *length* of this list, but rather on the way in which the singular propositions are generated. They are generated out of the propositional function by the normal mechanism of the word ' all '. The fact that in this case the propositional function '— used the library today ' does not cast its net very widely has nothing to do with the meaning of the word ' all ', or with the analysis of the universal proposition. It merely gives the clerk an alternative way of making reasonably sure that it is true.

This criticism of the way in which Russell expresses his thesis when he applies it to propositions like the one about the people using the library is only directed against part of what he says. It is not directed against his observation that, if you want to make reasonably sure of the truth of such a proposition without making an inductive inference, you will have to establish that your list of singular facts is complete, and that is another universal proposition. That observation is perfectly correct. However, when he goes on to use it to support his conclusion, that a general fact cannot be analysed into a set of singular facts, his argument contains a misleading suggestion. It suggests that the attempt to analyse a general fact into a set of singular ones starts off quite well, but cannot be completed unless it includes another general fact. But the real reason why the attempt to analyse a general fact into a set of singular ones inevitably fails is quite different, and has nothing to do with the way in which we are sometimes able to be reasonably sure of the truth of a contingent universal proposition without making an inductive inference. The real reason is that the word 'all' generates singular propositions in a universal way.[83]

If this is the real reason why general facts cannot be analysed into sets of singular facts, Russell's analysis of universal propositions will be saved from his own doubts. An examination of universal propositions which contain no restriction of space or time will confirm that it is the real reason. What Russell says about such propositions is this :

It is perfectly clear, I think, that when you have enumerated all the atomic facts in the world, it is a further fact about the world that those are all the atomic facts there are about the world, and that is just as much an objective fact about the world as any of them are. It is clear, I think, that you must admit general facts as distinct from and over and above particular facts. The same thing applies to ' All men are mortal '. When you have taken all the particular men that there are, and found each one of them severally to be mortal, it is definitely a new fact that all men are mortal; how new a fact appears from what I said a moment ago, that it could not be inferred from the mortality of the several men that there are in the world.[84]

In this passage Russell is extending his diagnosis of the reason why general facts cannot be reduced to sets of singular facts. He introduced it in a case where the universal proposition contained restrictions of space and time. Here he is extending it to universal propositions which contain no such restriction. But the extension runs up against the obstacle

[83] This is presumably the point of Wittgenstein's criticism of Russell's treatment of generality in *T.L-PH.* 5.521.
[84] *PH.L.A.* p. 37 (*L.KN.* p. 236).

which was mentioned earlier. If someone claimed to have made a complete list of the singular propositions which could be deduced from this kind of universal proposition, he would betray that he had not understood the meaning of the word 'all'. However, that does not make it impossible to explain the irreducibility of general facts. For even in the other kind of case the explanation did not really depend on the fortunate chance that the list of singular propositions could be completed.

CHAPTER XV

TRADITIONS

In the history of ideas anything that is said is likely to do some injustice to the things that are left unsaid. Certainly the truest single thing that can be said about Russell's philosophy is that it stands in the direct line of descent from Hume's, and much of this book has been devoted to analysing this heritage. Russell has been presented as the philosopher who gave empiricism an adequate logical framework. But, although this is truer than any other single comprehensive description of his work, it needs to be supplemented and qualified. For he was not the first British Empiricist to bring in logic. John Stuart Mill's logical theory was built into a psychological system which was very like Hume's, but his resources as a logician were far less than Russell's. Another point that ought to be mentioned is that, when Russell developed his logical empiricism, he cannot be represented as having succeeded in saying what Hume had really been trying to say. For a philosopher who works with an inadequate logical apparatus is not like an intelligent man with a poor grasp of a foreign language. Certainly Hume and Russell approached the same problems in broadly the same way, but the inadequacy of Hume's apparatus puts a gap between his philosophy and Russell's which cannot be described as a gap between his achievement and his intentions.

Another difference between them which needs to be pointed out is that Russell is a builder of systems, whereas Hume is not. This is a very vague contrast, which is often made vaguer by the use of the word 'metaphysician'. You might object that Hume is a sort of builder of systems. For he internalises the objects of knowledge, and constructs an elaborate psychological system, in which the laws of the association of ideas play much the same part as Newton's law of gravitation. That is true. But his system is egocentric, and the task of reconstructing empirical knowledge in a way that would explain how minds meet and communicate with one another is something that he never really attempts. However, that did not prevent him from constructing moral and political theories which presupposed that the task had been completed. So his system does not cover all the ground that he needs to occupy as a philosopher. Russell's system does, and it is in this sense that he is a builder of systems and Hume is not.

There are many explanations of this difference between them. Perhaps the most important single thing which explains it is the enormous advance of science. Russell set out to reconstruct scientific knowledge without serious loss of content. He certainly was not going to be satisfied with a philosophical theory which simply jettisoned the cargo in order to placate the sceptic. Nor would he accept a philosophy which was so wasteful that it would have to be shelved, in the way in which Hume shelved the destructive conclusions of the First Book of his Treatise when he went on to develop his moral and political philosophy. Russell thought that philosophy too must be scientific.

But this difference in Russell's outlook is not only the result of the period in which he lived. The greatest systems which have been produced since the Renaissance belong to the seventeenth century, and they all include a rational reconstruction of the science of their time. In fact, Russell's work was very much influenced by the system of Leibniz. His philosophical temperament combines in an unusual way the caution which is characteristic of British philosophers with the kind of speculation which, rather absurdly, we call 'Continental'. It is, of course, questionable whether the doctrines to which these two tendencies naturally lead can be combined. This is really the question which was raised in Chapter III. Can an impersonal system be built on a foundation of essentially private sense-data? Can such a foundation really support a reconstruction of empirical knowledge which is not egocentric? It is even doubtful whether an egocentric reconstruction will really stand up. Much of the later philosophy of Wittgenstein grows out of this doubt.

There is another influence which has not been adequately described in this book, the influence of G. E. Moore. Moore's article, ' The Nature of Judgement ',[1] had a profound effect on the development of Russell's ideas at the turn of the century. However, it would be tedious to prolong this list of omissions. They are mentioned only in order that silence should not be taken as a denial of existence. But there is one subject on which something more does need to be said, and that is the relationship between Russell and Wittgenstein. First, nothing that has been said about the similarities and connections between the work of the two philosophers applies to Wittgenstein's later writings. It was stated in the Introduction that criticisms of Russell's philosophy which were developed only after 1919 would be mentioned very briefly, and some of those criticisms were Wittgenstein's. For Wittgenstein's later philosophy really begins with a repudiation of the fundamental assumptions of logical atomism.

Secondly, the connections that have been traced in the period before 1919 between Hume and Russell and between Russell and Wittgenstein might be taken to suggest that Wittgenstein should be placed in the tradition of British Empiricism. But that would be absurd, and it is not implied by anything that has been said in this book. On the other hand, enthusiastic attempts to dissociate his early philosophy from Russell's, and to connect it exclusively with ideas of an entirely different kind usually go much too far in the other direction.

We can connect Wittgenstein's earlier theory of meaning with Russell's without making the connection depend on a shared theory of perception. As a matter of fact, Wittgenstein does seem to have shared Russell's views about the phenomenology of perception, and he was at least prepared to consider the identification of his ' objects ' with sense-data. But that is not important. For the way in which his theory of meaning developed out of Russell's does not depend on it.

[1] See p. 199, footnote 6.

Nor is it important to strike a balance between the sources of the *Tractatus*. Certainly the influence of Schopenhauer and from an entirely different direction, of Frege, are very clear in it. But so too is the influence of Leibniz, and that probably came through Russell, who himself did not stand squarely in the tradition of British Empiricism. Even the beginning of Wittgenstein's use of the distinction between science and mysticism can be found in Russell's writings.[2] But this is even less important, because the similarity of temperament which it seems to indicate is almost entirely illusory. What is important is that by chance Wittgenstein became a pupil of Russell's, and that thereafter they worked for some time on the same problems with much the same assumptions. The result is that their theories during this period are most easily understood together.

[2] *MYS. and LOG.* (*M. and L.* pp. 11-12).

BIBLIOGRAPHY

All the works to which reference is made in this book are listed here, and, if their titles are abbreviated in the footnotes in which reference is made to them, the abbreviations are given. An alphabetical list of these abbreviations is given on pp. 9-10. The books herein refer to British editions, since the author's page references throughout the text correspond to these editions.

PART I: BERTRAND RUSSELL

Some of Russell's earlier writings appeared in periodicals which are now very difficult to obtain. In such cases page-references will be given only to later, more accessible reprints. There is a complete list of his works, covering the period 1895 to September 1945, in *The Philosophy of Bertrand Russell*, edited by P. A. Schilpp (vol. v in *The Library of Living Philosophers*). The list which is given below is arranged in chronological order. It is not a complete bibliography, but only includes the works of Russell to which reference is made in this book.

1900. *A Critical Exposition of the Philosophy of Leibniz*: Cambridge University Press: 2nd ed. 1937.   *PH. of L.*

1903. *The Principles of Mathematics*: Cambridge University Press: 2nd ed. 1938   *P. of M.*

1904. '*Meinong's Theory of Complexes and Assumptions*': *Mind*, 1904.   *M.TH.C.A.*

1905. '*On Denoting*': *Mind*, 1905   *O.D.*
Reprinted in *Logic and Knowledge*: ed. R. C. Marsh; Allen and Unwin 1956   *L.KN.*

1906. '*The Nature of Truth*': *Mind*, 1906.
The first two sections of this paper are reprinted as '*The Monistic Theory of Truth*' in *Philosophical Essays* (see below, 1910).   *M.TH. of T.*

1910. *Principia Mathematica* vol. I: with A. N. Whitehead: Cambridge University Press: 2nd ed. 1935.   *P.M.*
'*On the Nature of Truth and Falsehood*'. This is the rewritten third section of '*The Nature of Truth*' (1906), and it is included in the next work.   *O.N.T. and F.*
Philosophical Essays: Longmans.   *PH.E.*

1911. '*Knowledge by Acquaintance and Knowledge by Description*': *Proceedings of the Aristotelian Society*, 1910-11.
     KN.A.KN.D.

Reprinted in *The Problems of Philosophy* **c. v.** (see below, 1912).

Reprinted in a longer version in *Mysticism and Logic* **c. x.** (see below, 1918).

1912. *The Problems of Philosophy*: Oxford University Press (page-references will be given to the 1946 reprint). *P. of PH.*

'*On the Relation of Universals to Particulars*': *Proceedings of the Aristotelian Society*, 1911-12. *R.U.P.*

1914. *Our Knowledge of the External World as a Field for Scientific Method in Philosophy*: Allen and Unwin. *O.KN.E.W.*

'*On the Nature of Acquaintance*': *Monist*, 1914. Reprinted in *Logic and Knowledge* (see above, 1905). *O.N.A.*

'*Mysticism and Logic*': *Hibbert Journal* 1914. Reprinted in the collection of essays entitled *Mysticism and Logic* (see below, 1918). *MYS. and LOG.*

'*The Relation of Sense-data to Physics*': *Scientia*, 1914. Reprinted in *Mysticism and Logic* (see below, 1918). *R.S.-D.PH.*

1915. '*The Ultimate Constituents of Matter*': *Monist*, 1915. Reprinted in *Mysticism and Logic* (see below, 1918). *U.C.M.*

1918. *Mysticism and Logic*: Longmans 1918 (page references will be given to this edition): Allen and Unwin 1929. *M. and L.*

'*The Philosophy of Logical Atomism*': *Monist*, 1918. Reprinted by the Department of Philosophy, University of Minnesota. *PH.L.A.*

Also reprinted in *Logic and Knowledge* (see above, 1905; page references will be given to both these reprints.)

1919. *Introduction to Mathematical Philosophy*: Allen and Unwin. *I.M.PH.*

'*On Propositions: what they are and how they mean*'; *Proceedings of the Aristotelian Society*, supplementary vol. 1919. Reprinted in *Logic and Knowledge* (see above, 1905). *O.P.*

1921. *The Analysis of Mind*: Allen and Unwin. *A.M.*

1922. *Introduction to Wittgenstein's Tractatus Logico-Philosophicus* (see part II of this bibliography). *I.T.*

1924. '*Logical Atomism*'. Included in *Contemporary British Philosophy* [*First Series*]: Allen and Unwin.

Reprinted in *Logic and Knowledge* (see above, 1905; page references will be given to both these collections).

1940. *An Inquiry into Meaning and Truth*: Allen and Unwin. *I.M.T.*

1943. '*Reply to Criticisms*': in *The Philosophy of Bertrand Russell* (see above). *PH.B.R.*

1948. *Human Knowledge, its Scope and Limits*: Allen and Unwin. *H. KN.S.L.*

Bibliography 275

1959. *My Philosophical Development*: Allen and Unwin. *M.PH.D.*

PART II: OTHER AUTHORS

ANSCOMBE, G. E. M. *An Introduction to Wittgenstein's Tractatus*: Hutchinson 1959. *I.W.T.*

AUSTIN, J. L. '*Other Minds*': *Proceedings of the Aristotelian Society*, supplementary vol. xx, 1946. Reprinted in *Logic and Language* (*Second Series*), ed. A. G. N. Flew, Blackwell 1953, and in J. L. Austin, *Philosophical Papers*, Oxford University Press, 1961.

AYER, A. J. *The Foundations of Empirical Knowledge*: Macmillan, 1940.

BLACK, M. '*Russell's Philosophy of Language*', in *PH.B.R.* (see above).

BRADLEY, F. H. *Appearance and Reality*: Oxford University Press, 1893 (page-references will be given to the 10th impression, 1946). *A. and R.*

FREGE, G. *Translations from the Philosophical Writings of Gottlob Frege*: by P. T. Geach and M. Black, Blackwell, 1952.

GEACH, P. T. *Mental Acts*: Routledge and Kegan Paul.

GRIFFIN, J. P. *Wittgenstein's Logical Atomism*: Oxford University Press, 1964. *W.L.A.*

HUME, D. *A Treatise of Human Nature* (page-references will be given to the Everyman edition). *T.H.N.*
Enquiry Concerning the Human Understanding: ed. L. A. Selby-Bigge, Oxford University Press (2nd ed 1902).
'*An Abstract of a Treatise of Human Nature*': in *Hume, Theory of Knowledge*, ed. D. C. Yalden-Thomson, Nelson, 1951. *H.TH.KN.*

JAMES W., '*Does "Consciousness" exist?*' in *Essays in Radical Empiricism*: Longmans, 1912.

KANT, I. *Critique of Pure Reason* (page-references will be given to the Everyman edition).

KNEALE, W. C. *Probability and Induction*: Oxford University Press, 1949.

KNEALE, W. C., and M., *The Development of Logic*: Oxford University Press, 1962.

LOCKE, J. *An Essay Concerning Human Understanding*, abridged edition by A. S. Pringle-Pattison, Oxford University Press, 1904.

MALCOLM, N. Review of Wittgenstein, *Philosophical Investigations*, *Philosophical Review*, 1954.

MEINONG. *Uber Annahmen*, Leipzig, 1902.

MOORE, G. E., '*The Nature of Judgement*', *Mind*, 1899.
'*External Relations*', in *Philosophical Studies*, Routledge and Kegan Paul, 1922.
'*Russell's "Theory of Descriptions"*', in *PH.B.R.* (see above).

PAUL, G. A. '*Is there a Problem about Sense-data?*' *Proceedings of the Aristotelian Society*, supplementary vol. 1936: reprinted in *Logic and Language (First Series)*, ed. A. G. N. Flew.

SEARLE, J. R., '*Proper Names*', *Mind*, 1958.

STRAWSON, P. F. '*On Referring*', *Mind*, 1950.
Introduction to Logical Theory: Methuen, 1952.
Review of Wittgenstein, *Philosophical Investigations*, *Mind*, 1954.
Individuals, Methuen 1959.

THOMSON, J. J. '*Private Languages*', *American Philosophical Quarterly*, 1964.

URMSON, J. O. *Philosophical Analysis*: Oxford University Press, 1956.

WARNOCK, G. J. *Berkeley*: Penguin Books, 1953.

WITTGENSTEIN, L. *Notes on Logic*, included as Appendix 1 of *Notebooks 1914-1916* (see below).   *N.L.*
Extracts from Wittgenstein's Letters to Russell, 1912-1920, included as Appendix III of *Notebooks 1914-1916*.
Notebooks 1914-1916, translated by G. E. M. Anscombe, Blackwell, 1961.   *N.B.*
Tractatus Logico-Philosophicus, translated by C. K. Ogden, Routledge and Kegan Paul 1922: translated by B. F. McGuinness and D. F. Pears, Routledge and Kegan Paul 1961.   *T.L-PH.*
'*Some Remarks on Logical Form*', *Proceedings of the Aristotelian Society*, supplementary vol. IX, 1929.   *L.F.*
The Blue and Brown Books: Blackwell, 1958.
Philosophical Investigations, translated by G. E. M. Anscombe, Blackwell, 1953.   *PH.I.*

WOLLHEIM, R. A. *F. H. Bradley*: Penguin Books, 1959.   *F.H.B.*

INDEX

277